INSECT SOUNDS

ASPECTS OF ZOOLOGY
SERIES

A BIOLOGY OF CRUSTACEA
J. Green, B.Sc., Ph.D.

INSECT SOUNDS
P. T. Haskell, B.Sc., Ph.D.

SOIL ANIMALS
D. Keith McE. Kevan, B.Sc.,
Ph.D., A.I.C.T.A.,
F.R.S.Edin.

In preparation
A BIOLOGY OF DRAGONFLIES
P. S. Corbet, B.Sc., Ph.D.

INSECT SOUNDS

by

P. T. HASKELL

B.Sc., Ph.D.

Deputy Director, Anti-Locust Research Centre

QUADRANGLE BOOKS CHICAGO

First published in 1961 by
QUADRANGLE BOOKS, INC., CHICAGO 1
H. F. & G. Witherby Ltd., London, W.C.1

Library of Congress Catalog
Card No. 61-6670

PRINTED IN GREAT BRITAIN BY
NORTHUMBERLAND PRESS LIMITED
GATESHEAD ON TYNE

PREFACE

THIS book was written with two ideas in mind; first to provide teachers and students with a short outline of present knowledge of insect sounds, and secondly in the hope that it would arouse some interest in the wealth of fascinating research problems waiting to be investigated. For the first purpose, I have tried to arrange a selection of the known facts around a functional framework, while for the second I have allowed myself the liberty of putting forward certain hypotheses and indulging in some speculations. I have been helped in this by discussions with many colleagues, and although any errors of omission and commission are mine, I should like to acknowledge the assistance I have had from them all. I must also thank the following for allowing me to reproduce certain illustrations and for giving me access to unpublished material: Dr. R. D. Alexander, Museum of Zoology, Michigan; Professor H. Autrum, Zoological Institute, Munich; Dr. R. G. Busnel, M. B. Dumortier, Mlle. S. Brieu and M. F. Pasquinelly, Laboratoire de Physiologie Acoustique, Jouy-en-Josas; Professor T. Eisner, Cornell University, New York; Dr. H. E. Hinton, Dept. of Zoology, Bristol; Dr. G. A. Horridge, Dept. of Zoology, St. Andrews University; Mr. D. Leston; Professor D. K. MacE. Kevan, Dept. of Entomology and Plant Pathology, McGill University, Canada; F. Ossiannilsson, Uppsala; Dr. J. W. S. Pringle, Zoology Dept., Cambridge; Professor R. J. Pumphrey, Dept. of Zoology, Liverpool; Professor E. O. Wilson and Mr. A. D. Grinnell, Biological Laboratories, Harvard. I am grateful to the following for helping with the systematics, illustrations and bibliography: Mr. E. B. Britton, British Museum (Nat. Hist.); Mr. J. W. Siddorn, Dept. of Zoology, Imperial College; Mrs. M. Siddorn; and Miss E. Hawkins, Miss K. M. Becker, Mrs. A. Greathead and Mrs. E. Blaxter, Anti-Locust Research Centre. Finally I must thank my wife, without whose constant encouragement and efficient secretarial help this book would never have been finished.

P. T. HASKELL.

Anti-Locust Research Centre,
1961.

v

CONTENTS

LIST OF PLATES

The following figures are reproduced as half-tone illustrations and are positioned as follows.

CHAPTER I

THE RECORDING AND ANALYSIS
OF INSECT SOUNDS

MAN has known for over a thousand years that insects make
sounds, and for some hundreds of those years naturalists have
been speculating as to how the sounds are made and arguing as to
whether they serve any useful purpose. Modern research has settled
some of the speculations and answered some of the arguments, but
the fact is that only the fringe of the problem has yet been touched.
It is true to say, however, that great advances in our knowledge of
all aspects of the problem have been made in the last twenty years,
although the main result of these advances has been to show in
which direction the most important problems lie and to indicate
the most profitable aspects for future research.

The aim of this book is to present in outline the present limits
of knowledge about insect sounds, which field must include that
of insect hearing and also the behaviour associated with the sounds.
No attempt at an exhaustive treatment has been made, but
examples have been chosen to illustrate those general principles
which at the present time seem to be the most important to the
subject itself and to its integration into the wider fields of ethology
and entomology.

Before embarking on a study of insect sounds some knowledge
of sound itself is required. Unfortunately, but understandably,
research on sound has always been conducted from the point of
view of man as the observer and receiver. Thus " sound " is defined
in most dictionaries as " the sensation produced through the ear;
what is or may be heard ". This anthropocentric attitude has direct
and unfortunate repercussions on the subject of insect sounds, since,
as will be seen later, the hearing organs of insects respond to sound
in a fundamentally different way to those of man. It happens that
the qualities of sound which human observers can detect and on
which they rely for their understanding of speech and their
appreciation of music are not those which appear to be significant
in the acoustic communications of insects. This difficulty brings

I   B others in its train; the definitions and concepts of acoustics have been formulated with the human ear in mind as the primary receiver. Thus the terms "sonic" and "ultra-sonic" apply to sounds of a frequency audible and inaudible, respectively, to the human ear; but the hearing organs of many insects respond to sounds of both types.

It is however impossible, even if it were desirable, to re-define all the qualities of sound to suit our present purpose, but since much confused thinking in connection with the study of insect sounds has had its genesis in this problem, it seems preferable to define our basic fields of interest, sound and hearing, in more suitable terms. For this purpose the definitions of Pumphrey (1940) can be used. Thus *sound* is defined as "any mechanical disturbance whatever which is potentially referable by the insect to an external and localized source". And *hearing* can be defined as follows: "an insect hears when it behaves as if it has located a moving object (a sound source) not in contact with it."

As far as the present study is concerned, we shall be dealing in the main with the propagation of sound in air, since very little is known of sound emission or reception by aquatic insects, and it will be useful to consider very briefly those theoretical aspects of airborne sound with which we shall be concerned. To begin with it will be of value to understand the physical events underlying the production of a sound wave. A mechanical disturbance in the air, such as the vibration of a tuning fork, sets up waves of compression and rarefaction which follow one another alternately; these waves are called longitudinal waves, because the air particles suffer an oscillatory displacement along the axis of propagation of the sound. By "particle" is meant an elementary air mass, very small, but containing many millions of molecules. In regions of compression, there is an increase in particle density and in regions of rarefaction, a decrease. It follows that in regions of compression, the sound pressure is at maximum, while the spatial displacement of particles is minimal; conversely in regions of rarefaction, pressure is minimal and displacement is a maximum. It is possible to plot graphically the displacement of air particles, with the convention that displacements in the direction of wave propagation are plotted above the horizontal axis of the graph, while displacements in the opposite direction are plotted below this axis. Fig. 1 shows such a displacement graph and the particle distribution from which it is derived. Since, as stated above, pressure is a maximum where displacement is minimal and vice versa, it is possible to draw on the graph the corresponding pressure wave of the sound.

Sound pressure is a scalar quality of sound, but displacement is a vector quality, that is, it has both magnitude and direction, and the maximum displacement is found normal to the wave-front. This fact has an important bearing on the directional qualities of sound receivers; if these are responsive to displacement, then, when they are rotated in a sound field, they will register a maximum effect when incident sound is normal to the plane of the diaphragm. As will become apparent later on, it seems probable that most insect hearing organs are displacement receivers and

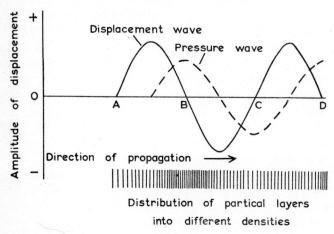

Fig. 1. Graphical representation of sound wave, showing particle layer distribution and related pressure and displacement waves.

thus will have a directional response to a sound source, which can be used in locating the latter.

The source of mechanical disturbance, or sound source, sets the air around it in motion by vibrating about its equilibrium position; the number of complete vibrations, or cycles as they are called, it makes in one second is called the frequency of the source, and also of the resultant sound, in cycles per second. In Fig. 1, a complete cycle stretches from the point A to the point C on the displacement wave, since in this time displacement has been effected in both directions about the equilibrium position B. As far as the human ear is concerned, the frequency of a sound determines its pitch; the higher the frequency of air particle vibration in a sound wave, the higher the sensation of pitch experienced by the human ear. However, if the frequency drops very low, to 5 or 10 cycles per second, the ear hears each vibration as a separate impulse, and only when the frequency rises to about 30 to 40 cycles per second are the vibrations heard as a continuous humming note. Increasing the frequency of vibration then increases the pitch of the note, and this continues until frequencies of about 15-20,000 cycles or 15-20 kilocycles per second are reached. Somewhere in this range of frequencies the sound becomes inaudible to the human ear, although by physical methods it can be demonstrated that sound energy is present. This band of frequencies, from 30 c/s to about 20 kc/s, is thus called the sonic band, or " the audio-frequencies", because sounds in this range are audible to the human ear. Sounds of frequencies above 20 kc/s are referred to as "ultra-sonic" sounds and are inaudible to the ear. Insect hearing organs, for the most part, have a wider range of frequencies to which they are responsive than human ears, and in the case of at least one organ the range includes the "sonic" band and extends into the "ultra-sonic" range as far as 200 kc/s. However, there is no counterpart in most insect organs for human discrimination of pitch; pure sounds, whatever their frequency, and provided their intensities are constant, sound the same to insects. One other point must be mentioned here, and that is the "time constant" of hearing organs. This may be defined as the time taken by the organ to reach a steady state when stimulated by a sound or to return to its original state when the stimulus ceases. In practice, it is found that if successive sounds impinge on a receptor and the intervals between those sounds are less than about four or five times the time constant of the receiver, then the sounds will not be heard separately but will appear as one confused sound. The time constant for the human ear is about 20 milliseconds, and thus sounds which follow one another at intervals of less than about $^{1}/_{10}$ second will not be distinguished from one another. Certain insect sounds consist of assemblages of sound pulses occurring at intervals far smaller than this; and in these cases the human ear will not distinguish the component pulses. On the other hand, the time constants of some insect hearing organs are very small, as low as 2 milliseconds or even lower, from which it follows that they can distinguish sounds separated by intervals as small as $^{1}/_{100}$ second. There are other important differences between human and insect ears which will be discussed later, but enough has been said for the present to show how dangerous it is to approach the study of insect sounds with notions based on the properties of the human ear.

So far we have only discussed sounds with a simple wave structure, as in Fig. 1. Such sounds are called "pure tones" because they consist of one periodic vibration only and are not further analysable; but all natural sounds are complex, that is, they consist of a number of vibrations of different frequencies. If the sound is not

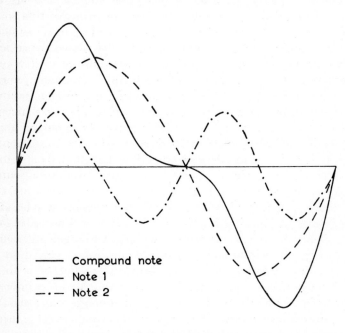

Fig. 2. Graphical representation of complex vibration and the sounds comprising it.

too complex, it can be analysed into constituent vibrations each with a simple wave form, and Fig. 2 shows such a complex wave broken down into its two fundamental vibration forms. It will be seen that note 2 is twice the frequency of note 1, but that the latter has a greater amplitude, and obviously plays more part in fixing the wave-form and frequency of the compound note. In complex tones, the constituent vibration of greatest amplitude and lowest frequency is called the "fundamental", the remaining notes being called "harmonics" or "overtones". We shall return to complex sounds later on, but must first consider some further fundamental properties of sounds.

Since the frequency of a sound depends only on the rate of vibration of the source, it is unaffected by distance or the state of the medium in which it is propagated. A change in frequency must mean that the vibration of the source has altered. There is one anomalous case here, and that concerns sound sources which are moving rapidly, and here the frequency may apparently alter as the source approaches towards or recedes from the observer, due to the Doppler effect; but since the speed of movement has to be relatively high, such considerations only enter into insect acoustics when attempting to record noises made in flight. Several aspects of the production of sound by mechanical vibrations of various types have a bearing on the variety of mechanisms used by insects to produce sounds; the anatomical details of these mechanisms will be discussed in the next chapter, but meanwhile there are two related phenomena which are of importance. As remarked above, any method of setting air into vibration produces a sound; the magnitude of the sound depends upon how large a mass of air can be set moving in a given time. A string hung from a nail with a weight at its free end will cause but a feeble sound when plucked; if, however, the string is stretched over two pieces of wood resting on a board, on plucking it quite a loud sound will be heard. The string communicates its mechanical vibrations to the board, which, being in contact with a large amount of air, causes many more air particles to move than before, consequently producing a louder sound. Such an arrangement, called a sounding board, is provided in many insects by the wings; the actual sound-producing mechanism transfers its vibrational energy to the wing, which in turn vibrates a large mass of air. A drawback to the sounding board is that the energy available from any given source is more quickly dissipated, but with a constant supply of energy this does not matter.

The second phenomena to consider is that of resonance; if two tuning forks of the same frequency are held near one another, and one of them is bowed so that it vibrates and produces a sound, the other fork will be found to be set in motion. The air waves from the bowed fork impinge on the second and set it in motion; they are able to do this because the forks have the same frequency and alternate compressions and rarefactions of the air produced by the first fork arrive at exactly the right moments to aid the gradual build-up of the movements of the second fork. If the forks were not of the same frequency, this timing would be wrong and the second fork would not be set in motion. This transference of energy between the forks is called resonance, and two bodies will only resonate together when both have the same natural frequency of vibration. However, it can happen that if a complex vibration is passed on to a solid body which has as a resonant frequency one of the components of that complex vibration, the body may vibrate at its own frequency, deriving its energy from the complex vibration. This phenomenon is found again in some insect sound mechanisms, when a complex mechanical vibration is passed on to a wing or similar surface; this resonates at its own frequency, and also acts as a sounding board, thus producing a comparatively pure note of high energy from a complex vibration. All vibrating systems are subject to a variety of resisting forces which cause decay of the amplitude of vibration, or "damping". The time of decay of the vibrations depends upon many factors, such as the internal friction of the body, its size and shape and so on; a bell, for example, vibrates a long time after being struck, but the biological materials concerned in insect sound mechanisms stop vibrating almost as soon as the supply of energy from the mechanical system—the muscles—ceases. This high damping affects the quality of certain sounds, since it facilitates production of short pulses of sound which can be rapidly repeated.

Having considered the frequency of a sound and some phenomena related to it, we must now discuss the intensity or loudness of sounds. The loudness of a sound depends upon the energy of vibration of the source, and there is for both human and insect ears a minimal energy which a sound wave must have in order to be audible. This value is known as the "threshold sensitivity" of the hearing organ, and it varies considerably with frequency. Thus for a sound of 1 kc/s frequency some insect hearing organs need 100,000,000 times as much energy for audibility as human ears, but at frequences of 10 kc/s the insect organ only needs about the same amount of energy as required by the human ear. The loudness of sounds can be measured in various units, but all are related to the concept of sound intensity, which is the rate of flow of energy per unit area normal to the direction of propagation of the wave. The unit is the erg per second per square centimetre. Unlike frequency, this quality is greatly affected by the distance between the sound source and the point of measurement. Consider a point source of sound which has a rate of production of

sound energy I_0 ergs per second. Assuming the sound spreads out
from the source in the form of an expanding sphere, it is clear
that, since the total energy is constant, it has to be distributed over
a greater and greater area as it travels away from the source.
Thus at x cm from the source (assumed small) the intensity I_x will be
$I_0/4\pi x^2$ and the sound intensity will decrease inversely as the square
of the distance from the source. This consideration explains the comparatively short ranges possible in acoustic signalling, for the energy
available is soon dissipated.

Sound intensity is also related to sound pressure in the following
way:

$$I = p^2/R$$

where I = sound intensity in ergs per sec. per sq. cm.
p^2 = sound pressure in dynes per sq. cm.
R = specific acoustical resistance.

Note the similarity to Ohm's law in this formula; I is analogous to
current, p to voltage and R to resistance. The acoustical resistance
R, is given by the relation

$$R = \rho c$$

where ρ is the density of the medium in gram per cc. and c is
the velocity of propagation of the sound wave in the medium in
cm per second. As has been said, we are mainly concerned here
with propagation through air; in this medium, although the
velocity of sound is unaltered by pressure changes, it is changed by
temperature, and of course density is altered when either pressure
or temperature alters. However, by defining conditions of temperature and pressure, that is 20° C. and 760 mm. of mercury, the values
of ρ and c become constants, being 0·0012 gm. per cc. and 34,400
cm. per sec. respectively, and under these conditions R=42 c.g.s.
units and

$$I = p^2/42 \text{ ergs per sec. per sq. cm,}$$

an approximation sufficiently accurate for present purposes. Thus
measurement of the sound pressure enables the sound intensity to
be calculated. This is most convenient since, as will be seen, most
physical instruments responding to sound are pressure recorders.
Threshold sensitivity for hearing organs can also be expressed in
terms of sound pressure and this is quite usual. But it must be
emphasized that sound intensity and pressure are two entirely
different things and it is wrong, strictly, to refer to "a sound

intensity of x dynes per sq. cm ", the dyne being a unit of force. However, since in practice it is extremely difficult to measure sound intensity directly it has been almost entirely abandoned in favour of terms using sound pressures such as "a sound level corresponding to an R.M.S. pressure of x dynes per sq. cm ".

A practical difficulty ensues at this point relative to such terms; the range of sound intensities and pressures to which the hearing organs of both vertebrates and insects respond is very large indeed, so much so that the ratio of the lowest to the highest pressures is over a million. The problem of finding suitable units in which to express such large quantities can be solved by the use of a logarithmic notation, the decibel scale. This scale can be used to express sound intensities or pressures by reference to the number of decibels a given intensity or pressure is larger or smaller than a standard reference intensity or pressure. As regards acoustics, the most general pressure standard used is that of the threshold sensitivity of human hearing for a note of frequency 1 kc; this lower limit is a pressure of 0·0002 dyne per sq. cm.

The relationship in decibels of a sound of pressure P_n to the standard pressure P_0 is given by the formula

$$n = 20 \log_{10} (P_n)/(P_0)$$

where n = number of decibels
P_n = pressure of sound in dynes/cm^2
P_0 = standard pressure 0·0002 dynes/cm^2

Throughout this book, any measurement of the level of insect sounds are given in decibels above a level where 0 db is equivalent to the standard pressure of 0·0002 dynes/cm^2. A very important qualification about such measurements must be mentioned here. As explained above, sound energy decreases inversely as the square of the distance from the source; any result expressed in decibels must therefore include the distance from the source otherwise comparative measurements are impossible. An example of a correct statement about sound level is as follows: "for the flight noise of a single male Desert Locust, the average sound level at the microphone 10 cms from the insect, in db above a reference level where 0 db $\equiv$ 0·0002 dynes/cm^2, was 67." It should be noted that the square of the ratio between two sound pressures gives the change in relative energy between them. Thus the change in relative energy between two sounds with pressures of 2 and 20 dynes/cm^2 is 100.

For subjective comparative purposes a few examples of loudness are given:

Threshold of hearing	o db
Quiet whisper at 5 ft.	10 db
Country house	30 db
City house	40 db
Large store	60 db
Factory	70-80 db
Hammer blows on steel plate at 2 ft.	120 db
Threshold of pain	130 db

Following our consideration of the energy of a sound and its measurement, we must briefly look at the ways in which this energy is attenuated during the passage of the waves through air. Apart from the diminution due to the effect of distance, energy is dissipated in three main ways. Air has a certain viscosity and when layers of it are in relative motion, as for instance in the zones of compression and rarefaction due to a sound wave, the viscous forces oppose this motion and energy is expended in overcoming this resistance. Also, when layers of air are compressed during passage of a wave, their temperature is raised, and there is a tendency for heat to be conducted away from such regions, causing a loss of energy. Thirdly, the difference in temperature between zones of compression and rarefaction results in the radiation of heat from the former to the latter, with a consequent loss of energy. With a full knowledge of the conditions of propagation and the frequency and intensity of the sound this attenuation can be calculated and allowances made for it. The losses increase as the frequency of the sound increases and in the ultrasonic range may become quite severe. The practical effect is to reduce even further the range of communication possible with sounds of given intensity and receivers of known sensitivity to less than that to be expected from the inverse square law. Sound, like light, can be reflected and refracted. The reflection of sound is obvious to anyone and the phenomenon of the echo is commonplace. Refraction is not so obvious, but nevertheless occurs and for exactly the same reason as light is refracted; that is, the sound wave suffers a change in velocity on passing from one medium to another, or from one region of a medium to another if they differ in temperature. For example, the velocity of sound in air increases by about 2 feet per second for every degree centigrade rise of temperature; a layer or mass of warm air will thus be a region of refraction, with consequent loss of energy to sound waves passing through it. Since, in nature, such temperature layers occur near the ground, this effect will seriously interfere with the propagation of sounds produced near the ground, as are the songs of many insects. Wind also interferes with the propagation of sound waves, sometimes increasing the range, sometimes diminishing it. All these phenomena interfere with sound waves in air, and result in anomalous propagation. The effect of this is important when considering the behaviour of insects in response to sound and will be discussed later. Brief mention can be made here of the propagation of sound in water; to begin with, the velocity of sound in water is about 4·3 times greater than in air, and consequently the wavelength of a sound of given frequency is 4·3 times as long. The specific acoustic resistance (R) of water at standard temperature and pressure is 147,000 c.g.s units compared with 42 c.g.s units for air; this means that to convey the same power the sound pressure in water would have to be sixty times as great as that in air. On the other hand there is very little dissipation of energy and a sound can travel about 1,400 times as far in water before losing a given fraction of its intensity as can a sound of the same frequency in air. Other advantages of the aqueous medium are its greater homogeneity and, all in all, underwater signalling would seem to offer great advantages over propagation in air.

We must now consider a further attribute of sound—" quality ". It is almost impossible to define " quality " except by saying it is related to the complexity of the vibration which produces the sound in question. In human acoustics it is of great importance, since man's ability to distinguish between complex notes of the same fundamental pitch is due to the difference in quality between them. When this matter is investigated further it is found that quality depends upon the frequency relationships in the complex sound. It very rarely happens that a sounding body produces a pure tone, and most natural sounds, including speech, are complex, that is, they are made up of a mixture of different frequencies. In most cases one frequency, the fundamental, or note of the lowest pitch, is present in the highest intensity, and other notes, called harmonics or overtones, are superimposed on this but with lower intensities. Often these overtones are simply related in frequency to the fundamental note (see Fig. 2) as has already been explained previously. Vertebrate hearing organs have the ability, by reason of their functioning as frequency discriminators, to recognize the two original vibrations of the compound wave when this latter falls upon the ear; this is not true of most insect hearing organs, which do not have this ability of frequency discrimination. Generally, when the several frequencies present in a complex sound bear a simple mathematical relationship to one another the sound may be characterized as "musical", but if very many frequencies are present, or if the mathematical relationship of frequencies is complex, the sound is said to be a "noise". The range of frequencies covered by the various components of a complex sound is called the "frequency spectrum" of the sound. The simpler the sound, the simpler the frequency spectrum and vice-versa; the limiting cases are of course a pure tone, which has one frequency in its spectrum, and "pure noise" which has theoretically an infinitely wide frequency spectrum.

Two further phenomena connected with the structure of complex sounds may be conveniently mentioned here, both being concerned in insect sound production; these are the phenomena of "beat" and "combination" tones. If two notes near to one another in frequency are sounded together their vibrations necessarily coincide at regular intervals and a periodical increase in intensity is thus produced, called a "beat". When the rate of production of the beat is low, then it is only perceived by human ears as a change in intensity, but if the rate of occurrence of the beats exceeds about 20-30 a second, then a low bass note may be heard over and above the original two notes. The phenomenon is said to occur in the sound production of certain mosquitoes and, as will be seen, may play an important role in their behaviour. The phenomenon of combination tones is somewhat similar; if two notes of different frequency are sounded loudly together, they give rise to a further two sounds. One of these is called the "difference tone" and is a note whose frequency is that of the difference between the two original frequencies, and the other the "summation tone", whose frequency is the sum of the original frequencies. Thus two sounds of say, 1,000 c/s and 1,500 c/s, if sounded together, would produce a "difference tone" of 500 c/s and a "summation tone" of 2,500 c/s. This latter is generally of low intensity and may not be perceived above the other three sounds; also, if the original frequencies are high, for example, 7 and 10 kc/s, the resultant summation tone of 17 kc/s is ultra-sonic for most human ears.

It will be appreciated from the above that knowledge of the frequency spectrum, intensity and waveform of a sound are essential to an understanding of its structure, and that any attempt at the classification and comparison of a series of sounds without knowledge of these qualities is impossible. This was the difficulty of the early workers on the sounds of insects; it was recognized that a knowledge of these qualities was desirable, but the data could not be obtained as the necessary techniques were not then available. Thus early biologists fell back on such methods as comparison with musical scales, using their own ears as detectors and frequency resolvers. Even some modern workers have attempted to categorize insect sounds with the aid of graphic symbols of their own invention. The difficulties and drawbacks of such systems are obvious: firstly, they depend on the human ear as a receptor and analyser, and as we have seen this has markedly different characteristics from insect hearing organs; secondly they do not take into account sound emission in the ultra-sonic range; and thirdly they cannot give in an easily assimilable form the complex data on waveform, frequency spectrum and intensity which are essential to any real knowledge of the sounds.

In short, the only answer to the problem is to submit the sounds to physical instrumental analysis, and describe them in terms of the parameters obtained during analysis. Even this process, however, is much more difficult than it sounds, not so much from the point of view of carrying out the analysis but of describing the sound accurately from the results. The fact is that the existing terminology of acoustics is really insufficient to cope with the task and a new and agreed one has not yet been decided upon by biologists. An attempt was made at the 1954 Paris Conference on the acoustics of Orthoptera to introduce such a terminology, but this has not been taken up by the majority of workers. It is really too early in the history of the subject to make such an attempt, and there is at present insufficient comparative data on sound production from the various insect orders on which to base such a terminology. There remains the practical problem of describing insect sounds in words when writing such a book as this or in scientific papers; for present purposes the problem has been tackled on an empirical basis, and there now follows an explanation of the derivation of various terms.

The waveform of a pure tone can be represented graphically and also appear on an oscilloscope screen in the form shown in Fig. 3A. By counting the number of complete waves occurring between the time markers, and converting this to "waves per second ", one obtains the frequency of the note; in the example it is 2 kc/s. Note that the amplitude of the wave is constant; it is possible, however, for the amplitude to vary, and if this happens periodically we get a waveform as shown in Fig. 3B. Notice that the frequency of the fundamental or "carrier" wave, as it is called, has not altered—it is still 2 kc/s. By counting the regular variations in amplitude of the carrier wave in the given time interval, we see it

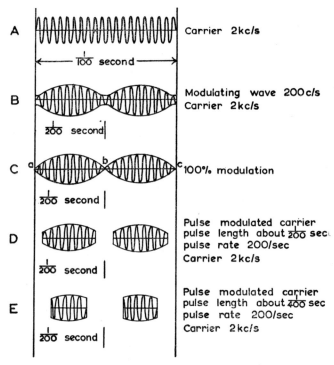

FIG. 3. Graphical representation of certain modulation patterns; for explanation see text.

is undergoing changes at a rate of 200 cycles per second. This figure is called the "modulation frequency" of the carrier wave. If now we increase the amplitude of the modulation itself, we get the picture of Fig. 3C; here the carrier is still 2 kc/s and again has a modulation frequency of 200 kc/s but the effect of modulation now is to reduce the carrier wave to zero at points a, b and c. When this happens the carrier is said to be 100% modulated; the carrier wave has been cut into sections, as it were, but each section starts exactly as the preceding one terminates. Imagine now that the beginning and end of each section is cut off, as in Fig. 3D; we have left sections of the 2 kc/s carrier, with gaps between them, but the sections still recur at the rate of 200 per second. This 2 kc/s waveform is now said to be "pulse modulated" at 200 c/s, and each wave train is referred to as a "pulse". Pulse modulation normally implies that the amplitude of the carrier does not change between pulses, but in insect song this is not always so, as will later become apparent. Notice that the specification "2 kc/s pulse modulated at 200 c/s" gives us no information as to the relative width of the pulses. In Fig. 3D they are not quite 1/200 second in duration, but if we reduce them to 1/400 second we still have the 2 kc/s pulse modulated at 200 c/s but each individual pulse is of course much shorter (Fig. 3E).

So far we have been describing this modulated carrier wave as a pure tone cut into pulses, and some insect songs are of this type, notably the songs of certain crickets. Fig. 77 is an example of this; it is one of the songs of the cricket *Oecanthus pellucens* and, as will be seen, consists of a carrier frequency of about 2·5 kc/s cut into pulses which recur at a rate of approximately 30 per second. The duration of these pulses is fairly constant and can be measured, as can the interval between them; this song could then be characterized as a carrier wave of 2·5 kc/s, pulse modulated at a frequency of 30 c/s, with pulse duration about 25 milliseconds and pulse interval about 16 milliseconds. The rate of occurrence of the pulses is known as the pulse repetition frequency, or "P.R.F." for short. However, most insect songs do not lend themselves so easily to this terminology. For one thing, the carrier wave is hardly ever a pure tone—even in the cricket example above, the note has harmonics in it—but is generally a very complex sound, containing many frequences, sometimes sonic, sometimes ultra-sonic or a mixture of both; any description of such a sound would have to include the frequency spectrum of the sound waves constituting the pulses.

Another important aspect of the problem is that the sound as heard by human ears may give no corroborative evidence as to what the oscillogram will look like, or to what an insect would hear. For example, Fig. 85 (facing p. 121) is an oscillogram of one song of the male of the bug *Sehirus bicolor*; it can be seen to consist of a number of sound pulses repeated with a regular pattern. Clearly the pulses are grouped into fours, and each group of four is repeated once every 1·4 seconds. Now, when this song is heard by the human ear, each of these multiple pulses is heard as one burst of sound every 1·4 seconds—the ear is incapable of responding to the separate pulses making up the group, because the time constant for the ear is longer than the interval between pulses. Thus as regards the ear, it is correct to call each assemblage of four sounds a "pulse"; but certain insect hearing organs are capable of resolving this pulse into the four constituents, and from this standpoint we ought to refer to the sounds as "a train of pulses" or some such term. In other songs of *Sehirus* the pulses are repeated more rapidly and to the human ear the song represented by Fig. 85c sounds like a continuous buzz. Logically, therefore, we ought to erect names for these various assemblages of pulses, but for reasons given above such an attempt may be regarded as premature. We shall therefore use the term "pulse" to indicate any sound or any connected series of sounds which clearly form the basic rhythmic unit in time of an insect song. Where such usage would be confusing, more detailed descriptions appropriate to the case will be given.

This description of the difficulties attendant on describing insect sounds—a necessary step before classifying them—should have re-emphasized that reliance on the human ear as an analysing instrument is useless. For reasonably accurate description, recourse must be had to the parameters obtained by instrumental analysis. But a practical difficulty in this respect at once emerges; it is in many cases difficult and in some impossible to carry out such an analysis unless the sound be permanently recorded in some form or other, so that the same sound, or part of it, can be examined by different instruments to measure all its qualities. It is for this reason that the recent developments of biological acoustics have gone hand in hand with the perfecting over the last ten years of simple portable recording devices of high fidelity. It is not too much to say that without the modern disc recorder, and, more particularly, the development of magnetic tape recording, very little progress could have been made in research on animal sounds. The development of recording apparatus has been accompanied by a similar development in analysing equipment, and nowadays it is comparatively simple to measure accurately most of the important features of a sound. These same measurements can also now be made, although with greater difficulty, on sounds of ultra-sonic frequency. To conclude this introductory chapter, we shall review the apparatus and methods commonly used to record and analyse insect sounds.

There are three practical systems of recording sound, mechanographic, photographic, and magnetic. Photographic sound recording is now virtually restricted to provision of sound track for films; of the other two methods mechanographic methods are still widely used, but magnetic recording has undergone great development during the last five years. Both systems have advantages and disadvantages, which depend in turn on the use to which the apparatus is to be put. From the point of view of recording insect sounds, both in the laboratory and the field, the magnetic tape recorder has very definite advantages over the disc machine, and it is probably true to say that at least 95% of all biological sound recordings are made on tape. The portability of the equipment, the fact that no processing is needed to produce a permanent recording, the economical use of the medium, all combine to make the tape recorder the instrument of choice.

There is no space in this book, even were it desirable, to contrast the merits and demerits of the various tape recorders now available in relation to the problem of recording the sounds of insects; but it may perhaps be useful to indicate some of the desirable qualities of a recorder in connection with this work in order to illustrate some of the attendant difficulties. At once we come up against the fact that the design theory of all present forms of recording and reproduction apparatus are related to human speech and hearing; for example, commercial magnetic recorders have amplifiers with the recording circuits adjusted for high-frequency correction. These correction circuits are based in theory on the average energy distribution of speech and music, and they produce higher amplification at high frequencies (say 7-8 kc/s upwards) than at low frequencies; when such a recording is played back, other correction circuits in the playback amplifiers "equalize" this initial correction. Since the average energy distribution of most biological sounds is not known, it is possible that serious distortion of some frequencies could be introduced by the correction circuits of the recording amplifier, and this fact must be remembered when using machines of this type for research.

The frequency response of the recorder should be as wide as possible, consistent with a reasonable tape speed. In general the higher the tape speed, the higher the upper frequency that can be recorded, but speeds above 15 inches per second are to be avoided

c

owing to the fact that the mechanical drive of the tape then needs to be of the highest quality, and the quantity of tape used becomes both uneconomical and difficult to handle. It is possible with careful design and good tape to obtain frequency responses of the order of 50 c/s to 20 kc/s at tape speeds of 15 inches per second, and this range is suitable for most purposes. In general, a range of 50 c/s to about 10 kc/s is adequate and this can be obtained with the economical tape speed of 7½ inches per second. The apparatus should have some arrangement whereby the operator can monitor the recording while it is in progress; some form of footage indicator for the tape is also very useful, since this enables the precise point on a tape where one recording ends and another begins to be noted, and this makes for economy of tape and also ease of replay and editing.

Turning to the amplifier of the apparatus, it is desirable that this should have a high gain, accurately controllable, and also a recording level indicator, which should be a meter and not a "magic-eye" indicator. The value of the H.F. bias applied to the tape should be variable, and it is an advantage if this can be read on the record level meter by appropriate switching, because is is then possible to adjust the bias for the particular type of tape being used. The amplifier should be able to work from low impedance microphones, as this arrangement allows the use of comparatively long microphone leads without excessive hum pick-up, an arrangement very useful for field recording. However, an alternative high impedance input is desirable to allow the use of a crystal microphone when maximum gain is necessary for recording sounds of low intensity.

The microphone is a most important link in the recording chain. but there is no space here to do more than mention some of the important points about the various types. With commercial recorders four types of microphone are used, crystal, moving coil, condenser and ribbon. The crystal microphone is the most sensitive, has reasonable frequency coverage and is omnidirectional, but it is rather fragile and needs a high impedance amplifier input with consequent danger of picking up hum and unwanted noise. The moving coil type is more robust, is omnidirectional, has a fair frequency coverage and has the advantage of having a low impedance and can be used with long field leads. It is probably the most widely used type for general purposes. Condenser microphones are now coming into prominence because of their wide frequency range, but again they are rather fragile and are high impedance instruments liable to interference. These three instruments are all pressure receivers, while the fourth type, the ribbon microphone, is a displacement receiver and consequently is very directional in use, with maximum pick-up when its diaphragm is perpendicular to the plane of the incident sound waves. It is rather fragile, but of low impedance and can sometimes be used to advantage for its directional properties in "picking-out" the wanted sound source from other adjacent sources. For field use, all these microphones can be mounted at the focus of a metal parabolic reflector to increase their range and directional effect; this method has been used a great deal in the recording of bird songs and is valuable in certain field situations when close approach to the animals is impossible or undesirable. A special problem is posed by the recording of the songs of aquatic insects. This interesting aspect of the subject has as yet hardly been tackled except for preliminary experiments in which the sounds of Corixids and Micronectids were recorded. Underwater microphones are available but are bulky and expensive; substitutes can be made however by placing a crystal microphone insert in a small glass tube, which is then filled with a light oil and the whole made watertight. Although unsatisfactory in several ways, such an improvised device enables the calls of the louder underwater stridulators to be recorded.

In addition to the amplifier of the tape recorder, it is sometimes advantageous and often necessary to have a pre-amplifier available; since the use of such an additional amplifier implies that more sensitivity is required, the amplifier should have a high impedance input suitable for a crystal microphone, the most sensitive general purpose type. With such a microphone and amplifier attached to the main amplifier of the tape recorder it should be possible to record in good conditions all but the feeblest of insect noises. Such pre-amplifiers can be made completely self contained and battery driven, and can be arranged to have a low impedance cathode follower output stage, which enables them to be carried about in the field and connected to the amplifier in the recorder with a long cable; the resulting flexibility is valuable for field work.

All the above apparatus is related to the recording of sounds in the audio frequency range, and for recording in the ultra-sonic range special instruments are required. The first essential is an adequate microphone; condenser microphones of a special type are used, and these can be obtained with a response up to the region of 100 kc/s, although at such frequencies the sound pressure required for operation is rather high. Amplification at such frequencies presents no problems, but the difficulty arises in the actual recorder. Here, by special design of the recording heads and by using a fast tape speed, recording up to about 150 kc/s can also be obtained; naturally, owing to the high degree of mechanical refinement required such recorders are much larger and more expensive than normal recorders and are suitable only for the laboratory. By the use of a frequency converter, however, a recorder of normal range can be used to record ultra-sonic noises within certain frequency ranges. In such an arrangement, the ultra-sonic signal after amplification is fed into a converter unit which changes it into a signal of audio frequency. Since all the ultra-sonic frequencies are altered in the same manner and to the same degree, the resultant recorded signal has all the characteristics of the original wave and as the transposition factor is known the facies of the original sound can be calculated. Such a device was used by Pierce (1949) in his pioneer work in the physical analysis of insect sounds.

The foregoing necessarily brief review of apparatus used in recording insect sounds must be qualified by some observations on certain practical difficulties. One of these is the recording of the sounds made by very small insects, such as some of the Heteroptera. The bug *Kleidocerys*, for example, makes a noise just audible to the human ear about 6 inches away; to record this satisfactorily without high background noise really requires a sound-proof room, a facility available to very few biologists. Any alternative device used must enable the insect to be kept at a reasonable temperature and light intensity, within view of the observer and constructed so as to allow the latter easy access to the insect. Haskell (1958) overcame the problem of recording *Kleidocerys* by constructing a small glass cage, about 2 inches cube, one side of which was closed by the microphone. The insects were inserted through a small hole, and could be watched through a binocular microscope and listened to on headphones. Although successful recordings were made, some frequency distortion of the sound was inevitable owing to reflection of sound within the enclosure, and many recordings were spoilt by pick-up of the sound of the insect walking. Such faults have some-times to be accepted in order to get recording at all, and as long as the nature of the distortion or deficiency is known the value of the recording for various purposes can be assessed. This example is quoted to emphasize the fact that in nearly all cases of the recording of animal sounds some compromise which departs from the ideal conditions must almost inevitably be adopted in order to get records at all. It is likely, as has been said above, that only a few workers will be equipped with a sound-proof room, and most will have to use their laboratory as it stands. Here the presence of reflections and echoes will at once complicate the situation. In the field, these unpleasant factors are generally absent, but instead one is plagued with background noises due to other animals, biotic disturbance ranging from cars to aircraft and, worst of all, noises due to wind. Again, the frequency of the noises to be recorded ought to be considered, and ideally for sounds in the very high sonic or ultra-sonic range the microphone should not be nearer to the source than about a yard, but if the sensitivity of the apparatus is low or conditions are poor the microphone must be placed as near to the source as possible. On the other hand, if the sounds to be recorded are of frequencies lower than about 500 c/s, then the microphone ought not to be placed too close because of wave disturbance near the source. Such difficulties could be multiplied endlessly, and the only solution is to get the best recording possible and to note very carefully all the conditions prevailing at the time, so that the probable nature and extent of any distortion can be estimated. Frequency distortion is the most common result of a compromise with ideal conditions, but it will become apparent later that for many purposes this is not a serious fault in recording of insect sounds.

There is another type of error connected with recording which must be mentioned here, because its effects are generally far more serious than those resulting from any deficiency of the apparatus, and furthermore it is an error completely dependent on the experimenter. This is that recordings, whether made in the laboratory or the field, are virtually valueless unless all data relating to them are noted, preferably on the tape, at the moment of recording. This data must include not only technical details of the apparatus, but also all the biological data as well. It cannot be too strongly emphasized that a recording apparently perfect in technical detail may be rendered valueless because data relating to the biological situation were not noted as well.

We must now turn to the question of the analysis of insect sounds, either directly as they are emitted or from previously recorded material. Three instruments are generally required to make a physical analysis of sound; these are a cathode-ray oscilloscope, a sound spectrometer and a sound level meter, or decibelmeter as it is sometimes called. It is advantageous if the oscilloscope is of the double beam type, since this facilitates the direct measurement both of the temporal arrangement and the frequency of the material to be analysed. This instrument can be used to determine the wave-form of the sound and in some cases the principal frequency or frequencies. If the sound consists of repeated pulses, the length of these pulses and the intervals between them can be measured. For example, Fig. 80 shows part of an oscillographic record of a grass-hopper song, which consists of a series of rapidly repeated pulses. By counting the number of pulses which occur in relation to a known number of time markers—in this case at $1/_{10}$ second intervals —the pulse rate and other factors can be measured with fair accuracy. By changing the speed of the oscillogram, measurements can be made of the temporal relations between the parts of a whole sequence of sounds which may last several minutes, and also of the details of variation in a single pulse lasting only a few milliseconds.

Most insect sounds are complex, made up of many frequencies, each with a different energy content. It is important to know the range of component frequencies—the frequency spectrum—of a sound, and this measurement can be made with a sound spectro-meter. There are two main types of spectrometer of use in connec-tion with insect sounds; one, the octave band analyser, gives a picture of the component frequencies of a sound and their relative energy over a short interval of time. The second type, the " Sona-graph " or " Vibralyzer " type of instrument, gives a picture of the change of frequency spectrum and related energy levels over a comparatively long period of time. The first type of spectrometer can be used with direct emission from the insect, or with recorded material. The instrument consists of a range of electrical filters corresponding to a number of set frequencies which cover in octaves the whole frequency range from 0-100 kc/s; when the signal is passed in, outputs will only be obtained from those filters which correspond to frequencies present in the sound, and this output is used to displace a spot on a cathode ray screen. The displacement of the spots is recorded photographi-cally and is arranged to be proportional to the energy of that frequency in the original sound; the greater the displacement the greater the energy. A series of typical records is seen in Fig. 79, together with the frequencies of the bands covered. An alternative form of this instrument is the heterodyne analyser; although the intermediate operations are different to the preceding apparatus the resultant data is displayed in a similar fashion as can be seen in Figs. 76 and 77. The drawback to both of these instruments is that they only indicate the frequencies present in the sound at a given moment and they do not show the change of frequency spectrum with time. Such information can be obtained from them by the costly and laborious process of photographing the cathode ray screen with a ciné camera while the whole sound sequence under investigation is passed through, and analysing the results frame by frame, but if this type of information is required, it is much easier to use the second type of spectrometer mentioned above. This machine, which is electro-mechanical in operation, automatically graphs the variation in frequency spectrum with time and also gives incidental information on the range of intensity fluctuations, but it suffers from the disadvantage that it can only make this analysis for a sound signal lasting about $2\frac{1}{2}$ seconds or less. Signals lasting longer than this must be analysed in short pieces and the results synthesized; because many insect sounds are comparatively long, this instrument has not been much used for their analysis, but for some investigations is capable of giving useful information. Fig. 84 shows an analysis of the songs of six species of cricket carried out with such apparatus.

The third piece of apparatus used in the physical analysis of sound is the sound-level meter, which measures sound pressure. As mentioned above, knowledge of sound pressure leads to the calculation of sound intensity. These instruments consist of a microphone and amplifier driving a meter; the instrument is calibrated in an anechoic chamber with sounds of known frequency and pressure. Most meters are graduated direct in decibels above the standard reference level where 0 db corresponds to a sound pressure of 0·0002 dynes/cm². Owing to valve noise and other difficulties, it is impossible to make a decibelmeter which reads down to 0 db, and generally the scale starts at something like 30 db above the threshold of hearing, and variable attenuators allow adjustment of the meter for louder noises. Meters can be obtained for measuring noise levels in both the sonic and ultra-sonic ranges. There is one important point about the use of some of these instruments constructed for the sonic range. For certain acoustic uses it is desirable that the frequency response curve of the apparatus should approximate to that of the human ear, and many meters are constructed with such characteristics; but for the analysis of the intensities of insect sounds it is desirable that the frequency response curve should be flat, and in the better type of meter a control is generally provided for this adjustment. It is essential, as pointed out before, when making sound intensity observations to measure the distance from the sound source to the microphone of the lever meter, since this is part of the required data. Measurement of sound intensities must always be made from natural material, since even if with recorded material the amplification or attenuation introduced by the apparatus is accurately known, the effect of extra noise and distortion produced by the act of playback cannot easily be overcome. The effects of various environmental noises are hard to overcome when recording in the field, and for this reason great accuracy can never be expected from sound level measurements. However, as will be seen the measurements are of value in arriving at the order of magnitude of the sound levels of various insect noises, and enable us to form some sort of picture of the sensitivity of insect hearing organs and the range of acoustic communication possible between certain insects in given environments.

It will be made clear in the following chapter that although the mechanical structure of the sound-producing apparatus of an insect may be known, it can be difficult to decide by deduction or direct observation exactly how it works. In such cases it is sometimes of value to employ a further technique, that of high speed cinematography with synchronized sound recording. It is then often possible by viewing slow motion pictures of the apparatus in action and listening to the recorded song to decide exactly how the sound is produced. The analysing instruments described above can be used with sounds of any frequency in the sonic or ultra-sonic range, and the information they supply about the physical structure of a sound is generally sufficient for it to be characterized for the purposes of biological acoustics.

Finally, the reproduction of recorded sounds must be considered, since the playing back of sounds to insects under various conditions has become an essential tool in work on acoustic behaviour. In this connection the tape recorder again offers great advantages over the disc machine in that it is also capable of playing back the recorded signal directly without intermediate processing. However, the reproductive fidelity of recorders is limited by several factors, the most serious of which is the loudspeaker. For reasons of space, if for no other consideration, the loudspeakers generally fitted in tape recorders are small permanent magnet instruments that can at best reproduce unequally across a frequency range of 100 c/s to 8 kc/s. While this is not a serious disadvantage in certain types of work it is no use as regards ultra-sonic experiments. This situation has recently been changed by the invention by Klein (1952), and subsequent production, of a new type of loudspeaker called the Ionophone. This instrument has no moving parts and sound waves are generated by the electrical propulsion of a small mass of air particles which is ionized by an electrical discharge. This speaker has the advantage of being aperiodic over a frequency range which covers both the sonic and ultra-sonic bands; it has the disadvantage that although small in itself it requires rather bulky ancillary equipment, but it has already been used to advantage in acoustic research on insects, notably on the continent. A further important point regarding loudspeakers used for playing sounds to insects is their size and container. Insect hearing organs, as will be seen, are displacement receivers and can orient accurately only on sources of sound which are comparatively small relative to the receptor organ. Large loudspeakers, or loudspeakers fitted with cones or baffles, often present effectively such a large sound source that the insect cannot orient to them; sometimes this can be got over by using a head-phone as the reproducer, despite the increase in distortion which this causes.

As far as the generation of artificial signals for acoustic stimulation is concerned, these present little difficulty; accurate beat-frequency oscillators and pulse generators now commercially available allow pure or interrupted tones, trains of pulses and other combinations to be used, but here again the limiting factor is always the ultimate reproducer, which, if an ordinary electro-magnetic loudspeaker, can introduce distortion. This can be detected and assessed by monitoring the signals, and such a precaution should always be taken in acoustic work.

REFERENCES

HASKELL, P. T. (1958) *Proc. zool. Soc. Lond.* **129**: 351-358.
KLEIN, S. (1952) *Bull. Soc. Radioélectr.* **32**: 314-320.
PIERCE, G. (1949) *The songs of insects.* Harvard Univ. Press, U.S.A.
PUMPHREY, R. J. (1940) *Biol. Rev.* **15**: 107-132.

CHAPTER II

SOUND-PRODUCING MECHANISMS IN INSECTS

I t is a task beyond the scope of the present volume to attempt a complete classification and description of all the methods of sound production known at present to exist amongst the insects. It would seem more profitable to erect a general classification of methods of sound production and to illustrate the various categories with a number of examples drawn from all orders of insects. The classification adopted is as follows:

1. Sounds produced as a by-product of some usual activity of the insect.
2. Sounds produced by impact of part of the body against the substrate.
3. Sounds produced by special mechanisms:
   (*a*) Frictional mechanisms.
   (*b*) Vibrating membrane mechanisms.
   (*c*) Mechanisms directly involving air movement.

Each of these categories will now be considered separately.

Before so doing however a point of terminology must be cleared up relating to the verb "to stridulate". The Oxford Dictionary definition of this verb is "make a shrill jarring sound by rubbing together of hard parts of body (cicadas, grasshoppers etc.)". This definition is, as it stands, incorrect. While many frictional mechanisms certainly make "shrill jarring" noises quite a number produce pleasant bell-like sounds; on the other hand, mechanisms other than frictional ones produce the type of sound definitively associated with the latter. Cicadas do not produce their sounds by a frictional method. The present usage restricts the employment of widely useful terms and it is suggested that the simplest way of avoiding these abuses is to define "stridulation" as "any sound produced by an insect"; hence such a term as "stridulatory mechanism" simply means "an insect sound producing mechanism". It is in the above sense that "stridulation" and its derivatives are used in the remainder of this book.

SOUNDS PRODUCED AS A BY-PRODUCT OF SOME USUAL ACTIVITY OF THE INSECT

It is quite obvious that in many insects the production of sound is an accidental phenomenon attendant on the carrying on of some usual activity; the most familiar examples of this are the sounds produced by insects in flight, such as the drone of bees and the whine of mosquitoes. Noises are also produced by feeding or cleaning reactions, but these may fairly be regarded as adventitious, and will not be further discussed, but evidence exists of the importance of flight noise in the life of several species of insects. The oscillatory movement of the wings of an insect sets up regions of compression and rarefaction as do the prongs of a tuning fork, and a sound is produced. The frequency of the sound will depend mainly upon the rapidity of the oscillations, and, as far as the human observer is concerned, the audibility will depend both on the frequency and on the intensity. The flight of insects has long excited the curiosity of the entomologist, and the investigation of wing-beat frequency has figured in much of the research. Interest has been focused on aerodynamic problems and little attention has been paid to the sound produced by flapping flight. It was soon realized, however, that the frequency of the resultant sound bears a direct relationship to the rapidity of wing movement, and early workers such as Landois (1867) attempted to evaluate the frequency of the flight noise of certain insects by aural comparison with frequency sources such as tuning forks. Advances in recording techniques have now made it possible to record and analyse flight noises with considerable accuracy, and from such analyses estimates of the wing-beat frequency can be made. It seems probable that in many insects the beating of the wings is not the only source of sound, since the whole thorax is intimately concerned with wing movement and vibrates during flight, and some workers have considered that this thoracic vibration is responsible for much of the sound energy produced. Thus the sound of the blow-fly *Calliphora* is said to be due to vibrations of the thorax caused by the friction of the wing bases against it, and the "piping" noises emitted by queen honey bees is believed by some biologists to be a result of the vibration of the thoracic sclerites.

The general range of wing frequencies in insects is between 4 beats a second to upwards of 1,100 beats a second, but certainly the acoustic output will contain higher harmonics of these frequencies produced by vibration and resonance in the wings and the thorax. Roeder and Treat (1957) recently showed that the flight noise of the moth *Prodenia eridania* includes noises of very high frequency although the wing-beat frequency is only about 40-50 per second. The noise produced during flight by grasshoppers of the group Oedipodinae is well known, but almost certainly a special mechanism is involved, which is discussed below. Wing collisions are probably the cause of the crackling noise emitted during flight by the locust *Disossteira*, which Pierce (1949) recorded; he was unable to decide on the mechanism, but thought the wings might hit the body. Haskell (1957) has recorded and analysed sounds made during flight by the desert locust, *Schistocerca gregaria*; during level flight the wing noise is very low, but under certain conditions flying locusts emit a clattering noise, said to be due to the hind wings hitting the hind legs. Several other locusts and grasshoppers emit noises during flight, but the mechanisms have only been guessed at; noises produced by certain moths and flies while in flight are due to special mechanisms and will be discussed in the relevant section.

A good deal of attention has been paid to the flight noise of mosquitoes, both because of their economic importance and also because it has been shown that this noise is a factor in mating behaviour. Kahn and Offenhauser (1949) recorded the wing noises of several species of mosquito and concluded that while they contain a well-defined fundamental frequency, ranging from 300 c/s in *Aedes flavicollis* to about 500 c/s in *Aedes aegypti*, overtones of higher frequency occur. Some mosquito sounds also show a beat effect, the rate being from 2-15 c/s, and Kahn and Offenhauser suggest that this may be due to the simultaneous emission of two sounds which form beats; there is no evidence as yet on the possible source of such sounds.

It will be clear from these few examples that a variety of insects produce special flight noises, but in no case has the mechanism responsible been clearly defined or described. This is clearly partly due to the difficulties of observing insects in flight, but the technique of high speed cinematography might produce some interesting data. Although, as will be seen in a later chapter, information is available on the structure of the sounds produced by some of these mechanisms, this throws but little light on the apparatus itself.

SOUNDS PRODUCED BY IMPACT OF PART OF THE BODY AGAINST THE SUBSTRATE

It can be imagined that many of the normal activities of insects will produce noises by the accidental impact of parts of the body against the substrate, but there are several insects which use this method to produce sustained sounds, which in some cases appear to be of significance in behaviour. The best known of these tapping insects are probably the furniture beetles *Anobium* and *Xestobium*, the so-called "death watch" beetle. The larvae of these insects bore into wood and live in a system of tunnels; the tapping noise is made only by adult beetles, and is thought by some workers to be a sexual call. The sound is heard most during April and May when mating occurs. The beetle jerks its whole body forward while in its tunnel, at the same time bending the head down, and so strikes the substrate with the lower part of the front of the head. There appears to be no special thickening of the head or any projections with which the beetle taps the wood. Tapping of the substrate with some part of the head, which again has no specialized organ, occurs in several species of termite; in colonies of *Leucotermes tenuis* numbers of individuals may hammer the ground in unison at a rate of about ten times a second, producing a faint drumming noise. Several species of ant are said to tap the substrate with their heads, the tapping being synchronous throughout the colony; this behaviour is discussed in Chapter 5. Another group of insects which produce sounds by tapping the substrate are the Psocoptera or Book lice. These primitive insects, which have some affinities with the termites, are best known from those species which are found in collections of books and papers; one of the commonest species is *Liposcelis*, and it has long been thought capable of producing a loud ticking sound, and has even been referred to as another "death watch" insect. However, only a few species of Psocids have so far been shown to produce audible sounds, including *Clothilla pulsatoria* and *Lepinotus inquilinus*. In *Clothilla* the sound is said to be produced by the insect tapping the substrate with a small knob near the apex of the ventral side of the abdomen. Sound production appears to be confined to the female and may be a mating call. Certain other Psocids are said to have frictional stridulatory organs, and these will be described below.

Amongst the Orthoptera, several species are recorded as producing noises by impact. Some of the Oedipodinae, for instance, are said to produce sounds by striking the ground with their tarsi, and Pierce (1949) has recorded the sound produced in this way by *Encoptolophus sordidus*. Sounds produced by striking the ground with the tip of the abdomen are said to occur in the Acridid *Aiolopus strepens* and in the Tettigoniid *Meconema thalassinum*, but recent work on the latter species is now thought to indicate that the sound is produced by the rapid drumming of one hind leg on the ground. In the Plecoptera, or Stoneflies, a drumming noise is produced apparently by tapping the end of the abdomen against the substrate. At the tip of the abdomen on the underside of the prolonged ninth sternite is found a small disc or hammer (Macnamara, 1926) with which the noise is presumably made; this apparatus occurs in at least five genera. Certain Tenebrionid beetles also produce sounds by drumming on the ground with the tip of the abdomen. Federley (1905) has described the production of sound by the larvae of the moths *Drepana curvatula* and *Drepana lacertinaria*, the caterpillars simply rubbing their anal segments against the leaf surface on which they are situated. There are two small chitinous hooks on these segments, said to be the rudiments of vanished anal legs, which produce the scraping noise. Larval stridulation has also been observed in Hymenoptera in *Vespa crabro*, the Hornet; Gontarski (1941) described how a scratching noise is produced by the larvae dragging their mouthparts along the papery walls of their cell.

SOUNDS PRODUCED BY SPECIAL MECHANISMS

(a) Frictional mechanisms

This category embraces a great diversity of types scattered all through the Insecta. In general, all these mechanisms are of similar construction and consist of two main parts; these are a surface bearing a series of ridges or projections, commonly called the " file ", and a hard ridge or knob called the " scraper ". The insect in its stridulation draws the scraper across the file, each tooth or ridge of the latter receiving an impact which throws the body surface into vibration, thus producing a sound. Such impact sounds almost always contain many frequencies with complex harmonics, and in some mechanisms the frequencies emitted will also depend on the speed with which the scraper is drawn across the file. The resonant frequency of the vibrating surface will also affect the frequency, especially when, as for example in most Orthoptera, it is an elytron or wing which is concerned. In insects, moreover, with their hard exoskeleton, a certain amount of vibrational energy will be transmitted to large resonant surfaces and thence radiated to the air even when the site of the actual frictional mechanism is apparently remote and localized, as for example in insects where sound is produced by the rubbing together of the antennae. The operation of these mechanisms may, through th*e* phenomenon of resonance, produce complex modulated sounds. When a scraper is drawn over a file which is situated on a surface such as a wing which has a very high resonant frequency, the principal frequency emitted will be the resonant frequency of this surface; in some Orthoptera this is an ultra-sonic frequency. This frequency will, moreover, tend to be modulated at a lower frequency, the value of which is determined by various factors such as the rate at which each individual tooth on the file is struck by the scraper. Analyses of such modulated sounds produced by these mechanisms and a more detailed description of the functioning of the apparatus will be found in a subsequent chapter.

The actual range of frictional stridulatory mechanisms is enormous. "By far the greatest number and variety of sounds emitted by insects are produced by this method," says Imms, and continues, "practically every external part of the body which is subjected to friction on an adjoining part has given rise to a stridulating organ in one or other insect." It is obviously impossible to catalogue all these mechanisms, and there now follows for the principal orders of insects descriptions of the main mechanisms occurring in the group, arranged to give some idea of the range of types.

Orthoptera

The Orthoptera have attracted the attention of entomologists as the principal sound-producing order of insects, and thus it is natural they should be the most documented group. Probably the best general paper on the subject is that of Kevan (1955), which lists 24 different fundamental frictional stridulatory mechanisms in these insects. Several Orthoptera produce sounds by friction of the head appendages, such as the rubbing together of the specialized third segments of the antennae in *Phyllium athanysus* and the mandibles in *Oedaleonotus fuscipes*. Others again use two sets of mouth-parts to produce the noise, such as the maxillo-mandibular stridulation described by Tindale (1928) in *Cylindracheta*. Fig. 4 illustrates this mechanism and shows the file situated on the maxilla and the scraper on the mandible. Mechanisms in which the file and scraper are situated on adjacent body segments are rare; they occur on the thorax in a few Orthoptera, but are probably primitive, and only in the dubious case of *Meconema* has an abdominal apparatus been suggested. As has been said above, it is now thought that the sounds produced by this insect are caused by drumming with one of the legs, the abdomen merely vibrating in sympathy with this movement. Frictional mechanisms exist, however, in which both the thorax and abdomen in conjunction with other parts of the body, such as elytra or legs, produce sounds. A method involving the rubbing of the abdomen by the femora of the hind legs is quite widespread in the Orthoptera, but notably in the Gryllacrididae. In this group the general form of the apparatus is as found in *Ametroides*; the second and third abdominal segments bear rows of tubercles (Fig. 5) while the interior face of the hind femur is roughened with many tubercles and acts as a scraper. The hind legs are moved up and down causing the scraper to rub over the abdominal tubercles and produce a noise. In the Gryllacrididae mechanisms of this sort are found in both sexes and also in the nymphal stages. Organs of this femoral-abdominal type are also found in several families of the Acridoidea. In *Pneumora sp.* the base of the abdomen carries stridulatory crests or ridges (Fig. 6) and these are rubbed by teeth on the inside of the hind femur; this mechanism is only found in the males of the Pneumorids, the females stridulating, it is said, by rubbing their elytra on the underside of the large pronotal shield. A mechanism similar to that of the Pneumorids is found in *Xyronotus aztecus* (*Xyronotidae*) and the Tanaoceridae. The mechanism borne by *Phonogaster cariniventris* (Fig. 7) is unique in having horizontal ridges along the abdomen, but the mode of action of all these types is of course similar.

It is when one considers the sound-producing apparatus involving the use of the elytra, wings and legs, that one appreciates the great variety of mechanisms evolved by the Orthoptera. Amongst these methods are found the two mechanisms which are most widespread in the Orthoptera—the so-called " orthodox " methods of stridulation. These are the elytral method, found in Tettigoniids and Gryllids, and the elytro-femoral methods found amongst the

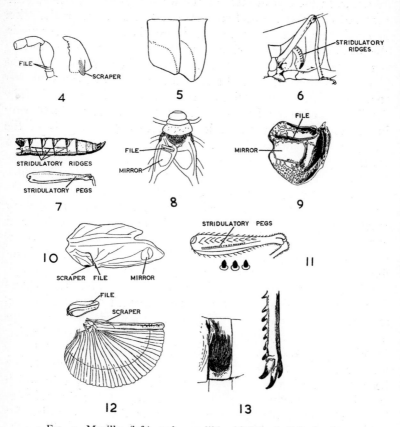

FIG. 4. Maxilla (left) and mandible (right) of *Cylindracheta arenivaga*. (From Kevan (1955) after Tindale (1928).) FIG. 5. Second and third abdominal segments of *Ametroides kibonotensis* showing rows of tubercles. (After Kevan, 1955). FIG. 6. Stridulatory apparatus of male *Pneumora* sp. (After Chopard, 1949). FIG. 7. Abdomen (above) and inner face of hind femur (below) of *Phonogaster cariniventris*. (After Henry, 1940). FIG. 8. Dorsal view of elytral mechanism of *Pterophylla camellifolia*. (After Pierce, 1948). FIG. 9. Underside of left elytron of male *Ephippiger bitterensis*. (After Busnel *et al.*, 1956). FIG. 10. Right elytron of male *Acheta domesticus*. FIG. 11. (above). Inner face of hind femur of grasshopper of tribe Truxalini; (below) enlarged view of some of the stridulatory pegs. FIG. 12. Dorsal view of elytron (above) and hind wing (below) of *Tridactylus thoracicus* male. (After Carpenter, 1936). FIG. 13. Sixth abdominal tergite and distal portion of the hind tibia of *Charora crassinervosa* male.
(After Henry, 1942).

D

Acridids. In the elytral method, the fore-wings or elytra have veins modified to act as file and scraper; one elytron overlaps the other and only one file and scraper come into play. To produce sounds, the insect moves the two elytra laterally across one another forcing the scraper over the file. The vibrations thus produced set the elytra in motion, and it is the resonant frequency of these surfaces that controls the principal frequency of the emitted sounds. The details of the mechanisms and the types of sound produced vary in an important way which is related to the phylogeny of the Tettigonioidea and Grylloidea. The Tettigonioidea comprise two main sub-groups which may be referred to here for convenience as the "winged" and "wingless" forms. In the former the elytra slope obliquely downwards and are generally fragile and membranous, the left usually overlapping the right, the stridulatory mechanism being contained in the cubito-anal area and the hind wings being generally longer than the elytra, although many apterous forms occur and include some of the largest species. Sub-families of this group are the Phaneropterinae, Pseudophyllinae, Copiphorinae, Conocephalinae and Decticinae. They are referred to commonly as "Katydids" because of the presumed onomatopoeic resemblance of the songs of certain species to the words "Katydid, Katy did"; the term is better restricted to the first two sub-families mentioned above. Fig. 8 is a drawing showing the stridulatory mechanism of *Pterophylla camellifolia*. Typically the left elytron bears the "file", a row of ridges on the stridulatory vein which is IA in the Comstock notation. On the edge of the right elytron is a small hard projection, the scraper; another modification for stridulation is found in the appearance of the clear disc-like area, called by some the "mirror". The size and shape of this area is very variable in all the groups; it is thought by some biologists to act as a resonator during sound production, and this suggestion is further discussed in a later chapter. During stridulation, the elytra are pivoted across one another, and the scraper engages the teeth on the stridulatory vein. In this group it seems that only the males sing, the elytra of the female being unmodified.

The second subgroup of the Tettigonioidea comprises the "wingless" forms, and in these the hind wings are absent and the elytra are reduced to sound-producing portions only. Subfamilies in this group include Bradyporinae, Hetrodinae and Ephippigerinae. The elytral morphology is the same as in the winged forms, but they are greatly reduced in size and virtually consist only of the file, scraper and mirror (Fig. 9). The mode of action of the mechanism is the same as in the "winged" group. In the Ephippigers, the pronotum is modified into a shield which protects the elytra; the modifications of the latter occur in males and females and both are able to stridulate. It should be noted that although in the "winged" group typically the elytra are asymmetrical, with the stridulatory vein greatly developed on the left elytron and the scraper and mirror appearing on the right, nevertheless there are several species with more symmetrically developed mechanisms, for example *Conocephalus fasciatus*. This underlines their affinity to the "wingless" group, in which symmetry is much more marked. A symmetrical elytral mechanism is also found in the Grylloidea (see below), and may perhaps be thought of as a primitive mechanism; it is therefore of great interest that Loher (1959) has recently described elytral stridulation in the Acridid *Schistocerca gregaria*, where the elytra are unmodified.

The second main group which produces sound by the elytral method is the Grylloidea; this superfamily is directly related to the Tettigonioidea and the closely similar method of stridulation bears witness to this. In the Gryllidae, or true crickets, the elytra lie flat on the abdomen and are bent over the sides of the latter; usually the right elytron overlaps the left. The stridulatory apparatus appears on both elytra, each of which has a file and scraper, and there is again a part of the wing said to be of special significance as a resonator, the mirror (Fig. 10). The method of stridulation is by rubbing the raised elytra together, as described above. Both males and females of this family possess the stridulatory apparatus, and it is certainly functional in some females, but the significance of this is not known; nymphs also possess the organs, and fourth and fifth instar male nymphs stridulate.

The curious group of the Gryllotalpidae, or Mole Crickets, which live a subterranean life, must also be included here; their elytral stridulatory mechanism is the same as that of the true crickets and operates in a similar manner.

The other large group of Orthoptera which produce sounds by causing the elytra to vibrate is the Acridoidea, or short-horn grasshoppers. Here the most widespread type of frictional stridulatory apparatus is one involving the femora of the hind legs and the elytra. The latter have one of the veins hardened and ridge-shaped, and on the inside of the femur is a ridge or a series of hard pegs. The insect moves the hind femora up and down and rubs the pegs over the veins, causing the elytra to vibrate and producing a harsh noise. This apparatus occurs in the subfamily Acridinae, but there are two variations of the basic morphology which Dirsh (1951) has used to separate two tribes. In the tribe Acridini, the stridulatory apparatus consists of a ridge on the inside of the hind femur and an irregular intercalary vein in the medial area of the tegmen. In the tribe Truxalini the femoral ridge is replaced by a row of stridulatory pegs (Fig. 11), the vena mediastina and vena radialis are ridge-shaped and the mediastinal area expanded. In the Acridinae the mechanism is found most fully developed in the males, and for long the opinion was held that only this sex stridulated. Recent observations refute this notion and show that many females not only possess the apparatus but also use it functionally. In certain grasshoppers, including several common species found in Britain, such as *Stenobothrus lineatus* and *Chorthippus brunneus*, the occurrence of female stridulation is of importance in mating behaviour. The later instars of many Acridinae are equipped with rudimentary apparatus, and various authors have reported hearing third and fourth instar nymphs stridulate, but whether this is of significance in their behaviour is not known.

Amongst the three main groups of Tettigonioidea, Grylloidea and Acridoidea there exist a number of other stridulatory mechanisms using elytra and hind wings. The elytra are rubbed against the pronotum in certain Pneumoridae, and in some Acrididae (e.g. *Romalea microptera*) sounds are made by scraping the elytra against the hind wings. In the Tridactylidae, the small elytra bear files and rub over scrapers on the hind wings (Fig. 12). The hind wings alone are also used as sound producers, and in this connection probably the best documented case is that of the Oedipodinae, which stridulate in flight. There is still controversy over the exact mechanism employed, but many workers, for example Uvarov (1928) and Jacobs (1953), agree with the original assertions of Karny (1908) that the sounds are produced by the partial opening and closing of the hind wings like a fan. The case of *Dissosteira carolina*, which also produces sounds in flight, has been dealt with above.

The hind legs are involved in many frictional mechanisms, besides the orthodox method found in the Acridinae. Probably the best known of these is the femoral-abdominal method which has been described above. Less well known are mechanisms like that of the tribe Porthetini of the Phamphaginae, which produce sounds by rubbing certain spines on the hind tibia across a specialized subcostal area of the elytra. Finally there is the tibio-abdominal method found in *Charora* and other genera, where certain tibial spurs are dragged across ridges on the abdomen to produce noises (Fig. 13).

There are many variations of the methods described above which only exist in a single species or genus of the Orthoptera, but the details given must suffice to indicate in a general way the vast range of sound-producing mechanisms in the group.

Hemiptera

The Hemiptera fall into two suborders, the Heteroptera (bugs) and the Homoptera, and one group of the latter, the Auchenor-rhyncha, has developed the most complex insect sound-producing mechanism of all, the tymbal organ; the details of this mechanism and its operation are described below. This appears to be the only sound-producing mechanism evolved in the Homoptera, except for a curious case among the Aphididae of a presumed frictional organ and a single instance in Psyllids. Williams (1922) described a rhythmic synchronous scraping noise emitted by colonies of the aphid *Toxoptera coffeae*. Eastop (1952) found that in this insect and two allied aphids the surface of the abdomen near the siphunculi was reticulated and the hind tibia bore modified hairs, shorter and stronger than normal, and suggested that the sound was produced by the scraping of these hairs over the abdominal reticulations.

Frictional mechanisms are found in several groups of the Heteroptera, and the basic types of these will now be described; this catalogue is incomplete because interest in these organs, and the certainty that they are true sound-producing organs, is quite recent. The classification of the terrestrial Heteroptera followed by Leston, Pendergrast and Southwood (1954) divides the group into Geocorisae, Hydrocorisae and Amphibicorisae, of which the first-named is divided again into two main series, the Pentatomomorpha and the Cimicomorpha. The Geocorisae have developed a diversity of frictional sound mechanisms comparable to that of the Orthop-tera, and sound production is widespread throughout the families which it comprises and is the subject of a recent review by Leston (1957). In the Pentatomomorpha one of the commonest mechanisms consists of a file on one of the veins of the hind wing which is rubbed by a scraper situated somewhere on the thorax or abdomen. Families possessing the apparatus include Piesmidae and Cydnidae, and other examples are found in certain Lygaeidae, Largidae and Tessaratomidae. A typical example of the mechanism is that of the

Lygaeid *Kleidocerys resedae* (Fig. 14). In Piesmidae and Cydnidae the apparatus is in general the same as in *Kleidocerys*, but the scraper is in these families situated on the tergum of the first abdominal segment. It is interesting to note that in the Cydnidae what are thought to be resonance chambers are formed by the depression of the first and second terga of the abdomen and the intucking of the third tergum under the second; it is perhaps due to these chambers that the sounds emitted by these bugs are relatively loud in comparison with those of other families (Leston, 1954).

The second type of stridulatory mechanism in the Pentatomomorpha consists of a strigil or file on certain abdominal segments which is acted on by a scraper situated on various parts of the legs. Such mechanisms are found in some Aradidae, the primitive shield bug subfamily Mecideinae and the Tetyrinae amongst others, and a typical example is that found in *Artabanus* (Fig. 15). Here longitudinal ridges in the third ventral segment of the abdomen are scraped by teeth on the hind tibia. In some South African Scutellerinae a mechanism has been described in which multiple rows of pegs on the dorsal side of the ninth segment of the abdomen are rubbed by a ridge on the conjunctival appendage of the genitalia, but its sound-producing function needs confirmation. However, a so-called sound-producing apparatus in Saldidae has recently been shown by Leston (1957) to be a male grasping organ! That it was originally described as a stridulating organ is not surprising in view of the rows of peg-like bristles present (Fig. 16). It may be mentioned here that sounds have been reported as being emitted by other groups of bugs of the Pentatomomorpha, particularly among the Pentatominae and a small group of Coreidae, but no apparatus has yet been found which appears capable of producing the noises.

In the Cimicomorpha, the stridulatory ability of the Reduviidae has long been known; the mechanism is present in nearly all genera, and in the later instars as well as the adults of both sexes. The apparatus is simple, almost an archetype of frictional mechanisms; the tip of the labrum is rubbed over a series of transverse ridges in the prosternal furrow. The same simple apparatus is found in the Elasmodemidae and Phymatidae. Amongst other families in the Cimicomorpha there is now doubt as to whether the so-called stridulatory mechanism in the Nabidae described by Ekblom (1926) is anything but a cleaning apparatus.

Of the semiaquatic bugs (Amphibicorisae) only the Veliidae have species which stridulate; the mechanism was described by Hungerford (1929) as consisting of a "stridular patch" on the inside of the hind femur which rasps against a row of pegs on a raised ridge on the side of the abdomen (Fig. 17). The organs are present in both sexes. Amongst the true water bugs (Hydrocorisae) stridulation occurs in Nepidae, Notonectidae, Pleidae and Corixidae. In the

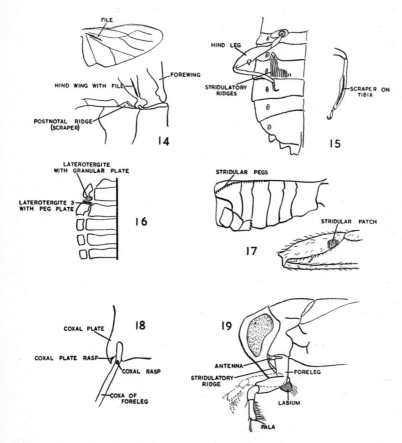

Fig. 14. *Kleidocerys resedae*, male; above, hindwing; below, lateral view of meso- and meta- thorax. Fig. 15. *Artabanus*; underside of abdomen and hind tibia (After Usinger, 1954). Fig. 16. *Saldula scotica* male; abdomen from above. (After Leston, 1957). Fig. 17. *Velia stridulata* male; lateral view of abdomen and inner surface of left hind leg. (After Hungerford, 1929). Fig. 18. *Ranatra quadridentata* male; left fore leg. (After Bueno, 1905). Fig. 19. *Corixa punctata* male; side view of head and thorax in stridulating position. (After von Mitis, 1935).

first-named family—water scorpions—Bueno (1905) described in *Ranatra quadridentata* what appears to be the typical mechanism. In this insect a rasp at the base of the coxa of the fore-leg rubs on a roughened area on the inner surface of the cephalic margin of the lateral plate of the coxal cavity (Fig. 18). A similar apparatus exists in *R. brevicollis*. Both adults and nymphs possess the apparatus and can stridulate in air or water, the typical squeaking noise being louder in the latter case. The exact nature of the stridulatory mechanism in the Corixidae has been the subject of long controversy. Kirkaldy (1901) described it as consisting of a comb on the tarsus of one anterior leg, which was drawn across a minutely toothed area on the inner surface of the femur of the opposite leg; this mechanism is only found in males. Von Mitis (1935), however, returns to the earlier suggestion of Carpenter, which was that a series of bristles on the inner side of the femurs of the forelegs are scraped against the side of the head. Von Mitis describes this type of mechanism in *Sigara striata* and *Corixa punctata*. In the males an area of thickened serially arranged bristles on the inner side of the femurs of the fore-legs is scraped against the sharp ridge on the head between the antennae and the labium (Fig. 19). The resultant sound is said to be amplified by the air sacs of the head. A simultaneous quick bowing by both femora produces a loud chirp, while a second type of noise can be produced by continuous friction. Recent unpublished work by Leston indicates that possibly these insects may use both types of mechanism. Von Mitis also described the stridulatory mechanism of *Micronecta meridionalis*. Here the strigil consists of a row of long chitinous rods pointing outwards and backwards, based on a curved chitinous disc situated on the sixth abdominal segment. Von Mitis assumed, but was unable to prove, that this strigil is somehow scraped by a part of the reproductive organs. His observations on living animals suggested that the right paramere acted as the scraper. This view was partly supported by Walton (1938) who, however, described two mechanisms in *M. poweri*; the first of these consisted of a roughened part of the eighth segment, which was rasped by the spiny aedeagus, and the second comprised the strigil on the sixth tergite, which he claimed was rubbed by the overlapping lobe of the superior tergite. Thus the true mode of stridulation of *Micronecta* is at present in some doubt; the mechanism is of interest because of the high intensity of the sounds produced by so small an insect.

Coleoptera

It may be surprising to some to discover the tremendous range of stridulatory mechanisms in beetles. They have been almost completely overlooked in recent research on insect acoustics, and yet they were paradoxically one of the first groups in which much concentrated work was carried out on the stridulatory mechanisms. Gahan and Arrow in England, Dudich and Marcu on the Continent, wrote between them about 70 or 80 papers on stridulation in Coleoptera, and Darwin, in the *Descent of Man*, dilated at some length on the meaning and significance of the sounds produced by beetles. One of the interesting things about the stridulatory mechanisms of Coleoptera is the uniformity of structure shown; they are all, or almost all, frictional mechanisms of the simplest type. However, what the organs lack in variety of structure, they make up in variation of position. As Gahan (1900) says: " Wherever any part of the external surface of the body is subjected to the friction of an adjoining part by the movements of the insect, there, in some species or other, these organs are almost sure to be found." The position and occurrence of stridulatory mechanisms seems far less related to phylogeny in the Coleoptera than they are, say, in the Orthoptera. The same or very similar structures, in identical positions, can be found in unrelated genera, while species of the same genus may have quite dissimilar mechanisms.

Stridulatory organs appear on the head in the Nitidulidae, Hispinae and Endomychidae amongst others. These consist of a single or double stridulating file on the top of the head, which is scraped by a small ridge on the underside of the front edge of the pronotum. In *Spilispa imperialis* (Hispinae) an interesting modification of this apparatus occurs, with the appearance of a flap-like projection of the front of the pronotum (Fig. 20); this does not act as the scraper, which is underneath the flap, and its role is at present unknown. In other genera, the apparatus, while still on the head, lies on the underside; generally the striate area lies on the gula, which is rubbed against a projecting ridge on the anterior edge of the prosternum. This is, in effect, a mirror image of the apparatus on the upper side of the head; it is found in Tenebrionids, amongst others. Another type of mechanism occurring on the head is the mandibular-maxillary apparatus found in the larvae of Scarabidae. The upper face of the stipes of the maxilla carries a series of teeth which rub over roughened granulose areas grouped on the lower face of the mandibles. The importance of the discovery of these organs in larvae lies in the fact that they constitute a challenge to Darwin's theory that all beetle mechanisms have evolved in direct relationship to their use in sexual behaviour.

Stridulatory organs involving parts of the thorax are many; they can in general be divided into mechanisms in which both file and scraper are on the thorax, and those in which the two parts are dispersed between the thorax and various appendages. An example of the first type is found in *Omaloplia brunnea*, where a process of the metasternum rubs across a transversely striated area on the inner face of the intercoxal part of the prosternum. In the Aseminae, Cerambycinae, Lepturinae and Lamiinae, sounds are produced by friction between the inner edge of the posterior margin of the prothorax and a specialized striated area on the median anterior elongation of the mesonotum. In *Cychrus rostratus* (Carabidae), a beetle producing very loud sounds, the mechanism seems in some doubt, although Gahan suggests that the ridged epimeral lobes of the prothorax are rubbed against the sides of the mesosternum to produce the noise. Mechanisms involving legs and thorax are found in the Carabidae and Bostrychidae. The organs of *Phonapate nitidipennis* (Bostrychidae) are particularly interesting, not only because they are well developed but because this appears to be the only case known in the Coleoptera in which the stridulating apparatus is confined to the female. The anterior femora bear striated areas near their tips which are scraped over a series of six or seven ridges developed along the hind end of the thorax (Fig. 21). In the Carabid *Siagona* the apparatus is similar, each side of the prothorax bearing a ridged carina, which is scraped by a striate area situated on the front femora.

A number of beetles have stridulatory mechanisms involving the abdomen. In certain Rutelinae a transversely striated ridge on the inner face of the posterior femur is drawn across oblique ridges on the side of the abdomen. A similar apparatus exists in the Heteroceridae, where a single narrow ridge on the upper face of the hind femora is rubbed against a striated area on the ventral plate of the first abdominal segment. Pocock (1902) describes an apparatus in the Carabid *Graphipterus variegatus* (=*serrator. Forsk*) in which a ridge on the upper surface of the hind femora rubs against the toothed edges of both the elytra and the abdominal sterna (Fig. 22).

Stridulatory mechanisms involving the elytra are widespread, being found in representatives of the Carabidae, Dytiscidae, Scarabaeidae, Tenebrionidae, Prionidae and Curculionidae. *Oxycheila* (Cicindelidae) typifies the elytro/femoral mechanism; here a narrow ridge along the edge of each elytron is finely striated, and is rubbed by a ridged area of the hind femur. A similar mechanism is found in the Tenebrionidae and some Prionidae. Variations occur in the

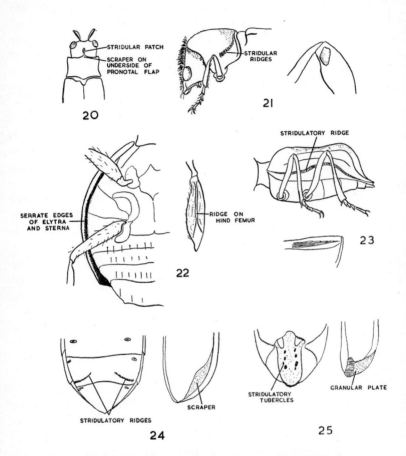

Fig. 20. *Spilispa imperialis* male; dorsal view of head and thorax. (After Gahan, 1900). Fig. 21. *Phonapate nitidipennis* female; lateral view of head and prothorax and inner surface of front femur. (After Gahan, 1900). Fig. 22. *Graphipterus variegatus* male, ventral view of thorax and abdomen and top surface of hind femur. (After Pocock, 1902). Fig. 23. *Cacicus americanus* male; lateral view of abdomen and inner surface of hind femur. (After Gahan, 1900). Fig. 24. *Blethisa multipunctata* male; dorsal view of apex of abdomen (left) and underside of left elytron (right). (After Gahan, 1900). Fig. 25. *Eupterus* sp. female; dorsal view of apex of abdomen (left) and underside of left elytron (right). (After Gahan, 1900).

position of the elytral ridge and Fig. 23 shows the mechanisms in
Cacicus americanus (Tenebrionidae), where the ridge is high up the
elytron and is curved. In some Carabidae, such as *Blethisa*, the
abdomen bears a series of very short ridges situated on each side of
the penultimate dorsal segment, and these are scraped by a striated
area on the underside of the edge of the elytra (Fig. 24). In the
Curculionidae also, the elytra and abdomen bear the stridulatory
mechanisms, but in this case the pygidium bears an area covered
with small tubercles which rubs a granulated area at the apex of
the elytra (Fig. 25). Several beetles have mechanisms of the type
which exist in *Encaustes gigas* (Erotylidae), where a striated area
on the wing is scraped by a roughened area at the tip of the elytra.
This type of apparatus is found also in Dytiscidae.

A most interesting type of stridulatory mechanism was described
by Schiödte (1874) from the larvae of certain Lucanidae, Passalidae
and Geotrupidae; it is confined entirely to the legs and consists of a
series of ridges on the coxae of the middle legs which are rubbed by
the scrapers on the trochanters of the hind legs. This apparatus is
particularly well developed in the larvae of Passalidae (Fig. 26),
where the hind legs are so modified that they can act only as
scrapers and are no longer of use in locomotion.

Pupal stridulation occurs in beetles; Gravely (1915) heard the
stridulation of the pupa of the Dynastid beetle *Oryctes rhinoceros*
and gives a description of the organ concerned. This appears to be
similar to the type described by Hinton from Lepidopterous pupae;
the latter author also observed that pharate adults of *Oryctes* and
Dynastes gideon may stridulate by friction between parts of the
pupal and adult cuticle, since sounds could be produced when these
pupae were manipulated by hand. Finally, mention must be made
of the family Elateridae, the so-called " click beetles ". Adult beetles
can leap in the air when lying on their backs, the action being
accompanied by a loud clicking noise. The mechanism is not fully
understood, but involves the prosternal process and the meso-sternal
cavity. The sound is almost certainly a secondary product of this
saltatory mechanism, the real purpose of which is still obscure.

Lepidoptera

A great deal has been written on sound production in the Lepidoptera, but much has been due to observations of a very superficial
nature. Various mechanisms have been described which may be
capable of producing sound, but observations of them in action are

rare indeed. The order appears to have evolved three methods of sound production involving special apparatus, the tymbal mechanism (see page 54), the "pulsed air stream" method of *Acherontia* (see page 54), and a variety of frictional mechanisms now to be described. These occur in all stages of development, larval, pupal,

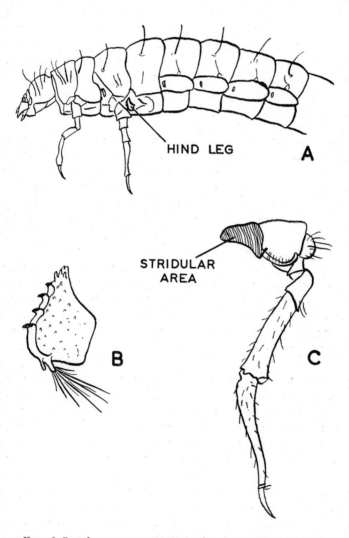

HIND LEG

A

STRIDULAR AREA

B

C

Fig. 26. *Passalus cornutus*; (A) adult larva; (B) modified hind leg, acts as scraper; (C) inner surface of middle leg, showing area of file. (After Schiodte, 1874).

and adult. Larval stridulation has been described by Federley (1905), who states that in *Telea polyphemus* sound is produced by rubbing the mandibles together, causing a loud rasping sound audible over several metres. In other larval Saturniids, notably *Rhodia fugax*, a noise is said to be produced by rubbing the back of the head against the rim of the prothorax (Packard, 1904). Certain larval Drepanidae, said to produce noises by impact, have been referred to previously. One of the most interesting aspects of sound production in Lepidoptera concerns noises made by pupae. The subject has been recently and exhaustively investigated and reviewed by Hinton (1948), and the following account is based on his paper. Lepidopterous pupae have four types of mechanisms for sound production; the body of the insect is knocked against the substrate or wall of the pupae; one or more pairs of abdominal segments are rubbed together; the abdomen is rubbed against the proboscis; and finally ridges on the pupae are rubbed against the walls of the cocoon. The first method seems the simplest and it is interesting to note that this type of mechanism is found in several of the Hesperiidae, thought to be a primitive group. The pupae have no structural modifications and the sound is produced by wriggling of the body when stimulated by touch. Hinton points out that it has yet to be determined if the insect wriggles to produce sound or whether the sound is an incidental product of wriggling. The second method, rubbing together of abdominal segments, is apparently the most common and widely distributed, being found in at least eight families. The mechanism consists typically of transverse ridges on the anterior margin of one segment, which are rubbed by raised tubercles on the posterior margin of the preceding segment. Fig. 27 shows this mechanism as found in *Lymantria viola*. The third method of pupal stridulation has so far only been described from one species, *Gangara thyrsis*. This pupa has twin ridges on the fifth abdominal segment and the exceptionally long proboscis, which is transversely ridged on the underside, lies between them. Contraction of the abdomen causes the two parts to scrape together producing a hissing noise. Stridulatory mechanisms involving cocoons are very widespread in the family Phalaenidae and two general types exist. In the majority of cases, the cocoon of hard parchment coloured silk is smooth inside; pupae in these cocoons have tuberculate areas on the head, thorax and part or all of the abdomen. The wriggling of the pupae on disturbance causes the tuberculate areas to scrape on the inside of the cocoon with the

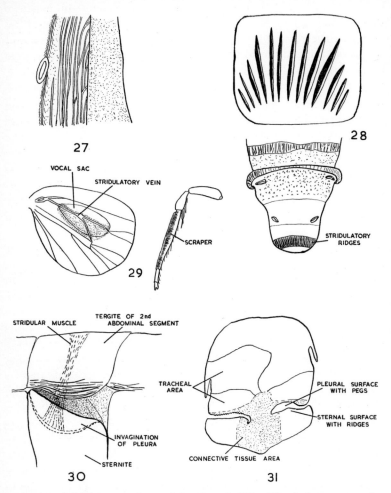

FIG. 27. Stridulatory surfaces of fourth and fifth abdominal segments of pupa of *Lymantria viola*. (After Hinton, 1948). FIG. 28. *Eligma hypsoides*; silken cocoon with ridges (above) and end of abdomen to same scale (below) showing ridges on 10th segment. (After Hinton, 1948). FIG. 29. *Thecophora fovea* male; hind wing and inner view of hind leg, with scraper on first tarsal segment. (After Hannemann, 1956). FIG. 30. *Lymantria monacha* male; semi-diagrammatic lateral view of 2nd abdominal segment, showing invagination and position of stridular muscle. (Redrawn after Kruger, 1913). FIG. 31. *Lymantria monacha* male; transverse section across 2nd abdominal segment, showing roughened surfaces of the invagination. (Redrawn after Kruger, 1913).

production of audible noises; it is said that the sounds produced by this mechanism in *Pseudoips bicolorana* can be heard several feet away. In the second type of cocoon mechanism, the silk case has ridges on the inside walls, which are so placed as to be above the tenth abdominal segment of the pupa. On the dorsal surface of this latter is a row of short transverse ridges, and the pupae can wriggle so as to scrape one set of ridges over the other. The apparatus as found in *Eligma hypsoides* is shown in Fig. 28. The sound produced by a related species *E. narcissus*, has been compared by Hemmingsen to that of a grasshopper, although the noise was produced at a slower rate and "the tone was more hissing". The significance of pupal stridulation will be discussed in a later chapter.

Amongst adult Lepidoptera a number of interesting frictional mechanisms have evolved. In several butterflies and moths both fore and hind wings bear some raised veins, and the action of opening scrapes these veins over the opposing wing surface and produces a hissing noise. Well known in this connection is the Peacock Butterfly (*Nymphalis io*), but several related species such as *N. antiopa* also possess the same apparatus. A number of Lepidoptera stridulate by rubbing ridges on the wings with some part of the legs. This is the mechanism in the Noctuid moth *Thecophora fovea* (Fig. 29), where a specialized nerve on the hind wing set above a small depression or sac, is scraped by the modified tarsus of the hind legs. Jordan, and more recently Hanemann, have described several similar mechanisms in some detail, especially in Noctuid moths. All are basically of the leg/wing type, but the details vary slightly. Whereas in *Thecophora* the hind wing is rasped by the hind leg, in *Pemphigostola synemoristis* a modified fore-wing vein is rasped by a file on the middle leg (Hannemann, 1956), while in *Musurgina laeta* a raised vein on the fore-wing is rubbed by a file on the hind tarsus (Jordan, 1921). Probably the most primitive of these wing/leg mechanisms is that described by Jobling (1936) from *Parnassius apollo*. The sound is only made by gravid females, who cling to a grass stem, open their wings wide and simply rattle the hind legs over the base of the hind wings, thus producing a noise audible for 4-5 yards. Males of the moth *Aegocera tripartita* (Agaristidae) fly at dusk making a loud clicking noise at intervals of about a second. According to Hampson (1892) this noise is produced by friction of the greatly enlarged tarsal spines of the front legs rubbing over a transversely ridged patch on the underside of the fore-wing, which is situated at the costal edge and devoid of scales.

The moth *Hecatesia* has a different type of wing apparatus, described by Nicholson (1955); during flight, part of the wing membrane clicks in and out when the wings are knocked together. This is, as far as our present classification goes, a unique method of sound production, and might be considered as a "vibrating membrane" apparatus, but is inserted here as it clearly has affinities with other wing mechanisms. Finally, one finds in the males of certain Lymantriid moths (e.g. *Lymantria monacha, Stilpnotia salicis*) an abdominal mechanism of an interesting type (Fig. 30). The apparatus, described by Kruger (1913), is situated on the second segment and consists of a cavity formed partly from the sternite and the pleural membrane. Under the action of certain abdominal muscles, the ridged sternal part of the mechanism rubs against the opposite pleural face of the cavity, which is roughened with small pegs (Fig. 31). This apparatus is present in about 50% of male moths only and does not occur at all in the related *L. dispar*, while in *Stilpnotia* it is only weakly developed.

Other orders

Frictional stridulatory mechanisms in the Hymenoptera have been observed mainly in the ants. The Ponerine and Myrmicine ants have an organ consisting of a ridge on the petiole which can be rubbed over a series of transverse striations at the base of the first tergite of the gaster (Fig. 32). The noise thus produced is generally very weak, although that of the large tropical Ponerines is audible to humans. It has been suggested that some smaller Myrmicine species emit ultra-sonic noises. Stridulatory organs also

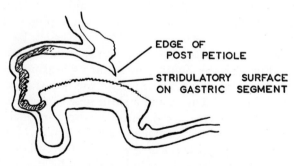

EDGE OF
POST PETIOLE

STRIDULATORY SURFACE
ON GASTRIC SEGMENT

FIG. 32. Median section of gaster of *Myrmica laevinodis* showing stridulatory organ. (After Janet, 1893).

E

occur in the Mutillid wasp *Mutilla europaea*; the organ is very similar in position and structure to that found in ants and is present in both sexes. Pupal stridulation occurs in the Hymenoptera and is particularly developed in the Ichneumonid *Phytodictus polyzonias*, where Lyle (1911) describes the noise as loud enough to be heard in the room when the pupae stridulated in a drawer. In males the tip of the abdomen, in females the end of the ovipositor, is scraped on the inner surface of the cocoon.

In the Psocoptera, Pearman (1928) has described a so-called coxal stridulatory mechanism of a frictional type found on the hind legs of certain species. It consists of a nearly circular rugose area (the "file") and a round chitinous window (the "mirror"). This organ is found only in adults and shows much variation between families, some losing the mirror and some the file. No observations have been made of this organ in use, and its possible sound-producing function must therefore remain hypothetical. This is also the case with the organs reported in certain Thysanoptera by Hood (1950). The mechanism is found only in males, and consists of a file on the outer surface of the fore coxa, which is rubbed by a thin flange at the base of the fore femur. The organ occurs in fourteen species of the three genera *Diceratothrips*, *Sporothrips* and *Anactinothrips*. These cases are cited to show that the habit is still prevalent of reporting as "stridulatory organs" any discovery of friction between cuticular surfaces, even if the alleged mechanism has not been observed or heard to function as a source of sound. The danger is not only that we shall amass a list of spurious stridulatory organs, but that if sound production be accepted as the function of the organ described the chances of discovering its real purpose will be correspondingly reduced.

In contrast to these rather dubious examples, Asahina (1939) describes both the mechanism and the sounds produced by the larvae of a species of dragonfly, *Epiophlebia superstes*. Here a series of ridged stridulatory areas exist on the sides of abdominal segments 3-7 (Fig. 33); the number of segments bearing these areas varies with the larval instar. These patches are rasped by the ridged inner side of the hind femora and a shrill tone is generated, which is heard when the larvae are disturbed. True frictional mechanisms occur in the Diptera amongst the fruit flies (Trypetidae). Monro (1953) worked with *Dacus tryoni*, the Queensland fruit fly, and recorded and analysed the sound produced by the mechanism, which is an alary/abdominal one. The cubito-anal area of each wing vibrates in a dorso-ventral movement across two rows or combs of large bristles situated one on each side of the third abdominal tergite. The combs are found only on male flies and consist of 20-24 bristles. The wing venation of male and female flies differs, that of the former probably being specialized for stridulation. Recent work suggests that the power of sound production may be quite widespread amongst the Trypetidae, although the mechanism may not be always as described above. It would be possible to extend the list of orders of insects suspected of having sound-producing mechanisms of a frictional type with many more references; most of these, however, describe structures presumed to be stridulatory

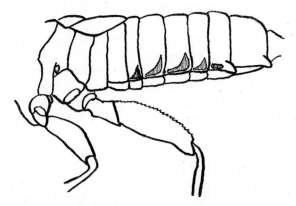

FIG. 33. Last instar larva of *Epiophlebia superstes*, showing stridulatory patches on abdominal segments 3-7 and ridged inner side of hind femur. (After Asahina, 1932).

purely on morphological grounds, and since they are of types identical to or very similar to those already described above, no purpose would be served by including them.

(b) Vibrating membrane mechanisms

What is certainly the most elegant and also one of the most efficient methods of sound production in insects is, not surprisingly, restricted to one fairly small group, the Homoptera Auchenorr-hyncha, although an apparently similar type of organ is found in some Lepidoptera, and will be referred to later. The Cicadas have been famous for their powers of sound production for centuries, and it has been suspected for some time that various other members of the Auchenorrhyncha were capable of sound production, but not until the publication of Ossiannilsson's classical paper *Insect Drummers* (1949) did it become clear that the ability was widespread throughout the group and that the apparatus was essentially similar and probably homologous in its parts. In its essentials the mechanism is simple, as the schematic diagram (Fig. 34) shows. A nearly circular membrane, the tymbal, is supported around its edge by a heavy chitinous ring, and is normally bowed outwards; a large muscle, the tymbal muscle, is attached to the tymbal near its centre. The contraction of this muscle pulls the tymbal inwards and its distortion produces a sharp click—a single pulse of sound, analogous to the sound produced when the lid of a tin is forced in by the fingers. When the muscle relaxes, the tymbal springs back to its original position by virtue of its own elasticity, and in so doing produces another sharp pulse of sound. If the muscle contracts and relaxes at a rapid rate a noise will be produced which will sound continuous to the human ear. Pringle (1954) has investigated the mode of action of this sound-producing organ, and has shown that the frequency of contraction of the tymbal muscles in the species examined ranges from 120 to 480 per second.

These tymbal organs are paired, and occur on the dorsal-lateral surface of what appears to be the first abdominal segment. Fig. 35 is a transverse section across the abdomen of *Neophilaenus campestris*, with soft parts except muscles removed. One of the pair of tymbals and its large associated muscle can clearly be seen, and a number of small muscles attached to the edge of the membrane are also shown. These muscles, according to Pringle's work on Cicadas, serve to increase the curvature of the tymbals and in this way increase the volume of sound emitted at each distortion of the tymbal. In so doing, however, they reduce the repetition frequency of the sound pulses and thus alter the character of the song (see Chapter 4). Also associated with the tymbal organs in many of the Auchenorrhyncha are large tracheal air sacs, which are open to the exterior; in Cicadas, Pringle found that the cavity of these sacs had resonant frequencies nearly the same as the frequency of tymbal vibration and a set of muscles existed by means of which their resonance could be adjusted. When the tymbal muscle contracts, and the tymbal is buckled, it is thrown into vibration and the frequency of the sound so produced is determined by the natural frequency of the membrane, which in turn depends on its size, elastic modulus and other specific characters. This natural frequency of vibration of the tymbal is pulse modulated at the rate of contraction of the tymbal muscle, but variations in the sound pattern occur due to the actions of the tensor muscles of the tymbal membrane and also of the muscles controlling the resonance of the air sacs. Ossiannilsson's work suggests that in many of the Swedish Auchenorrhycha examined by him the same complex

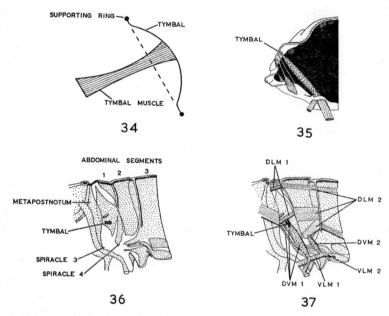

FIG. 34. Schematic diagram of Homopteran tymbal mechanism. FIG. 35. Transverse section of right half of first abdominal segment of male *Neophilaenus campestris*, seen from the front, with soft parts except muscles removed. (After Ossiannilsson, 1949). FIG. 36. Right half of hind part of metathorax and base of abdomen of male *Neophilaenus campestris*, seen from inside, with soft parts removed. FIG. 37. Same as 36 but with muscles drawn in. D.L.M. = dorsal longitudinal muscle. D.V.M. = dorso-ventral muscle. V.L.M. = ventral longitudinal muscles. 1, 2 = first and second abdominal segments. (After Ossiannilsson, 1949).

mechanism exists. An idea of the complexity of the musculature is given by Figs. 36 and 37, which show sagittal sections of a Cercopid with and without musculature. The variation in sound patterns which can be produced by this system will be illustrated in Chapter 4. It has been widely supposed that only males produce sounds, the females being silent or only possessing rudiments of the apparatus, but recent work suggests that some females may possess functional tymbal organs; it seems probable that the nymphs cannot sing, but since many of them live subterranean lives, this is not surprising.

Hinton has recently applied the name "tymbal organs" to certain mechanisms found widely distributed amongst the Lepidoptera. The organ, situated in the thorax of certain Arctiidae and Syntomidae, is a modification of the metepisternal sclerite, which forms a membranous covering over a cavity. This membrane, the tymbal, is said to be vibrated by rapid alterations of the shape of the cavity, probably brought about by contractions of the dorsoventral flight muscles. The noise produced by the insect when on the wing is a crackling sound, and in certain genera, such as *Setina*, is said to be audible over considerable distances.

(c) Mechanisms directly involving air movement

In some ways methods of sound production involving the expulsion or vibration of air directly, as opposed to indirect movement by vibrating bodies, are the most interesting of all the various mechanisms used by insects, because the human voice and many musical instruments operate on this principle. Unfortunately this method is by far the least investigated in insects and the evidence for its occurrence is in many cases dubious and confusing. One well-known case, however, is that of the Deaths Head Hawk Moth, *Acherontia atropos*. The sound-producing ability of this moth has been known for centuries, as the volume of literature testifies, and a large number of suggestions have been advanced as to the mechanism. The concensus of opinion at present is that the description of Prell (1920) is substantially accurate and the recent work of Busnel and Dumortier (1959), in which they recorded and analysed the sounds, confirms most of Prell's suggestions. Fig. 38 is a drawing of a sagittal section through the head of the moth. The essential part of the apparatus is the epipharynx; the pharynx with its associated muscles serves to suck or blow air in and out through the proboscis. This air flow passes between the floor of the pharynx and the epipharynx and is interrupted by movements of the latter. The effect is to produce a pulsed air stream, the frequency of which will be related to the resonant frequency of the pharyngeal cavity. The proboscis may act as an amplifier, but plays no part in sound production; similarly, the pharynx acts only as an air pump. It is clear that sound production is only possible when the pharynx is

empty of food. One interesting aspect of this mechanism is that it
so closely parallels the human method; the pulsed air stream
method of sound production is one of the most efficient known,
giving very loud sounds for comparatively low energy inputs, and
this probably accounts for the loud squeaks that the moth can
produce. This specialized pharyngeal anatomy is found only in
atropos; other species of the genus are apparently dumb and the
sound-producing power may be due to very small anatomical
changes in the epipharynx. The persistence of this mutation argues
some advantage to the moth with vocal powers, and these possi-

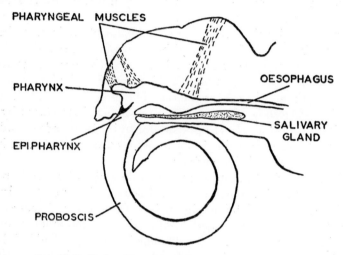

FIG. 38. Sagittal section through head of adult *Acherontia
atropos*. (After Prell, 1920).

bilities are discussed in a later chapter. An analysis of the cry of
Acherontia will be found in Chapter 4.

Although similar mechanisms have not been observed or suspected elsewhere in insects, Lovett (1881) recorded that a specimen
of *Arctia caja* produced a loud squeaking sound several times while
crawling on his arm, the noise being as loud as and similar to that
of *Acherontia*. It seems possible that in moths with similar pharyngeal anatomy to that of *Acherontia*, the occasional aberrant form
may be capable of sound production, but it is unlikely that this is
widespread. There is, however, another possibility in the case of
Arctia, suggested by the observations of E. Burtt in Tanganyika, as
reported by Carpenter (1938). Burtt observed that two species of

Arctiidae, *Rhodogastria bubo* and *R. lupia,* when touched emitted a
mass of evil-smelling froth from the prothoracic collar and *R. bubo*
at the same time produced an audible squeaking sound. *Pseudo-
hypsa speciosa* (Hypsidae) also when touched exudes froth with a
very audible sizzling sound, and the emission of froth bubbles is
synchronous with vibrations of the metapleura. In an addendum to
this note of Carpenter's, Eltringham says that both *Rhodogastria
bubo* and *R. lupia* emit froth and stridulate when touched, and
goes on to describe the stridulatory organ, which is a ridged, air-
filled, drum-like mechanism with a thin chitinous membrane,
found on the metapleuron. The noise is produced by this being
rubbed against the next anterior segment. However, Hartland-
Rowe (1959) describes stridulation in males of *R. bubo* as being
produced by a rapid forward and backward movement of the hind
coxae. Thus for Lovett's observation on *Arctia* there seems to be
two possible explanations; one, that it possesses stridulatory organs
and uses them without production of froth. The other is that
emission of froth by *R. bubo* and other insects is produced by air
expulsion from the spiracles and accompanied by sounds caused by
this expulsion; here again *Arctia* would use the spiracular mechanism without the emission of froth.

There is no doubt that many insects do emit poisonous froth or
unpleasant liquids through certain spiracles, and that such emission
can be accompanied by audible noises. Duncan (1924) quotes the
case of the grasshopper *Taeniopoda picticornis,* and amongst other
Acridids with this power a notable one is the large Florida lubber
grasshopper *Romalea microptera*; in this latter species the mechanism seems uncertain, to say the least. Sometimes froth is emitted
without sound, sometimes sound without froth; the stimulus to
produce either response is very variable, being sometimes a light
touch and at others rather severe handling. The mechanism, which
is presumably defensive, may be adapted to the type of stimuli
likely to be received from typical predators, so no conclusions may
be drawn from these few observations. Other Orthoptera, notably
the Pyrgomorphinae, have the ability to emit an unpleasant fluid,
and in the case of *Dictyophorus* this emission is accompanied by a
hissing sound audible to human ears several yards away. Chopard
(1938) records audible expulsion of air in *Gromphadorhina* (Blat-
todea), and similar observations have been made for some beetles
of which the most famous is undoubtedly the Carabid *Brachynus
ballistarius,* the Bombardier Beetle. This beetle, when attacked,

emits a spray of fluid from certain abdominal glands, the emission being accompanied by an audible sound. In this case it is probable that the production of sound is a secondary feature of the mechanism, which has now been shown by Eisner (1958) to be a defensive adaptation. Simultaneous sound production may add to the deterrent effect, but no clear evidence is as yet available on this point.

Of more interest are those cases where emission of air with production of an audible sound, generally through the spiracles, appears to be a primary feature. Landois (1867) comments on this phenomenon, which occurs in several groups of Diptera and also in Coleoptera and Hymenoptera. Landois ascribed the sounds emitted by various Diptera to the vibration of a series of lamellae situated in the tracheae close to certain spiracles; the lamellae are set in motion by the passage of air produced by respiratory movements. He describes the production of such sounds in *Calliphora* and states that the head, wings, legs and abdomen of the fly can be removed without alteration to the note, but if the thoracic spiracles are blocked the sound stops. But Bellesme (1878) observed that in certain Diptera and Hymenoptera sound emission continued after removal of the wings and stoppage of the spiracles. Harris (1903), however, gives a very detailed account of the mechanism of sound production in *Eristalis tenax*, the apparatus being in essence that described by Landois. Unfortunately, no modern work has been carried out on this possible spiracular mechanism in Diptera, and the whole matter must remain a problem for the future.

Several biologists, past and present, have ascribed the well-known sound-producing powers of queen bees to the spiracular expulsion of air; this has been strongly denied by others, such as Armbruster (1922), who stated that the sounds were produced by the wings, and Snodgrass (1925), who suggested that vibration of the wing-base sclerites caused the sounds. However, the piping of queen honey bees has been investigated in some detail by Woods (1956, 1959), who recorded and analysed the sounds in question. From his analysis, which showed the noise to be a nearly pure tone of between 290 and 380 c.p.s., Woods showed that of the various mechanisms suggested —wing vibration, wing-base vibration, vibration of the spiracular valves and " organ pipe resonance " in the tracheae—none had the physical characteristics necessary to produce the qualities of the very pure note recorded. After further work Woods produced a new hypothesis—that of the " pulsed air stream ". He considers that the piping queen vibrates her wings at a frequency determined by muscular development, and the size and weight of the wings—and hence slightly variable for different insects according to their development. The frequency of this movement, detected by proprioceptors, determines the rate of opening and closing of the spiracular valves; whenever air is passing into or out of the spiracles —as determined by the respiratory movements—the air stream will be modulated at the wing-pendulum frequency and will produce a pulsed air stream at that frequency. Using these ideas as a basis, Woods constructed a mechanical model of a spiracular modulating system, in which a series of holes equal in number and size to the spiracles of a queen bee were opened and closed 350 times per second. When an air stream was passed through the holes a note very similar to the queen piping was produced. While this ingenious theory requires to be examined more critically, at least it appears to accord with the necessary acoustic and physical criteria far more satisfactorily than any previous one, and can be used as the basis for future research.

This brief survey, although incomplete, gives some idea of the great range of sound-producing mechanisms evolved by the insects; this alone should suggest the importance that sound plays in their biology, an influence very much overlooked in past studies of behaviour and life history. Because the approach used here has been a functional one, it may perhaps lead to certain facts being overlooked, namely that several different mechanisms have evolved in the same orders of insects, and that sound-producing mechanisms may have evolved many times over during the phylogeny of a group. Therefore to remedy this in part and to close the chapter, a table is given showing the types of sound-producing mechanisms and their distribution amongst the modern orders of insects (Table I).

Occurrence of Stridulatory Mechanisms in Insects

Order and Stage	Sounds produced as by-product	Sounds produced by impact against substrate	Special mechanisms		
			Frictional	Vibrating membrane	Air movement
COLEOPTERA					
Larva			+		
Pupa			+		
Adult		+	+		+
DIPTERA					
Adult	+		+		+?
HETEROPTERA					
Nymph			+		
Adult			+		
HOMOPTERA					
Nymph				+?	
Adult			+	+	
HYMENOPTERA					
Larva		+			
Pupa			+		
Adult	+	+	+		+?
ISOPTERA					
Adult		+			
LEPIDOPTERA					
Larva		+	+		
Pupa			+		
Adult	+		+	+	+
ODONATA					
Nymph			+		
ORTHOPTERA					
Nymph			+		
Adult	+	+	+		+
PLECOPTERA					
Adult		+			
PSOCOPTERA					
Adult		+	+?		
THYSANOPTERA					
Adult			+?		

REFERENCES

ARMBRUSTER, L. (1922) *Arch. Bienenkunde.* **4**: 221-259.

ASAHINA, S. (1939) *Zool. Anz.* **126**: 323-325.

BELLESME, J. (1878) *C. R. Acad. Sci. Paris.* **87**: 535-536.

BUENO, J. R. (1905) *Canad. Ent.* **37**: 85-87.

BUSNEL, R. G. and DUMORTIER, B. (1959) *Bull. Soc. ent. Fr.* **64**: 44-58.

CARPENTER, G. D. H. (1938) *Proc. zool. Soc. London.* A. **108**: 243-252.

CHOPARD, L. (1938) *La Biologie des Orthoptères. Encycl. Ent.* (A.) **20**: 541 pp.

DIRSH, V. M. (1951) *Eos.* 1950: 119-248.

DUNCAN, C. D. (1924) *Pan-Pacific Ent.* **1**: 42-43.

EASTOP, V. F. (1952) *Entomologist.* **85**: 57-61.

EISNER, T. (1958) *J. ins. Physiol.* **2**: 215-220.

EKBLOM, T. (1926) *Zool. Bidr. Uppsala.* **10**: 31.

FEDERLEY, H. (1905) *Jour. N.Y. ent. Soc.* **13**: 109-110.

GAHAN, C. J. (1900) *Trans. Ent. Soc. Lond.* 1900: 433-452.

GONTARKSI, H. (1941) *Natur. u. Volk.* **71**: 291-292.

GRAVELEY, F. H. (1915) *Rec. Indian. Mus.* **11**: 483-539.

HAMPSON, G. F. (1892) *Proc. zool. Soc. Lond.* 1892: 188-193.

HANNEMAN, H. J. (1956) *Dtsch. ent. Z.* **3**: 14-27.

HARRIS, W. H. (1903) *J. Queckett micr. Cl.* **8**: 513-520.

HARTLAND-ROWE, R. C. B. (1959) *Proc. Roy. ent. Soc.* (C). **24**: 18.

HASKELL, P. T. (1957) *J. ins. Physiol.* **1**: 52-75.

HINTON, H. E. (1948) *Entomologist.* **81**: 254-269.

HOOD, J. D. (1950) *Proc. ent. Soc. Wash.* **52**: 42-43.

HUNGERFORD, H. B. (1929) *Jour. Kansas. ent. Soc.* **2**: 50-59.

JACOBS, W. (1953) *Z. Tierpsychol. Suppl.* 1-228 pp.

JOBLING, B. (1936) *Proc. R. ent. Soc. Lond.* (A) **11**: 66-68.

JORDAN, K. (1921) *Nov. Zoologicae.* **28**: 68-74.

KAHN, M. C. and OFFENHAUSER, W. (1949) *Amer. J. trop. Med.* **29**: 827-836.

KARNY, M. (1908) *Stettin. ent. Z.* **69**: 112-129.

KEVAN, D. K. MacE. (1955) *Colloque sur L'Acoustique des Orthoptères. Ann. Epiphyt.* (tome hors serie): 103-141.

KIRKALDY, G. W. (1901) *Entomologist.* **34**: 9.

KRUGER, P. (1913) *Zool. Anz.* **41**: 505-512.

LANDOIS, H. (1867) *Z. wiss. Zool.* **17**: 105-186.

LESTON, D. (1954) *Ent. mon. Mag.* **90**: 49-56.

LESTON, D. (1957) *Proc. zool. Soc. Lond.* **128**: 369-386.

LESTON, D., PENDERGRAST, J. G., and SOUTHWOOD, T. R. E. (1954) *Nature. Lond.* **174**: 91.

LOHER, W. (1959) *Proc. R. ent. Soc. Lond.* (A) **34**: 49-57.

LOVETT, E. (1881) *Entomologist.* **14**: 178.

LYLE, G. T. (1911) *Entomologist.* **44**: 404.

MACNAMARA, C. (1926) *Canad. Ent.* **58**: 53-54.

MITIS, H. VON (1935) *Z. Morph. Oekol. Tiere.* **30**: 479-495.

MONRO, J. (1953) *Austr. J. Sci.* **16**: 60-62.

NICHOLSON, A. J. (1955) *Proc. R. ent. Soc. Lond.* (C). **20**: 13.

OSSIANNILSSON, F. (1949) *Opusc. Ent. Suppl.* **10**: 1-145.

PACKARD, A. S. (1904) *Jour. N.Y. ent. Soc.* **12**: 92-93.

PEARMAN, J. V. (1928) *Ent. mon. Mag.* **64**: 179-186.

PIERCE, G. W. (1949) *The songs of insects.* Harvard Press, U.S.A.

POCOCK, R. I. (1902) *Ann. Mag. nat. Hist.* **10**: 154-158.

PRELL, H. (1920) *Zool. Jahrb. Abt. Syst. Geog. Biol. Tiere.* **42**: 235-272.

PRINGLE, J. W. S. (1954) *J. exp. Biol.* **31**: 525-561.

ROEDER, K. D. and TREAT, A. E. (1957) *J. exp. Zool.* **134**: 127-158.

SCHIODTE, G. C. (1874) *Nat. Tidsskr.* **9**: 227-376.

SNODGRASS, R. E. (1925) *Ann. Rept. Smithsonian Inst.* (1923): 405-452.

TINDALE, N. B. (1928) *Rec. S. Austr. Mus.* **4**: 1-42.

UVAROV, B. P. (1928) *Locusts and Grasshoppers: a handbook for their study and control.* London. 325 pp.

WALTON, G. A. (1938) *Trans. Soc. Brit. Ent.* 1900: 433-452.

WILLIAMS, C. B. (1922) *Entomologist.* **55**: 173-176.

WOODS, E. F. (1956) *Bee World.* **37**: 185-195, 216-219.

WOODS, E. F. (1959) *Nature, Lond.* **184**: 842-844.

CHAPTER III

INSECT HEARING

BEFORE studying the actual sounds produced by the various mechanisms described in the previous chapter, we must consider the hearing ability of insects. This is in certain fundamentals different from the hearing of vertebrates and since this difference is of importance in relation to the investigation of the structure of insect songs it will be considered first before any attempt is made to describe the songs themselves. It may be as well to recall here that definitions of the words "sound" and "hearing" for the purpose of this book were given in the first chapter. Thus hearing in insects was defined as follows: "an insect hears when it behaves as if it has located a moving object (a sound source) not in contact with it." Hearing organs, then, may be understood as any receptors which will mediate the behavioural responses mentioned above. It will at once be appreciated that no sharp distinction is drawn between organs which respond to airborne sounds and those which respond to vibrations of the substrate.

This is intentional, since recent work has demonstrated the existence of organs which encompass both these responses, and moreover, there is some evidence to show that both modalities of reception may be concerned in the response behaviour of certain insects to acoustic stimuli. The reception of water-borne stimuli may also be fitted into this scheme, although at present there is little information on the responses of aquatic insects to sound.

Early naturalists derived their knowledge of insect hearing almost entirely from behaviour experiments, such as those described by Kirby. "I was once observing," he writes, "the motions of an Apion (a small weevil) under a pocket microscope; on seeing me it receded; upon my making a slight but distinct noise, its antennae started. I repeated the noise several times, and invariably with the same effect." Such experiments convinced many entomologists of the existence of a sense of hearing in insects, and it was then natural to look at a variety of apparently sensory structures in order to determine which was the seat of the ability to hear. This produced many conflicting opinions; various authors, such as Muller (1826), who was probably the first in the field, observed structures such as tympanal organs and ascribed auditory functions to them on morphological grounds, perhaps because of the slight resemblance they bear to vertebrate ears. Other workers such as Newport (1838) became convinced from behavioural evidence that the antennae were the principal hearing organs. This era of confusion was gradually brought to a close by the careful behaviour work of a few entomologists, outstanding among whom were Regen, Minnich and Mayer. The former showed clearly that in various Orthoptera the main seat of hearing was in the tympanal organs, although some slight sensitivity to sound remained when these were destroyed. Minnich demonstrated the ability of certain hair organs of caterpillars to respond to airborne sounds, while Mayer showed that the long hairs on the antennae of some male mosquitoes were resonant to certain frequencies and concluded that their vibrations might stimulate Johnston's organ in the antennae. It thus became clear that more than one type of organ was concerned in insect hearing.

However, the work of many anatomists and histologists had demonstrated that although the external morphology of receptors known to be responsive to sound varied considerably, the sensory cells of many of them appeared to be the same or similar. Siebold (1844) seems to have been the first to describe these sense cells, but most work on them was completed by Graber in a series of classical papers from 1872-82; he named these cells "chordotonal organs" in the erroneous belief that they acted like stretched strings and resonated to acoustic stimuli. These sensillae, nowadays thought to be derived from campaniform sensillae through elongation, are made up of three cells (Fig. 39) the cap cell, sheath cell and the primary sense cell. Attached to the latter by the terminal filament is a long rod, the scolopale or sense rod. From this rod is derived an alternative name for these cells, the scolopidia. It seems likely from physiological work that activation of the primary nerve cell depends upon displacement of the scolopale with respect to the terminal filament. This type of sensillum is found widely distributed in both larvae and adults of all groups of insects, and is very variable in the fine details of its structure, as Fig. 39 shows. In the great majority of cases the distal or cap cell is either inserted into the hypodermis of the cuticle, or the whole receptor lies in a strand of tissue which stretches between two parts of the body wall. These facts suggest that the original function of these sensillae was to register the relative motion of parts of the integument; in other words, the organs are proprioceptors. In many cases, however, these sensillae have become associated with other structures, such as the tympanic membrane, which render them sensitive to airborne sounds.

There exist five main types of hearing organs in insects, as far as present knowledge goes. These are:

(a) Tympanal organs
(b) Johnston's organ
(c) Sub-genual organs
(d) Scattered chordotonal sensillae
(e) Hair sensillae of various types.

Of these five groups all but the last two consist of various structures associated with groups of chordotonal sensillae.

(a) Tympanal organs

These organs are characterized by the presence of a tympanum or membrane, so called from the Greek " tumpanon ", a drum; associated with the tympanic membrane, which is exo-skeletal in derivation, are chordotonal sensillae and large air sacs. Tympanal organs are always paired structures and only occur in the Orthoptera, Lepidoptera and Hemiptera as far as is known at present. In the Orthoptera, the organs occur in the first segment of the abdomen in the Acridoidea (Fig. 40) and in the tibia of the forelegs in the Grylloidea (Fig. 41) and the Tettigonioidea (Fig. 42). They appear in all these groups in the nymphs, but are probably only fully functional in the later instars and the adults, where they are equally developed in both sexes. The Acridid tympanum is the simplest type, and Fig. 43 shows the organ of a locust *Locusta migratoria* as seen from within the insect. The large membrane supported on a chitinous ring is exposed to the air, and the group of chordotonal sensillae are applied somewhere near the centre of the membrane in Muller's organ. The auditory nerve from the organ passes down the body wall to the metathoracic ganglion. Applied to the inner surface of the tympanum is a large air sac, and in most Acrididae these sacs meet across the median body line (Fig. 44) and thus connect the organs acoustically. The functions of these sacs is probably to decrease the damping of the membrane which would occur if it came into contact with body fluids or tissues. However, as Pumphrey (1940) has pointed out, the presence of these air sacs enables sound to impinge on the tympanal membranes from both sides instead of, as in mammalian receptors, only on one side of the membrane. Such an arrangement suggests that the tympanum may respond to the displacements of air rather than to the pressure change associated with sound waves, a hypothesis pursued in more

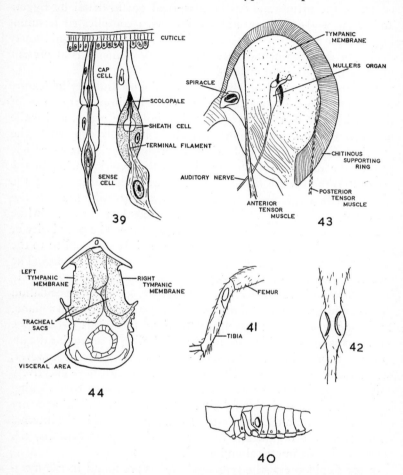

FIG. 39. Structure of two types of chordotonal sensillae. (After Wigglesworth, 1939). FIG. 40. Acridid tympanal organ in first segment of abdomen. FIG. 41. Inner opening of Gryllid tympanal organ on tibia of fore leg. FIG. 42. Front view of symmetrical openings of Tettigoniid tympanal organ in tibia of fore leg. FIG. 43. Simplified drawing of tympanal organ of *Locusta migratoria* seen from within the insect. FIG. 44. Transverse section of typical Acridid in tympanal region showing juxtaposition of air sacs. (After Schwabe).

detail later. There is always at least one muscle associated with the tympanal organ, the so-called " tensor tympani ". However, its function has never been investigated and is not clear; in some Acridids a second muscle, very thin, appears attached to the other side of the membrane. The distribution of chordotonal sensillae at the centre of the membrane has been worked out in detail by Eggers and other workers for several species and a complicated terminology for the various groups of sensillae exists. As the significance, if any, of this fragmentation of the sensory elements is at present unknown, details will not be given here.

The tibial tympanal organs of Tettigonioidea and Grylloidea are much more complicated than the relatively simple structures of the Acridoidea. The tibia are dilated to hold the organ, and while in the Gryllids the membranes may be completely exposed to the exterior (Fig. 41), in the Tettigoniids two heavy folds of cuticle protect the membranes, the opening to the exterior being in the form of two forward facing slits (Fig. 42). The structure of the organ can be appreciated from Figs. 45 and 56, which shows the twin tympanal membranes separated by the enlarged trachea while the latter are separated by a hard sheet of tissue. The peculiarity of these organs is that the chordotonal sensillae are not applied to the membranes, but along the anterior edge of one of the trachea. The fact that the size of the chordotonal sensillae gets progressively smaller from above downwards (see Fig. 56), led to the speculation that they formed a series of resonant elements, like strings in a piano, enabling the organ to respond differentially to various frequencies. The organs of Grylloidea are in general similar in all major details to those described for the Tettigonioidea; the structure is, however, rather variable between species. Some (e.g. *Cophus*) have effectively only one opening to the exterior, and in *Gryllotalpa* this opening is protected by a cuticular fold. Generally the outer tibial aperture is much larger than the inner one, and this is reflected in the internal structure of the organ, but in some species (e.g. *Oecanthus*) the apertures are symmetrical and equal.

In the Lepidoptera, the tympanal organs are found in the metathorax in the Noctuoidea and in the first or second segment of the abdomen in Pyralidina and Geometroidea, except for the peculiar family Axiidae, where it occurs in the seventh segment. Fig. 46 is a schematic drawing of the organs in the metathorax of a Noctuid moth; this shows the arrangement of the air sacs and secondary tympanal membranes which effectively connects the two organs and allows sound to impinge on both sides of the primary tympanal membrane. The structure of the organ in Lepidoptera is in general similar to that of the Acridoidea, but shows great variation, particularly as regards the external openings and the associated air sacs. Insufficient data on hearing in Lepidoptera are available to assess the significance, if any, of this variation.

In the Hemiptera Homoptera tympanal organs of the general type found in Orthoptera and Lepidoptera only appear to exist in

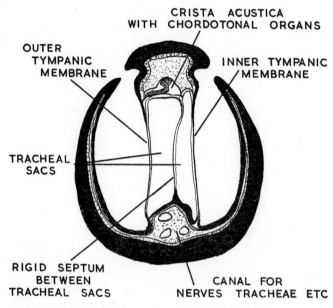

FIG. 45. Transverse section across tibia of *Decticus* in region of tympanal organ. (After Schwabe).

the Cicadas. Although the remainder of the Auchenorrhyncha possess tymbal organs homologous with those of the Cicidas, according to Ossiannilsson the tympanal organs are lacking. The thoracic organ in Cicadas has been described by Vogel (1923), and is in its essentials similar to that of all other groups possessing such receptors (Fig. 47). A variation is found in the fact that chordotonal sensillae are situated in a "Tympanalcapsule", and their distal ends are inserted near or at the edge of the tympanic membrane. In these insects, the tracheal space behind the membrane is continuous between the organs on either side of the thorax, an arrangement producing the same acoustical result as the juxtaposition of air sacs in the Acridoidea.

Organs described as tympanal organs have been found in several of the Hydrocorisae. Fig. 48 shows the organ as found in *Plea atomaria*. It consists of a membrane, the tympanum, in communication with the external (aqueous) medium; on the inner surface of

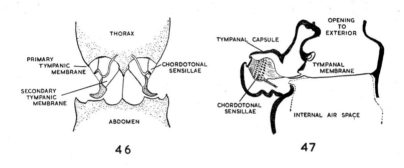

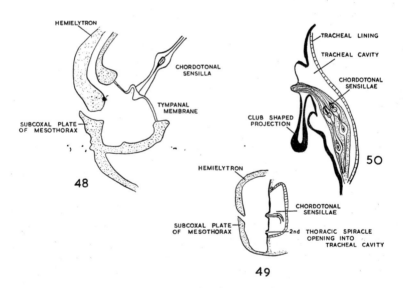

FIG. 46. Schematic horizontal section across metathoracic region of Noctuid moth. (After Eggers). FIG. 47. Horizontal section of tympanal organ of *Cicadetta*. (After Vogel). FIG. 48. Transverse section of mesothoracic tympanal organ of *Plea atomaria* (After Eggers). FIG. 49. Transverse section of mesothoracic tympanal organ in *Corixa punctata* (Redrawn after Eggers). FIG. 50. Horizontal section of tympanal organ of *Corixa punctata*.

the membrane is inserted the end of a bundle of chordotonal sensillae, the point of juncture being marked by a cone. This organ, in various forms, many of which have no membrane, is found in the Corixidae, Notonectidae, Pleidae, Nepidae and Naucoridae. It is situated in the mesothorax, near the articulation of the elytra,

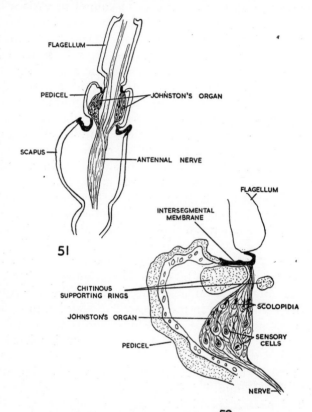

FIG. 51. Section of antenna of *Triphosa dubitata*. (After Eggers). FIG. 52. Section of pedicel of *Agrotis baja*. (Redrawn after Eggers).

and the second thoracic spiracle is situated closely adjacent to it. In *Corixa punctata* (Fig. 49) the organ is situated in a tracheal cavity which communicates with the exterior through the second thoracic spiracle. In this species also, a large club-shaped projection is attached near the sensory cone (Fig. 50), but experimental evidence to be recounted later suggests that this plays no fundamental part in the responses of the receptor.

(b) Johnston's organ

This organ is named after Johnston, who first described it in the mosquito *Culex*. It now appears that this receptor, in a variety of modifications, is found in all insects and is a most labile structure, mediating responses to several types of stimuli in various insects. It has been clearly shown however that it is the principal organ of hearing in mosquitoes, and probably other Diptera, and thus must be included in the present survey. The organ is situated in the second segment or pedicel of the antennae and comprises a variable number of chordotonal sensillae arranged in a radial fashion (Fig. 51). These are attached to the wall of the pedicel and terminate at their upper end in the intersegmental membrane between the flagellum and the pedicel (Fig. 52). The sensillae are thus placed to register the changes in the motion of the antennal flagellum relative to its base. This organ and its occurrence in insects has been studied in detail by Eggers (1928) and more recently by Risler (1953); it appears from the work of the former that even in primitive insects (e.g. *Lepisma saccharina*) Johnston's organ is present in a fairly well-developed form. It is, however, in the Chironomidae and the Culicidae that the organ is most highly developed, the large number of chordotonal sensillae completely filling the greatly enlarged second segment (Fig. 53). It seems significant that in these groups the other chordotonal sensillae and the campaniform sensillae normally found in the antennae in addition to Johnston's organ are absent, and there is evidence from other insects which suggests that the reduction of the former organs is related to the enlargement of the latter.

Since the organ is in general a proprioceptor responding to movements of the flagellum, it is involved in a variety of responses; in the beetle *Gyrinus* it is said to respond to changes in the curvature of the water surface, in certain Diptera it controls the adjustment of wing-beat in relation to air-speed, while in ants it mediates the response to gravity. The stimuli able to excite the organ are therefore many and varied, and it would be premature to consider it acts or can act as an auditory organ in all or even many insects. The recent work of Tischner (1953) on the physiology of the organ in mosquitoes supports the behavioural work of Mayer mentioned above, and leads to the conclusion that in the Nematocera, if not in all Diptera, the organ is auditory. The morphological work of Risler (1953) has clarified the mechanical structure of the organ in mosquitoes where, as will be seen later, it plays an important role in the response physiology of several species. As Risler shows (Fig. 53) there are two main sets of chordotonal organs which, together with several more receptors such as those under the basal plate, make up Johnston's organ. The inner and outer rings of chordotonal sensillae can apparently register the vertical and horizontal movements respectively of the flagellum, while perhaps the remaining receptors are proprioceptors involved in endogenous movements of the flagellum.

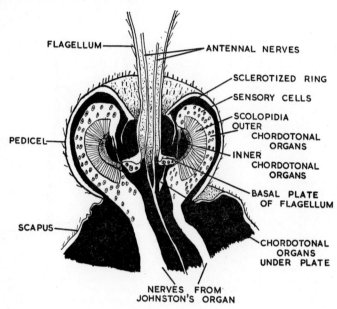

FLAGELLUM

ANTENNAL NERVES

SCLEROTIZED RING

SENSORY CELLS

SCOLOPIDIA
OUTER
CHORDOTONAL
ORGANS

INNER
CHORDOTONAL
ORGANS

PEDICEL

BASAL PLATE
OF FLAGELLUM

SCAPUS

CHORDOTONAL
ORGANS
UNDER PLATE

NERVES FROM
JOHNSTON'S ORGAN

FIG. 53. Section through pedicel of male *Anopheles stephensi.*
(After Risler).

(c) *The sub-genual organs*

These interesting receptors, consisting of groups of chordotonal organs, are found in the proximal region of the tibia of the legs in many orders of insects, including Orthoptera, Plecoptera, Lepidoptera, Hymenoptera and Hemiptera, and respond to vibrations of the substrate. In all orders of insects, of course, many chordotonal organs are present in all sections of all legs which presumably act as proprioceptors, and in some cases, for example in Coleoptera and Diptera where true sub-genual organs are lacking, it has been shown that these organs can mediate detection of low frequency vibrations of the substrate. Acoustic stimuli of low frequency and sufficient intensity to set the substrate in motion could also probably be detected by these organs. But the true sub-genual organs referred to above are distinguished from these general chordotonal sensillae by the facts of their appearance and position. Sub-genual organs, in the strict sense, consist of a number of closely packed chordotonal sensillae whose cap cells are embedded in an "end-bundle" or mass of connective tissue which is finally attached at one point only to the integument; these receptors never appear to

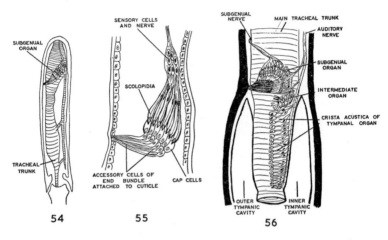

FIG. 54. Frontal section of tibia of fore leg of female *Formica sanguinea*. (After Eggers). FIG. 55. Enlarged view of subgenual organ of *Formica sanguinea*. (After Eggers). FIG. 56. Longitudinal section through fore tibia of *Decticus*, showing tympanal organ, subgenual organ and intermediate organ. (After Schwabe).

be associated with joints. Figs. 54 and 55 illustrate the typical position and structure of these receptors as seen in *Formica sanguinea*. In the Orthoptera the organs are particularly well developed, and in the fore legs of the Grylloidea and Tettigonioidea are in close physical association with the tympanal organ (Fig. 56), although the separate identities of the two receptors is emphasized by their separate innervation. Physiological experiments, however, show that the proximity of the organs may in this case have some effect on acoustic responses, and this possibility will be discussed later. Sub-genual organs are only moderately well developed in the

Lepidoptera and Hymenoptera and poorly in the Hemiptera, but in all these groups maintain the same general form and properties.

(d) Scattered chordotonal sensillae

It should be emphasized here that many chordotonal sensillae present in the body of insects may on occasion respond to air-borne stimuli. It is clear that when a mechano-receptor of the chordotonal type is attached to the integument of an insect, perhaps as a proprioceptor or for other purposes, and a sound of sufficient intensity falls upon that area of the integument, the receptor may be stimulated and give rise to nervous responses. It is probably true to say, however, that the threshold in such cases would be very high and that such reception does not normally enter into the pattern of insect communication by sound. Exceptions to this rule may occur in aquatic insects, where the degree of coupling afforded by the dense aqueous medium may render a tympanal membrane unnecessary. Reference to experimental evidence on this point is given below.

(e) Hair organs

The bodies of insects are covered with a great variety of hairs, and some of these have been shown to be capable of responding to stimulation by air-borne sounds. The most generalized hair organs are those commonly supposed to be tactile, and the structure of the base of such an organ from the larva of *Vanessa urticae* is shown in Fig. 57. In these organs the sensory element is a bipolar sense cell which appears to have its distal process—which may include a scolopale—attached to or lying near the margin of the hair socket; stimulation of the sense cell is caused by the hair moving in the socket. This basic structure, or something similar, is found in all insects, but it is not always safe to assume that because certain of these organs in some insects have been shown to mediate responses to sound that all have this property in some degree. It is probably true that by the use of signals of sufficient intensity a response to air-borne stimuli could be obtained from most hair organs, but such experiments do not accord with natural conditions. Minnich (1925, 1936) investigated the acoustic sensitivity of a number of Lepidopterous larvae having such generalized hair organs and obtained responses, measured by the behavioural re-actions of the insects, to sounds of reasonable intensity. From this and other work it seems clear that in certain insects generalized body hairs do respond to sounds of such intensity as to make it probable that they could detect the natural emission of other insects. Haskell (1956) has demonstrated this in the case of certain body hairs of some grasshoppers, but here the threshold was such that the natural emission of the insects could only be detected by these organs over ranges of a few centimetres. Sensitive hair organs have been described by Sihler (1924) from the anal cerci of a number of Orthoptera. Fig. 58 shows the basal structure of such hairs, which are very long and loosely articulated as they occur in *Gryllus campestris*; they appear to be present in a greater or lesser degree on the cerci of nearly all Orthoptera, and they have been shown in several species to be very sensitive mechanoreceptors.

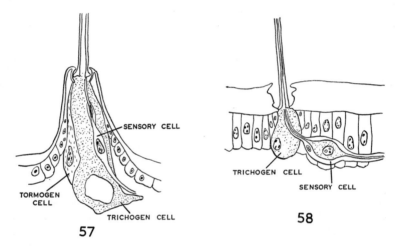

Fig. 57. Base of tactile hair of *Vanessa urticae*. (After Hsü). Fig. 58. Long hair sensilla from anal cercus of *Gryllus campestris*. (After Sihler).

The physics and physiology of the receptors

The relationship between displacement and pressure in a sinusoidal sound wave has already been remarked on; to detect sound waves, receptors may be responsive to changes in one or other of these parameters. As regards pressure detectors, these must be designed to respond to the force which is produced by the difference between the sound pressure to be measured and the steady atmospheric pressure. A detector of this type, a crystal microphone for example, must have one side of the diaphragm exposed to the sound waves and the other in contact with an enclosed volume of

air at steady atmospheric pressure. Fig. 59 is a diagram of this
type of system; a small breather hole may be provided in the
rigid enclosing framework to ensure that the internal pressure is
always equal to the atmospheric pressure. The human ear is also
an example of this sort of receptor; the drum acts as the diaphragm,
and the pressure in the nearly closed inner ear is kept at atmospheric
level by connection to the exterior via the Eustachian tubes. Most
microphones in common use are of this type. The force exerted on
the diaphragm of this type of instrument is independent of the
frequency of the stimulating sound, provided that the diameter

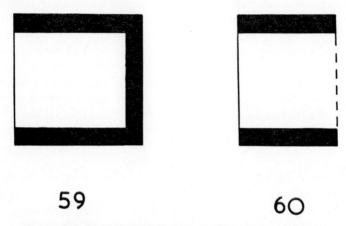

59   **60**

FIG. 59. Schematic diagram of elements of a receptor sensitive to
pressure changes; the thin line is the diaphragm. FIG. 60. Schematic diagram of a receptor sensitive to displacement; thin line
is the diaphragm and broken line indicates open back of casing.
(After Pumphrey).

of the diaphragm is very small compared with the wavelength of
all frequencies in the working range. Moreover, since pressure is a
scalar quantity, the orientation of the receptor with respect to the
source of sound produces no alteration in the force exerted on
the diaphragm.

The design of a receptor to respond to displacement is shown in
Fig. 60; here the essential feature is that both sides of the diaphragm
shall be exposed to the operating force, which is achieved in practice by having an open back to the rigid framework supporting the
diaphragm. A ribbon microphone is an example of an instrument
of this type. Under these conditions the diaphragm is exposed to
a force which is proportional to intensity in a sound of constant

frequency, and to frequency in a sound of constant intensity. Displacement is a vector quantity of sound, and thus the diaphragm of such a receiver will experience maximum effect when its plane is normal to the incidence of the stimulating sound; such a property confers upon this type of receptor the ability to detect the direction of propagation, and hence the source, of the stimulating sound. Pumphrey (1940) in an important review of this subject, points out that the structure of all insect hearing organs makes it probable that they are displacement receivers. In all types of tympanal organ, as we have seen, there is an arrangement which ensures that the primary membrane shall be exposed to the stimulating sound on both sides; in Gryllids, Tettigonids and Lepidoptera this is done by the use of two tympanic membranes open to the atmosphere, and in Cicadas and Acridids, by an arrangement of air sacs which results in virtually the same arrangement. Nowhere do we find the typical, rigid, enclosed structure demanded by a pressure receiver. As far as Johnston's organ and hair receptors are concerned, it is clear that they most operate as displacement receivers, since they have no associated enclosed air volume. The experimental evidence available in all cases supports the conclusion that the acoustic receptors in insects are displacement receivers.

This experimental evidence is derived in two ways, one by direct physiological experiment on the receptors and the other by observing the behaviour of intact insects to acoustic stimuli. Although because of technical difficulties, use of the latter preceded the former, the two methods are or should be complementary. Behavioural evidence was accumulated to support the fact that insects can hear sounds both sonic and ultra-sonic, but much of the earlier work used sounds of great intensity to elicit responses from the insects, and the results did not as a rule indicate whether the sounds made by insects themselves could in fact be heard by them. Moreover, the behavioural reactions studied were often brief motions of the antennae or of the body, and gave no clear idea of what receptors were involved. However, in a series of papers from 1902 to 1930, Regen showed clearly that in crickets and long-horn grasshoppers the tympanal organs were the principal, but not the only, receptors of acoustic stimuli, and his work was extended to many other insects, although in a rather uncritical way, by Baier (1920).

The work of Regen was most important for two reasons; in his work on the cricket *Liogryllus campestris* (1913), he was able to attract a female cricket to a telephone-receiver relaying the chirping of a male cricket, but only if the female was mature and unmated. This important proviso on the physiological state of the experimental insect was unknown beforehand, and doubtless explains much of the confusion of earlier work, and has been greatly neglected since with similar consequences. Secondly Regen showed that in the long-horn grasshopper *Pholidoptera aptera* (1926), it was possible to make a newly moulted male sing in alternation with a variety of artificial stimuli, but that males which had already sung in concert with members of their own species could not be induced to sing thus. This finding meant not only that learning played some part in the song behaviour of these insects, but that the older males could somehow distinguish the song of their species from the artificial signals. On the other hand, the female crickets were attracted to the sound of the males chirping through a telephone, even though the resultant sound was so distorted that it was hardly recognizable to the human ear. The behavioural evidence of hearing in other groups of insects was likewise puzzling. Thus, although Fabre (1911) had failed to produce any effect on singing cicadas by the noise of a cannon discharge nearby, yet Myers (1928) thought that the cicada song was part of a communication system. In the Lepidoptera as well conflicting behavioural evidence was amassed. A number of moths were shown to react to artificial sounds (Turner and Schwarz (1914), Eggers (1925). Eggers held that reactions were only obtained from Lepidoptera which possessed tympanal organs, but Turner and Schwarz obtained responses from Saturniids, which lack tympanal organs, and Collenette (1928) described the behaviour of the butterfly *Ageronia* as responding regularly to the noise made by birds.

This conflicting evidence was to a large extent reconciled by physiological work on tympanal organs, which had come to be regarded as the principal insect hearing organ. In 1933 Wever and Bray published the results of the first electrophysiological experiments on insect hearing organs, appropriately entitled "A new method for the study of hearing in insects". They inserted a wire electrode into the fore legs of various crickets and long-horn grasshoppers and amplified the electrical responses obtained from the nerve of the tympanal organ when the latter was stimulated by pure tones from an oscillator and loud-speaker. They found in this way that the tympanal organs of certain crickets responded to pure tones over the range 250-10,000 c/s, while the range for long-horn grasshoppers was even larger, 800-45,000 c/s. They found also that the frequency of discharge of nerve impulses was asynchronous, that is, the impulse frequency of the discharge was not affected by the frequency of the stimulus and bore no simple relation to it. Wever (1935) later used the electrophysiological technique to investigate the responses of the tympanal organ of the grasshopper *Arphia sulphurea,* and found the same type of discharge was present. In this experiment Wever measured the intensity of the stimulating sound, and thus was able to plot the threshold curve of sensitivity against frequency. These preliminary experiments were quickly followed by the classical work of Pumphrey and Rawdon-Smith in England, who, in a series of papers from 1936 to 1939, described investigations with refined technique on the physiology not only of Acridid tympanal organs but also of certain hair organs as well. In 1940 Autrum in Germany published work on the tympanal organs of Tettigoniids, agreeing in most particulars with the findings of the English investigation. There the whole matter rested until recently, when Pringle (1954) investigated the responses of the tympanal organs of Cicadas, Haskell (1956 a, b) published work relating to Acridid tympanal organs, and Haskell and Belton (1956) and Roeder and Treat (1957) investigated the responses of the tympanal organs of certain moths. It will be most convenient to consider all these results together, irrespective of their dates.

As far as tympanal organs are concerned, the range of frequencies they respond to is very large with the following approximate limits: in Acridids from 100 c/s to probably 50 kc/s, in Tettigoniids from 1-100 kc/s, in Gryllids from 200 c/s to 15 kc/s, in the Lepidoptera (Noctuidae) from 1-150 kc/s, and in the Cicadas probably from 100 c/s to at least 15 kc/s. In all cases the nervous discharge to stimulation by pure tones was asynchronous, the frequency of the discharge being merely a function of the intensity of the stimulus and having no relation to its frequency (Fig. 61). The impulse pattern was similar in most organs, there being a resting discharge in the nerve under conditions of zero stimulation, which increases to a maximum with stimulation above the threshold. Most work so far has been done on the responses of whole nerves, single fibre responses having as yet been little investigated, and as a result compound action potentials were recorded. Initially, the amplitude of these impulses increase as the intensity of stimulation increases, presumably as more and more fibres fire, but soon a stimulus level occurs when the amplitude remains steady. In the case of Cicadas and Lepidoptera, a marked "after discharge"

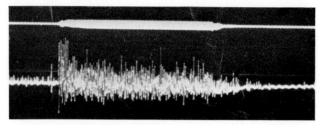

FIG. 61

Volley of impulses in tympanic nerve of *Locusta migratoria migratorioides* (lower trace) on stimulation with pure tone of 1 kc/s (upper trace). Note resting discharge prior to stimulation, the marked "on-effect" and short after-discharge.

(a)

(b)

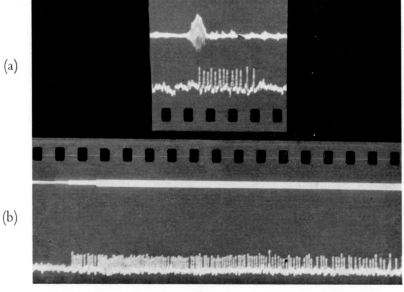

FIG. 62

(a) Volley of impulses in tympanal nerve of *Phalera bucephala* (lower trace) on stimulation by brief pulse of high frequency sound (upper trace) ; note considerable after discharge.
(b) Volleys of impulses in tympanal nerve of *Arctia caja* (lower trace) on stimulation with pure tone of 3 kc/s (upper trace). Note increase in discharge frequency when intensity of stimulus is increased and then slow adaptation.

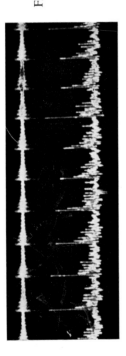

FIG. 64 Responses in tympanic nerve of *Locusta migratoria* (lower trace) to repetitive sound pulses (upper trace).

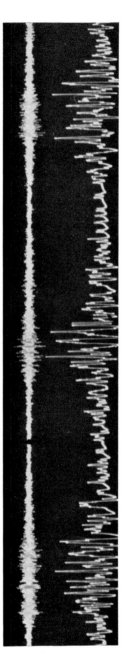

FIG. 65

Fast oscillogram showing responses in tympanic nerve of *S. lineatus* (lower trace) to stimulation by normal song of male *O. viridulus* (upper trace) of which three pulses are seen.

phenomenon is noticed when stimulation ceases, and in the latter group slow, incomplete adaptation also occurs (Fig. 62A and B). The threshold intensities at various frequencies have been measured for several insects, and Fig. 63 is a graph showing some of these plotted against the curve for the sensitivity of the average human ear. From this it can be seen that at low frequencies the ear is more sensitive than the insect organ, but at frequencies above

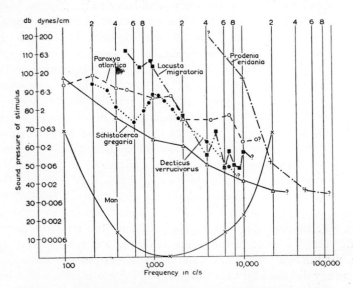

FIG. 63. Threshold intensities of tympanal organs of various insects compared with that of man, for a pure tone stimulus. The figures are not accurate to more than ± 5 dbs because of the variety of calibrations used by various workers. Man: combination of figures of Wegel and Munson. *Paroxya atlantica*: Wever & Vernon (1957). *Locusta migratoria*: Pumphrey & Rawson-Smith (1936). *Decticus verrucivorus*: Autrum (1941). *Schistocerca gregaria*: Haskell (1957) *Prodenia eridania*: this graph is very approximate, constructed from a few measurements of Roeder & Treat (1957).

about 15 kc/s the tympanal organs become more sensitive. That such a comparatively simple receptor should have such a high sensitivity is most interesting, and Pumphrey (1950) has pointed out that this may be in part due to the possibility that the system is regenerative; he is of the opinion that the resting discharge is due to sensory cells firing spontaneously due to some feedback excitation.

It has already been stated that the response of tympanal organs to pure tones is asynchronous, and this seems to rule out the possibility that frequency discrimination by them is accomplished, as in the human ear, by having a number of nerve endings each of which responds to a different frequency component in the stimulating sound. The structure of the organs also militates against this as a possible mechanism, there being no graduation in size of the respective end organs, except in the crista acoustica of Tettigoniid and Gryllid receptors, where the resemblance to the human basilar membrane is purely fortuitous. In some cases in the Lepidoptera, as with the Notodontid moths investigated by Haskell and Belton, only one sensilla is present, as is suggested by the spike pattern of the discharge (Fig. 62), and thus frequency coverage by such a method would be, to say the least, inadequate. And yet, as described previously, the experiments of Regen on Tettigoniids and Gryllids, later confirmed in other groups, showed that these insects were capable of discriminating between sounds which differed quantitatively; how were they able to do this? Pumphrey and Rawdon-Smith (1939) advanced a hypothesis to explain this observation; in their experiments they stimulated the tympanal organs of *Locusta migratoria* with a carrier frequency of 8 kc/s, amplitude modulated at frequencies up to 300 c/s, and were able to show electrophysiologically that the temporal pattern of nervous discharge in the tympanal nerve was synchronous with the modulation frequency, and that alteration of the carrier frequency did not affect the discharge so long as it remained within the acoustic range of the receptor. They concluded from this that as far as insects with tympanal organs were concerned it is the modulation pattern of a sound which is reflected in the impulses in the auditory nerve. Fig. 64 shows the discharges in the tympanic nerve of *Locusta* on stimulation with repetitive square wave pulses passed through a small loudspeaker near the insect, while Fig. 65 is a fast oscillogram showing valleys of impulses in the tympanal nerve of *S. lineatus* on stimulation by the normal song of a male *O. viridulus*. This important hypothesis at once gave an explanation of why Regen was able to attract a female cricket by an apparently distorted signal from a telephone-receiver, since the distortion produced by such a transducer is frequency distortion and the modulation of the sound would remain unaffected. The above observations of Pumphrey and Rawdon-Smith on the tympanal organs of *Locusta* have been verified for the tympanal organs of Cicadas by Pringle (1954), of the Desert Locust and several Acridid grasshoppers by Haskell (1956a, b, 1957), and of certain moths by Haskell and Belton (1956) and Roeder and Treat (1957). All this work was carried out by recording electrical activity in the complete auditory nerve, and the impulse frequencies in single fibres, and the nature of their response to acoustic stimuli, have been determined only in one case, referred to later. It is likely that this mechanism would enable insects possessed of tympanal organs to discriminate between various sounds provided their modulation patterns were different; it thus seems significant that the songs of at least three groups investigated so far, Orthoptera, Homoptera and Heteroptera are characterized not so much by different frequency spectra as by different forms and speeds of amplitude modulation, which differences would thus form a basis for discrimination. These differences between various insect songs will be discussed in the next chapter. It also seems possible, however, that the form of the modulation of the sound may affect the nervous response of a tympanal organ, and Busnel and his co-workers, in the course of a series of experiments (summarized in a paper in 1956), have become convinced that it is essential for stimulating signals to contain " transients " (very rapid increases or decreases in intensity) for the insect to react to them. These various possibilities are discussed in Chapter 5.

Very recently Katsuki and Suga (1958) have recorded single fibre responses from tympanic neurones of the Tettigoniid *Gampsocleis buergeri*. Impulse frequency increased with the intensity of the sound stimulus for sounds of constant frequency and with sounds of constant intensity increased with frequency up to a maximum and then declined. These observations confirm the previous work on tympanal organs as displacement receptors with the added suggestion that some rudimentary form of frequency discrimination— probably to high and low pitched sounds—may be founded on the differential responses of individual chordotonal sensillae in Muller's organ. This suggestion is supported by the observations of Horridge (1960) on tympanal organs of *Acheta*, *Locusta* and *Schistocerca*, in which rough frequency discrimination between low and high pitch sounds was found.

There is as yet very little data as to how insects can measure or compare the intensities of acoustic signals. The change of intensity of a stimulus is reflected in the rate of discharge of nervous impulses, the greater the intensity the higher being the impulse frequency; because of the refractory period and other limitations of

F

a single nerve fibre, there is a limit to the range of intensity which it can indicate in this way, and intensity range is then increased by having a number of fibres—and end-organs—with overlapping ranges. Under optimum conditions, as Pumphrey (1950) has pointed out, a collection of n end-organs, each with a working range of m units of intensity, will have a group working range of m^n units. Clearly, receptors with few end-organs—such as the tympanal organs of some Lepidoptera and Heteroptera which have only two or three chordotonal sensillae—will have less potential discrimination of intensity than those with large numbers of end-organs, such as the tympanal organs of Acrididae with up to 100 sense cells and those of Cicadas with upwards of 1,500 sensillae. Nevertheless, the increase in intensity obtainable by even a small number of end-organs is impressive; for example, a receptor with four end-organs, each capable of responding over an intensity range of 10 units, might have a group intensity range of 10,000 units. Even supposing the increase to be only half this, the extension in range is enormous. An example of a system with two receptors of different threshold is that of the tympanal organ of the moth *Prodenia*, investigated by Roeder and Treat (1957). However, it must be realized that the optimum conditions for increasing the receptor range are that the impulses from each end-organ are transmitted to a common nervous centre where their effect is additive. No such centre has been demonstrated physiologically in insects as yet, but anatomically, in all hearing organs consisting of collections of chordotonal sensillae, the neurones pass together to a ganglionic centre; with hair receptors, on the other hand, this is not normally so, although there are cases of groups of hairs (e.g. on the anal cerci of some Orthopteroid insects) where it occurs. The behavioural evidence available on intensity discrimination is meagre but interesting. In a general sense the range of average intensity of natural sounds is lowest in moths, and highest in cicadas, with orthopteroid insects in between, and the comparative theoretical potentiality of intensity discrimination of the hearing organs of these groups, as outlined previously, is thus in line with actual requirements in the field. Experiments indicate that several Orthoptera can distinguish between two identical songs on an intensity basis when the difference is of the order of 5 dbs over a range of several yards, which is no mean performance for a comparatively simple receptor. Nor is there any reason to suppose that this is likely to be the limit of discrimination, since the data of Hughes (1952) shows that in *Dytiscus* an acoustically sensitive end-organ exists, which, at its optimum frequency, increases its discharge rate by 20% for each 1 db increase in stimulus intensity above the threshold, suggesting that such small increments could be recognized. The ability to detect small increments of intensity is of importance in regard to localization of sound sources by tympanal organs, as will be seen below. Present data on intensity discrimination by insects is so meagre that while we can recognize as a strong probability the existence of intensity discrimination of wide range and considerable sensitivity in a variety of insects, only

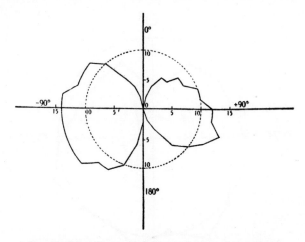

Fig. 66. Polar diagram of the sensitivity of an isolated tympanal organ of *Locusta* as a function of the angle of incidence of the sound stimulus; the sensitivity is arbitrarily zero at the origin, the 0–180° line is the sagittal axis of the insect, and the + and − signs indicate the external and internal face of the tympanal membrane respectively. (After Pumphrey).

further experiment can indicate the range and mechanism of the process.

A further important property of tympanal organs must now be examined; this is their directional sensitivity. There is abundant and conclusive evidence from experiments on behaviour that in insects with tympanal organs localization of and orientation to a source of sound is accomplished by these organs. Quite accurate localization over distances of up to 30 metres has been reported, and this is maintained while the insects are travelling over rough ground towards the source. Furthermore, if the insect is deprived of one receptor, it can still orient to and reach the sound source, although with more difficulty. Such evidence at once disposes of the possibility that localization is carried out by a difference of intensity, timing or phase of the incident sound on the two organs (as in vertebrate hearing), and leads to the conclusion that each organ is in itself directional. It has been pointed out that it is highly probable that tympanal organs are displacement receivers, and that displacement is a vectorial quality of sound; here then is a possible mechanism, and this aspect of the responses of the receptors has been investigated by Pumphrey and Rawdon-Smith (1940) for

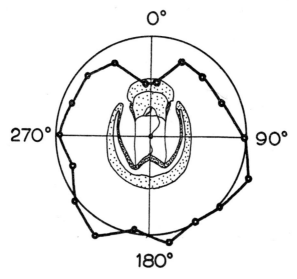

Fig. 67. Polar diagram of sensitivity of a tibial tympanal organ of *Tettigonia viridissima* as a function of the angle of incidence of the sound stimulus; the sensitivity is maximal at the origin. (After Autrum).

Acridids and Autrum (1940) for Tettigoniids. The former, using a monophasic transient sound, stimulated an isolated tympanal organ of *Locusta migratoria* at various angles of incidence, and determined the intensity required to produce a response in the auditory nerve as a function of this angle. They found that the organ was most sensitive when the source of sound was approximately at right-angles to the sagittal plane of the insect, which is to be expected on considering the theoretical situation (Fig. 66). It is therefore interesting that for the tibial tympanal organs of Tettigoniids Autrum (1940) found a different relationship. In this group, a graph of sensitivity as a function of the angle of incidence (Fig. 67) showed that sound was heard most strongly when it impinged either on the inner or outer faces of the organ from a very restricted zone. Fig. 68 illustrates this; a sound source anywhere within the black zone would be poorly heard, but if it is moved to either of

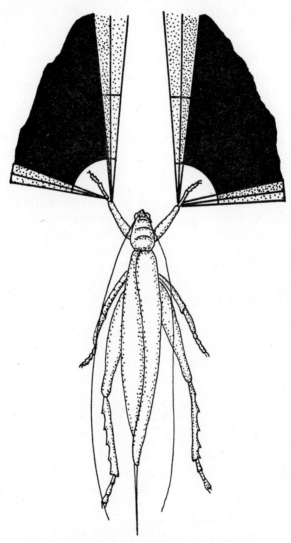

Fig. 68. Hypothetical sensitivity field of tibial tympanal organs of *Tettigonia cantans*; for explanation see text. (After Autrum).

the stippled zones it would be heard much louder. Autrum has developed from these observations a theory of sound location in Tettigoniids; as the insect moves forward, each fore-tibia will alternately sweep out an area of about 120° each side of the longitudinal axis of the insect. During these leg movements, one tibia—that on the side nearest the sound source—will be arrested by the insect when it sweeps across the critical zone barrier, that is, when the intensity of the sound perceived undergoes a sudden change. The opposite tibia will still make a full movement, since no change in the intensity will be perceived, and this will tend to swing the whole insect round towards the source of sound. The insect will continue to move thus, constantly correcting its motion until the angle between its longitudinal axis and the source becomes zero, when it will be moving directly towards the sound emitter. The geometry of the response characteristics of these Orthoptera would imply that the Tettigoniid organ is capable of more accurate sound location than that of the Acridid, and this is borne out by the behaviour of the two groups of insects. This would particularly apply when the insects approach close to the source of sound, when the angle subtended by the source at the tympanal organ grows relatively large; in this case apparently the Acridid receptor would become less accurate much quicker than the Tettigoniid organ, and in fact may be useless at distances nearer to the source than about 10 cm. This may explain why a blinded female Acridid usually experiences great difficulty in locating a singing male, while a blinded Tettigoniid can still accurately locate its partner. No direct evidence on directional response has yet been obtained for the tympanal organs of Cicadas or Lepidoptera, but it is hard to imagine that these organs, so similar in other responses, do not in this quality also resemble Orthopteroid types. However, since, as can be clearly seen in the Acridids and Tettigoniids, the geometry of the receptors and their associated structures markedly influences the mode of directional response it would be unwise to speculate on this matter until experimental evidence is available. However, the work of Roeder and Treat (1957) does afford an indication that in *Prodenia* the organ acts directionally. As was remarked above, the ability to discriminate small changes of intensity will be concerned in the accuracy of localization, since the insect must be able to recognize the moment of reception of peak sound level as it moves its receptor diaphragm in the sound field. In any feed back system, such as must be involved in the movement of an insect towards a source of sound, the sensitivity of the sensory element is the main factor determining the accuracy of the result and also in minimizing the "scanning" or "searching" of the insect for the path of maximum intensity.

Finally we must refer to the time-constant of tympanal organs; as already noted in a previous chapter, this is an important characteristic of hearing organs, limiting as it does the ability to recognize individual constituents in a train of stimuli if these are separated by an interval less than four or five times the time constant. From electrophysiological work done on a number of tympanal organs it is clear that their time constant is considerably smaller than that of the human ear, probably averaging 4-5 milliseconds and in some cases perhaps being less than one millisecond. From this it follows that the tympanal organ will recognize as a separate entity each pulse in a train of pulses, even with repetition frequencies up to several hundred times a second. The limit of this discrimination also depends upon the intensity of each pulse and for maximum discrimination each sound has to be well above the threshold of sensitivity. Investigations of nervous response to pulsed sounds indicate that recognition of pulse elements ranges from about 90 pulses per second for small grasshoppers like *Stenobothrus lineatus* (Haskell, 1956) to 300 pulses per second for *Locusta migratoria* (Pumphrey and Rawdon-Smith, 1939). The practical implications of this small time constant is that sounds which appear continuous to human ears may be resolved into their constituent pulses by tympanal organs; as an example of this, the normal song of *Sehirus bicolor* (Fig. 85) has already been referred to in a previous chapter. In those few species where evidence is available at present, the range of pulse repetition discrimination more than covers the pulse repetition frequencies found in their stridulation.

Although Pumphrey remarked in 1940 that the possibility that Johnston's organ mediated sound reception "needed further investigation", a further thirteen years were to pass before Tischner in 1953 afforded direct physiological evidence of the auditory function of these receptors in mosquitoes. Using *Anopheles subpictus*, he recorded potentials at the base of their antennae, near Johnston's organ, in response to stimulation with pure and beating tones. Although the impulses recorded—the so-called electroantennagram —were not shown to be solely derived from Johnston's organ, the general picture of responses agrees so well with that to be expected on analysis of the physical and mechanical characteristics of the organs, and so convincingly explains the behavioural responses obtained by Roth and Mayer, that there can be little doubt that the receptors operate, in outline at least, as Tischner suggests. Tischner and Schief (1954) repeated these experiments with *Aedes aegypti*; when the voltage of the male electroantennagram is plotted against the frequency of a pure tone stimulus from 100-550 c/s—the response range of the receptor—the curve obtained is typical of a resonant structure, with a sharp peak at a resonant frequency of

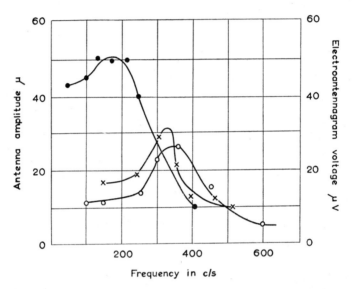

Fig. 69. Responses of antennal receptors in a male *Aedes aegypti*; x−x, electroantennagram voltage plotted against frequency of sound stimulus; o−o amplitude of male antennal movement in *μ* as a function of frequency of a constant intensity sound stimulus; •−•, as previously, for females.

about 325 c/s at 21° C. (Fig. 69). The resonant frequency rises with temperature from this figure to about 390 c/s at 35° C. Fig. 69 also shows graphs of the amplitude of antennal movement of both sexes in relation to the frequency of a constant intensity sound stimulus, and it will be seen that for males this figure is again in the form of a resonance curve, with the resonant frequency reasonably near to that obtained from the electroantennagram. This frequency corresponds quite well in *A. aegypti* with the principal frequency of the female flight note at the same temperature. Tischner also showed that the impulse volleys were apparently synchronous with the stimulating sound, although frequency doubling, when the frequency of the impulses was twice that of the stimulus, also occurred. This effect may be due to fibre interaction similar to that described by Pumphrey and Rawdon-Smith (1936b) from the cercal fibres of the cricket, but in any case the implication is that discrimination of sounds on the basis of frequency is possible. The organs act as displacement receivers, and Tischner (1953) elaborates an explanation of how each antenna alone or both together can act as directional detectors. Tischner and Schief, observing how male *Aedes* responded to female flight noise and artificial sounds, investigated the polarization of the emitted sound near the female, and concluded that flying males responded only to sounds of the correct frequency emitted in a polarized field, that is, one with marked displacement gradients arranged in a regular pattern in relation to, and nearby, the source of sound. Thus stimulation with a tuning fork of the correct frequency would be attractive, as Roth (1948) showed, and mosquitoes would also fly to a small loudspeaker without a reflector. But a loud-speaker set in a baffle has a more even sound field without the necessary displacement gradients to which the receptors are responsive, and this explains Roth's failure to attract mosquitoes with such a device. It seems likely that in some mosquitoes the "beat tone" observed during flight could also play a part in helping the male to orientate correctly towards the source of sound (the female) because of intensity differences in the sound field. Tischner and Schief (1954) and Risler (1953) have attempted to relate this physiological evidence to the morphology and anatomy of Johnston's organs, and while the results are interesting it is clear that further investigation will be needed before a clear insight into the function of the receptors can be attained.

Burkhardt and Schneider (1957) have more recently recorded impulses in the antennal nerve of *Calliphora erythrocephala*, which apparently have their origin in the receptors of Johnston's organ. While in the fly this organ principally responds to air movements, it is also sensitive to sounds in the range 50-500 c/s and the nervous discharge is synchronous with the stimulus. Between 150-250 c/s, the range of the wing-beat frequency of *Calliphora*, the sensitivity of the organ is about equal to that of the human ear; evidence of the directional properties of the receptors was also obtained. However, these authors reject the hypothesis that the acoustic sensitivity of these organs mediates meetings of the sexes in this species by responding to female flight tone, on the ground that the organ could not distinguish between the closely similar male and female flight tones.

Johnston's organ may play a part in the acoustic behaviour of aquatic insects and also in those predacious insects, such as ant-lions, which detect the presence of prey by vibrations transmitted through the substrate. The lability of Johnston's organ has been emphasized above, but it can hardly be doubted any longer that in certain insects, notably amongst the Diptera, it is capable of responding to and discriminating between low-frequency air-borne sounds.

All insects have a number of chordotonal sensillae scattered throughout the body, and while most of these clearly act as proprio-ceptors, many are so placed in relation to the external cuticular surface that they may in some circumstances act as acoustic receptors; this might well occur in aquatic insects. Thus Hughes (1952) while investigating abdominal mechanoreceptors in the aquatic beetle *Dytiscus marginalis* found certain receptors which responded like proprioceptors in that they discharged synchron-ously with the respiratory movements of the insect and like extero-ceptors in that they responded to sound stimuli of low frequencies. They appeared to be sharply tuned to frequencies about 100 cycles per second, and the discharge was asynchronous with the stimulus, but the frequency increased as the stimulus intensity increased. This finding emphasizes the fact that sound communication in aquatic insects does not necessarily demand the evolution of a receptor with tympanal membranes or similar structures; pressure or displacement waves impinging on the cuticle of a sub-merged insect can probably be detected by unmodified chordotonal sensillae attached to that cuticle. Thus it seems likely that the apparent lack of a membrane in some of the so-called tympanal organs of the aquatic Heteroptera does not seriously reduce the efficiency of these organs while submerged. This is borne out by the work of Schaller and Timm (1951) on the hearing ability of *Sigara striata*; males ready for copulation reacted to whistle sounds of 2-10 kc/s with a chirp and to ultra-sonic tones of 20, 30 and 40 kc/s with a long-drawn grinding noise. If the tympanal organs on both sides were completely destroyed, the reaction disappeared; unilateral extirpation had no effect, nor did removal of the "Kolben", the projecting club-like structure (Fig. 50), reduce the response. The work of Hughes and Schaller and Timm is virtually the sum total of knowledge of sound reception in aquatic insects, a field of infinite possibility.

Pumphrey and Rawdon-Smith (1936a) recorded responses in the abdominal nerves of *Locusta migratoria* to air-borne sound. The form of the response curve (Fig. 70) suggested a resonant structure and they attributed the response to short hairs on the thorax and

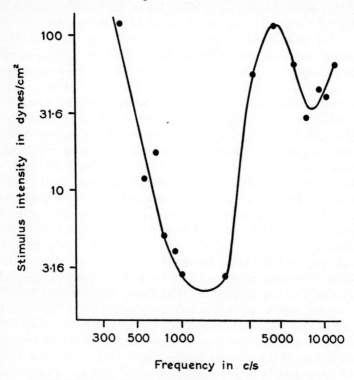

Fig. 70. Threshold curve for acoustic receptors with fibres in abdominal nerves of *Locusta migratoria*. (After Pumphrey & Rawdon-Smith).

abdomen. Pumphrey (1940) later revised this view and was inclined to think the responses were due to segmental chordotonal sensillae. Haskell (1956) has investigated the problem in certain grasshoppers and concludes that certain hair organs are the receptors concerned; this work is referred to in more detail later when hair sensillae are considered as a group.

The last type of organ involving chordotonal sensillae and concerned with hearing is the sub-genual organ, the structure and distribution of which has already been discussed above. We owe almost all our knowledge of the responses of these organs to Autrum and his colleagues (1941, 1948), who have studied them very fully; the receptors are specially adapted to perceive vibrations of the substrate, and their sensitivity is very high, but they cannot distinguish between different frequencies. Fig. 71 is a graph showing the threshold amplitudes of vibration at various frequencies in a range of insects. It will be seen that in some insects very small vibrations indeed can be detected; in *Periplaneta* for example, the smallest amplitude detectable is about 0·004 mμ, a figure comparable to atomic magnitudes. The organs respond to frequencies in the range 100 c/s to 10 kc/s. Haskell (1955) has shown that the process of stridulation in certain grasshoppers sets up vibrations of the substrate which might be perceived by the sub-genual organs. The organs can also perceive air-borne sounds, providing these are of low frequency and sufficient intensity to produce vibrations of the substrate, but it seems doubtful whether this is of much use under natural conditions, because most insect noises are deficient in frequencies below 1 kc/s, even as harmonics. Autrum has demonstrated in certain Tettigoniids that the presence of the sub-genual organ near the tibial tympanal organ has an effect on the threshold response of the latter; tympanal organs whose companion sub-genual organs have been destroyed undergo a reduction in their frequency response range and suffer a great decrease in sensitivity, particularly to low frequencies. The reason for this inter-action of the organs, which are separate anatomically, is not known. Subgenual organs proper are absent in Diptera, Coleoptera and certain Hemiptera, and in these groups Autrum has shown that responses to vibrations of the substrate are mediated by hair sensillae on the tarsal joints and by tibio-tarsal chordotonal sensillae. These organs respond only to low frequencies between 50 and 400 c/s and to comparatively large amplitude vibrations of the order of several microns.

The remaining major group of insect hearing organs to be considered is the hair sensillae. Minnich (1925, 1936) investigated the response of a number of Lepidopterous larvae to stimulation by the note from a tuning fork, the criterion for response being a behavioural one. For example, the caterpillars of *Vanessa antiopa* contract the dorsal longitudinal muscles when stimulated by certain sounds, and this causes the front end of the larvae to rise from the ground. The same muscular contraction can be demonstrated on

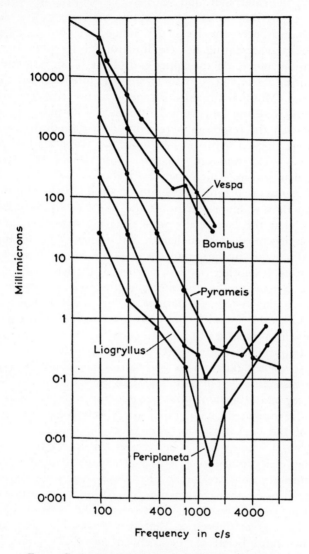

FIG. 71. Responses of sub-genual organs of a number of insects; the graphs are threshold amplitudes of vibration of the substrate over a range of frequencies. (After Autrum & Schneider).

pieces of the caterpillar, and by this method Minnich was able to map the distribution of the receptors concerned. The response was obtained over the frequency range 32-1,000 c/s, the lower frequencies representing not the limit of the receptors but of the stimulating source. At the upper end of the band, responses could be obtained above 1 kc/s by increasing the intensity, but the effect was small. Minnich provided strong evidence that the receptors concerned were the long body hairs of the caterpillars by demonstrating that the responses were reduced or disappeared when the hairs were clogged with water or flour, but reappeared when these substances were removed. In later observations the work was extended to species which had relatively few body hairs and the same response as before was obtained, although the threshold for the smooth was higher than for the hairy caterpillars. Minnich thought that the body hairs were resonant structures, and their response depended on their length and diameter; he attempted to demonstrate this by fatiguing the response to one frequency and then testing at another frequency, when, if the hairs were resonant and the fatigue was in the receptors themselves and not in the central nervous system, the fatigue of one group should not affect other groups. He found in fact that low frequency fatigue tended to inhibit the responses to high frequencies, but that fatigue with a high frequency had little effect on the responses at the lower end of the frequency range. This observation could not be explained on the resonance hypothesis, and had to wait for the work of Pumphrey and Rawdon-Smith (1936b) for interpretation. These workers investigated oscillographically the responses of the cercal nerve of the cricket *Acheta domesticus* on stimulation by pure tones from a loud-speaker. The cerci of this insect bears, amongst a number of receptors, long, loosely articulated hairs (see page 74), and Pumphrey and Rawdon-Smith showed these to be the receptor concerned in the acoustic reaction by coating them with vaseline, when the nervous response disappeared. The responses of these organs is of great interest in that they respond to pure tones in a manner reminiscent of the cochlear nerve of mammals. The nervous discharge is synchronous up to about 800 c/s, but at higher frequencies this synchronism only persists for the first fraction of a second of stimulation. Sometimes, on stimulation with lower frequencies, Pumphrey and Rawdon-Smith obtained results which they termed "frequency-doubling" and "frequency-halving"; thus on stimulation with a tone of 400 c/s a short-lived response of

800 c/s was occasionally obtained. At slightly higher frequencies, say 600 c/s, a short response at 300 c/s was obtained in some records. Pumphrey and Rawdon-Smith interpreted these results as demonstrating the phenomenon of "alternation"; each nerve fibre responds to every other stimulus wave, but because the responses in certain fibres are 180° out of phase, the resultant effect is one of synchrony with the stimulus. Such summation does not always

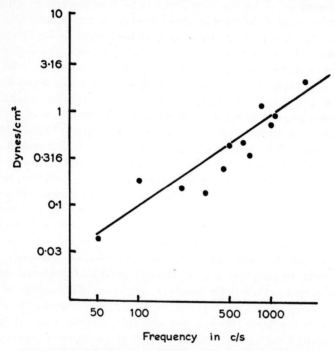

FIG. 72. The points represent the threshold of a long hair sensilla on the anal cercus of *Acheta domesticus* for a range of pure tones; the line corresponds to a constant displacement of the hair of 560 Angstrom units. (After Pumphrey & Rawdon-Smith).

occur however, because fibres often fire in phase, and this accounts for the short-lived appearance of the effects noted above. Pumphrey and Rawdon-Smith plotted the threshold curve for these receptors (Fig. 72), and were able to show from this that the hairs act as displacement receivers over the range investigated. On the basis of this graph, Pumphrey (1940) pointed out that on the assumption that the hair receptors investigated by Minnich had properties like those of the cercal sensillae, the fatiguing phenomenon demonstrated by the latter could be explained by the fact that for stimuli of equal intensity the lower frequencies would be relatively louder for the caterpillar than the higher, and therefore more likely to fatigue responses to higher frequencies. Most Orthoptera bear acoustically sensitive sensillae on their anal cerci, which are sensitive both to gross air movements (Fig. 73A) and also to low frequency sounds up to a few hundred cycles per second (Fig. 73B).

As mentioned above, Pumphrey and Rawdon-Smith obtained responses from abdominal segmental nerves of the Acridid, *Locusta migratoria*, and believed the receptors concerned to be short hair sensillae. Pumphrey later revised this view and considered the responses were obtained from segmental chordotonal sensillae. However, Haskell (1956 a, b) has demonstrated the existence in several species of Acridid grasshopper of organs on the thorax and abdomen capable of responding to air-borne stimuli, and adduces evidence that these receptors are in fact hair organs. The discharge from these organs was synchronous with regard to the stimulating sound, but an increase of stimulus intensity caused an increase in the number of fibres firing and the frequency of the discharge. These organs did not fatigue or show accommodation after prolonged stimulation. The threshold sound pressure for response in these receptors was 7 dynes/cm^2, and this high value probably precludes them from use as acoustic receptors for detecting the sounds of other grasshoppers, since such sound pressures exist only very close to a stridulating insect. Haskell produced evidence which suggests that certain hair sensillae on the sternal borders of the pleura are probably the organs concerned, but the matter needs further investigation. Haskell was also able to demonstrate that the hair sensillae on the sternites of certain grasshoppers responded to vibrations of the substrate, but the threshold response was not investigated. The question of the acoustic response of insect hair sensillae needs much further attention before any generalization can be made. Although in certain insects what appear to be generalized body hairs respond to acoustic stimuli, this is no warrant for assuming that any insect with similar hairs has some sensitivity to sound. In investigations of this problem care must be taken to control the intensity of stimulus to a level which is related to natural conditions, since it may be quite easy to obtain behavioural responses to sound of very high intensities which the insect would normally never encounter. The problem of hair receptors must also be investigated in relation to the responses of chordotonal sensillae

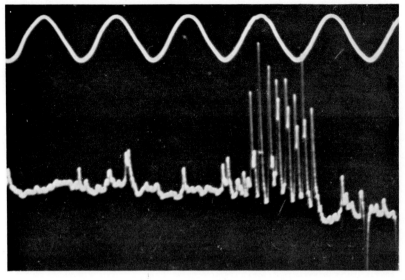

FIG. 73 (a)

Discharge in cercal nerve of O. *viridulus* to puff
of air from pipette 3 feet from the preparation;
timing wave 50 c/s.

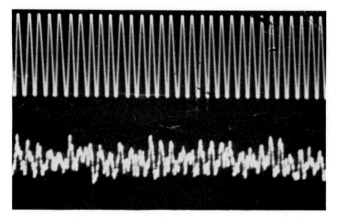

FIG. 73 (b)

Synchronous discharge in cercal nerve of S.
lineatus (lower trace) on stimulation with pure
tone of 250 c/s (upper trace).

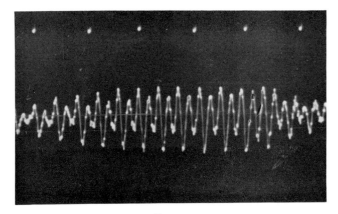

FIG. 74

Oscillogram of flight tone of a mosquito
(*Aedes* sp.); timing marks 1/100 second.

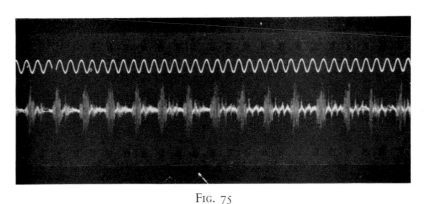

FIG. 75

Oscillogram of wing-beat noise of single
Desert Locust; timing wave 50 c/s.

in the body; the possibilities of confusion in this direction have been referred to above.

It should now be apparent that there are a number of types of hearing organ in insects, whose existence has been demonstrated physiologically or ethologically, and whose responses are in some cases known. The evidence is as yet very incomplete and imperfect, and does not permit any generalizations about hearing in the class Insecta as a whole. Nevertheless, it can be said that where carefully controlled behaviour experiments with insects suggest the presence of an acoustic sense, this should not be denied simply because the receptors concerned cannot be located and demonstrated. A case in point concerns certain Heteroptera investigated by Leston (1957) and Haskell (1958); these workers have studied the sound-producing mechanisms, the sounds produced and to some extent the behaviour associated with them, and the evidence points strongly to the possibility that the insects do communicate by sound although no specific hearing organs have as yet been described. Again, the response of bees (Frings and Little, 1957) to sounds has been demonstrated, although here the sound pressures required to produce a reaction are so great as to make it unlikely that air-borne sounds play any great part in the normal biology of these insects. However, the "piping" and "honking" of the queen bee as recorded and analysed by Woods (1956) seems to have some effect on other bees, and it would be most premature to state that bees cannot hear. In fact, having regard to the evidence now available on the variety of acoustic receptors possessed by insects, it is as well to bear in mind Pumphrey's warning that "it is necessary to regard experiments purporting to show that the sounds produced are not perceived by other individuals of the same species with great reserve".

A summary of the types of insect hearing organs, their distribution in the main orders, and some data on their performance is given in Table II.

G

Table II

Insect Hearing Organs

Receptor	Distribution	Position	Preferred Stimulus	Approximate Frequency Range (Kc/s)	Nervous Response
1. TYMPANAL ORGAN	*Orthoptera:* Acridoidea	1st segment abdomen	Air-borne sound	0.1-15	All tympanal organs so far investigated show responses asynchronous to pure tones but synchronous to modulation
	Tettigonioidea	Tibia of fore leg	ditto	1-100	
	Grylloidea	Tibia of fore leg	ditto	0.2-15	
	Homoptera Cicadidae	Metathorax and base of abdomen	ditto	0.1-50	
	Lepidoptera Noctuoidea	Metathorax	ditto	1-150	
	Pyralidina	Abdomen	ditto	—	
	Geometroidea except	1st or 2nd seg. abdomen	ditto	—	
	Axiidae	7th segment abdomen	ditto	—	

TABLE II—*continued*

Receptor	Distribution	Position	Preferred Stimulus	Approximate Frequency Range (Kc/s)	Nervous Response
1. TYMPANAL ORGAN (*cont.*)	*Heteroptera* Corixidae, Notonectidae, Pleidae, Nepidae, Naucoridae	Mesothorax	Water-borne sound, perhaps air-borne as well	2–40 — — — —	
2. JOHNSTON'S ORGAN	All insects	2nd segment of antenna	Many types of stimulus but in many Diptera, particularly Nematocera, air-borne sound	0·05–0·5	In several mosquitoes and *Calliphora* discharge synchronous with pure tone stimulus
3. SUB-GENUAL ORGANS	Orthoptera, Plecoptera, Lepidoptera, Hymenoptera, Hemiptera	Generally the proximal region of the tibia of all legs	Vibrations of the substrate	0·1–10	Asynchronous to pure tones

TABLE II—continued

Receptor	Distribution	Position	Preferred Stimulus	Approximate Frequency Range (Kc/s)	Nervous Response
4. SCATTERED CHORDOTONAL SENSILLAE	All orders	Almost anywhere in the body	Probably general proprioceptors, but when attached to cuticle could respond to air or water borne sound or substrate vibration	Probably 0·05-1	In one case asynchronous to pure tones
5. HAIR SENSILLAE	All orders	Almost anywhere. Found particularly on thorax and abdomen of Orthoptera and Lepidoptera and on anal cerci of Orthoptera	Generally tactile sensillae, but respond to fairly high intensity airborne sound	0·05-10	In several cases discharge synchronous with stimulus

REFERENCES

AUTRUM, H. (1940) *Z. vergl. Physiol.* **28**: 326-352.

AUTRUM, H. (1941) *Z. vergl. Physiol.* **28**: 580-637.

AUTRUM, H. and SCHNEIDER, W. (1948) *Z. vergl. Physiol.* **31**: 77-88.

BAIER, L. J. (1920) *Zool. Jahrb. Abt. allg. Zool. Physiol.* **47**: 151-248.

BURKHARDT, D. and SCHNEIDER, G. (1957) *Z. Naturf.* **126**: 139-143.

BUSNEL, R. G. (1956) *Insectes sociaux.* **3**: 11-16.

COLLENETTE, C. L. (1928) *Ent. mon. Mag.* **64**: 178-179.

EGGERS, F. (1925) *Z. vergl. Physiol.* **2**: 297-314.

EGGERS, F. (1928) *Zool. Bausteine.* **2**: 353 pp.

FABRE, J. H. (1897) *Souvenirs entomologiques* **5**. Paris.

FRINGS, H. and LITTLE, F. (1957) *Science.* **125**: 122.

GRABER, V. (1882) *Arch. mikr. Anat.* **20**: 506-640.

HASKELL, P. T. (1955) *Nature, Lond.* **175**: 639.

HASKELL, P. T. (1956a) *J. exp. Biol.* **33**: 756-766.

HASKELL, P. T. (1956b) *J. exp. Biol.* **33**: 767-776.

HASKELL, P. T. (1957) *J. ins. Physiol.* **1**: 52-75.

HASKELL, P. T. (1958) *Proc. zool. Soc. Lond.* **129**: 351-358.

HASKELL, P. T. and BELTON, P. (1956) *Nature, Lond.* **177**: 139-140.

HORRIDGE, G. A. (1960) *Nature, Lond.* **185**: 623-624.

HUGHES, G. M. (1952) *Nature, Lond.* **170**: 531.

KATSUKI, Y. and SUGA, N. (1958) *Proc. Jap. Acad.* **34**: 633-638.

LESTON, D. (1957) *Proc. zool. Soc. Lond.* **128**: 369-386.

MINNICH, D. W. (1925) *J. exp. Zool.* **42**: 443-469.

MINNICH, D. W. (1936) *J. exp. Zool.* **72**: 439-453.

MULLER, J. (1826) *Zur vergleichenden Physiologie des Gesichtsinnes des Menschen und der Tiere.* Leipzig.

MYERS, J. H. and MYERS, I. H. (1928) *Psyche.* **8**: 40-57.

NEWPORT, G. (1838) *Trans. Ent. Soc. Lond.* **2**: 229-248.

PRINGLE, J. W. S. (1954) *J. exp. Biol.* **31**: 525-60.

PUMPHREY, R. J. (1940) *Biol. Rev.* **15**: 107-132.

PUMPHREY, R. J. (1950) *Symp. Soc. Exptl. Biol.* **4**: 1-18.

PUMPHREY, R. J. and RAWDON-SMITH, A. F. (1936a) *Nature, Lond.* **137**: 990.

PUMPHREY, R. J. and RAWDON-SMITH, A. F. (1936b) *Proc. Roy. Soc.* B, **121**: 18-27.

PUMPHREY, R. J. and RAWDON-SMITH, A. F. (1939) *Nature, Lond.* **143**: 806.

PUMPHREY, R. J. and RAWDON-SMITH, A. F. (1940) *in* Pumphrey, R. J. (1940).

REGEN, D. J. (1913) *Pflüg. Arch. ges. Physiol.* **155**: 193-200.

REGEN, D. J. (1926) *Sitzb. Akad. Wiss. Wein. Math-Nat. Kl. Abt.* 1. **135**: 329-368.

RISLER, H. (1953) *Zool. Jahrb. Abt. Anat. u. Ontog. Tiere.* **73**: 165-186.

ROEDER, K. and TREAT, A. E. (1957) *J. exp. Zool.* **134**: 127-158.

ROTH, L. M. (1948) *Amer. Mid. Nat.* **40**: 265-352.

SCHALLER, F. and TIMM, C. (1951) *Z. vergl. Physiol.* **33**: 476-486.

SIEBOLD, C. T. (1844) *Arch. Naturg.* **10**: 52-81.

SIHLER, H. (1924) *Zool. Jahrb. Anat. Oent. Tiere.* **45**: 519-580.

TISCHNER, H. (1953) *Acustica.* **3**: 335-343.

TISCHNER, H. and SCHIEF, A. (1954) *Verhandl. deut. Zool. Ges.* 1954: 444-460.

TURNER, C. H. and SCHWARZ, E. (1914) *Biol. Bull.* **27**: 275-293.

VOGEL, R. (1923) *Z. ges. Anat. Abt. 1. Z. Anat. Entw.* **67**: 190-231.

WEVER, E. G. (1935) *J. cell. comp. Physiol.* **20**: 17-20.

WEVER, E. G. and BRAY, C. W. (1933) *J. cell. comp. Physiol.* **4**: 79-93.

WEVER, E. G. and VERNON, J. A. (1957) *Proc. Nat. Acad. Sci. Wash.* **43**: 346-348.

WOODS, E. F. (1956) *Bee World.* **37**: 185-195; 216-219.

CHAPTER IV

THE SONG PATTERNS OF INSECTS

THE techniques of recording and analysing insect song described in a previous chapter enable the physical make-up of the sounds emitted to be determined in terms of frequency range, intensity and general waveform and modulation pattern. Some insect sounds are devoid of a pattern, others have only a very simple one; others again, such as those of some of the Orthoptera, have such a complex structure that special names have been given to the various parts of the song as shown in physical analysis. The analysis of song structure is important for two reasons. First it may help in the understanding of how the sound-producing mechanism of the insect functions. In the case of wing noises, this is not so difficult, but in the case of a complex mechanism like the tymbal organ of the Homoptera the sound pattern is of great assistance in determining the exact mode of action. Secondly, the analysis of the song of an insect assists in the interpretation of ethological observations concerning that insect and is necessary for the formulation of proper conditions for further behaviour experiments. Control of intensity, for example, is of great importance. It has been already pointed out that by using sounds of sufficiently high intensity it is often possible to obtain reactions from isolated sense organs or whole insects which were previously thought not to be acoustically sensitive. Clearly the intensity of stimuli used in behaviour experiments should be limited to that occurring under natural conditions, otherwise spurious responses may be obtained; the knowledge of the range of intensity, and that relating to other parameters of the song, can only be obtained by analysis of the natural sounds. However, knowledge of the structure of the stridulation and of the functioning of the sound-producing mechanism is not sufficient for the student of behaviour; he wants to know under what conditions and in response to what stimulus, interior or exterior, the song is produced, whether more than one song exists, and if so when the alternatives are used, whether the song is modified by learning and so on. Thus to characterize the song of an insect completely requires both physical and ethological detail; it must be admitted at once that only in the Orthoptera and Hemiptera has real progress been made in collecting such data, observations on all other groups being very meagre. In this chapter a few insect sounds will be described in some detail in an attempt to give a broad outline of the type and range of variation that exists. In order to preserve the two-fold functional and comparative approach, the divisions of Chapter 2 will be retained; thus for example all sounds made by frictional mechanisms, as in the Orthoptera, Lepidoptera and Heteroptera, will be considered under one heading. This will help to emphasize the variety of sounds which can be produced by one basic type of apparatus.

I. SOUNDS PRODUCED AS A BY-PRODUCT OF SOME USUAL ACTIVITY OF THE INSECT

As was pointed out previously, for all practical purposes this category is limited to flight noises. Noises made during feeding or by cleaning movements are almost certainly adventitious and no case has yet been investigated which has shown them to be otherwise. The flight noise of insects is one aspect of the present subject which has attracted considerable attention amongst entomologists, although their aim has generally been fixed on some aspect of flight physiology and interest in the sounds themselves and their biological significance has come a poor second. It does not seem to have been clearly realized that the terms "flight note", "flight tone", and "flight noise" need not mean the same thing. In all flying insects the motion of the wings set the surrounding air in motion and this may generate a "sound" within our present definition. In insects with very slow wing-beat frequences, such as those of 5-10 per second found in some butterflies, the sound will be infrasonic. As the wing-beat frequency increases, an audible sound will be heard, and it is clear that in many insects, such as bees and flies and mosquitoes, the fundamental frequency of this "flight tone" will be equal to the wing-beat frequency, and it is possible to deduce the latter from the former, as many workers have shown, notably Sotavalta (1947). But two further points arise; first, the wings themselves may vibrate at their own resonant frequency or harmonics of this frequency, and thus a complex tone is produced in which the fundamental frequency is still that of the wing-beat frequency, but in which exist harmonics of higher or lower frequency. Sotavalta and other workers realized this, and some determinations of the sound frequency spectrum of certain insect flight-tones have been made. An oscillogram of such a sound (Fig. 74) reveals a fairly simple pattern in which the fundamental can clearly be seen and in which the presence of harmonics can be deduced by the irregularities present. Such a sound may reasonably be termed a "flight tone", since it bears a direct relationship to wing-beat frequency. As far as present data goes, the probable frequency range of the fundamental note in such sounds ranges from some 6 per second in such Lepidoptera as *Pieris rapae*, through the 35 per second of Odonata such as *Aeschna juncea*, and the 220-250 per second of the honey-bee, up to the 587 cycles per second of the mosquito *Aedes cantans* and the 2,000 cycles per second of the midge *Forcipomyia*. The frequency of such flight tones will naturally vary somewhat from individual to individual, and may be altered by age or by environmental conditions, notably temperature. For example, in *Aedes aegypti* Tischner and Schief (1954), showed that in general the fundamental flight tone of the female at 23° C. was 385 ± 30 c/s, a fairly small variation; but the change with age was much greater, from about 220 c/s at 12 hours after emergence to perhaps 430 c/s three to four days later. In *Drosophila*, according to Sotavalta, the rate changes from 150 c/s at 10° C. to 250 c/s at 37° C. In the Tsetse fly *Glossina palpalis* the common name is said to be onomatopaeic for the sound made by the fly while feeding, and Kartman *et al.* (1946) pointed out that at low air temperatures the flight is noiseless, but at high temperatures a characteristic buzzing is heard.

In contrast to these comparatively pure sounds there are certain sounds connected with flight in insects which have a considerably more complex structure, and in which the wing-beat frequency is concerned in a manner different from that described above. Haskell (1957) investigated the flight noises of the Desert Locust and showed that when in free flight with the legs tucked up near the body, the flight noise was of the type referred to above, the wing-beat frequency appearing as a fundamental in a note of very low intensity. But during certain stages of flight, just after taking off or when preparing to land, when the legs were lowered, the noise changed to a much louder sound, which he termed the "wing-beat noise", and which was apparently due to the hind wings hitting the hind legs. The sound now had a far more complex structure, as seen from the oscillogram in Fig. 75; the noise can now be regarded as pulse modulated at the wing-beat frequency of about 17-20 cycles per second, but each pulse is a complex sound in which frequencies of from 60 c/s to 6·4 kc/s were detected by audiospectrographic analysis. Similarly Roeder and Treat (1957) found in the moth *Prodenia eridania* that while the flight noise was apparently of a fairly simple type with a frequency of about 50 cycles per second, corresponding to the wing beat, a pulse of high frequency sound, containing components at least up to 15 kc/s, was emitted at a fixed phase of the wing stroke. This case emphasizes the need for analysis of apparently simple sounds, since it was shown that in this moth the high frequency pulse might play an important part in acoustically oriented flight behaviour. In view of these findings, it may be desirable to use the term " flight tone " to indicate a sound resulting from flight activity, when that tone is of comparatively simple structure and in which the fundamental frequency is that of the wing-beat frequency of the insect; the term " flight noise " could then be used to indicate that the sound output caused by flight was of a complex form, bearing no simple relation to wing beat. The matter is further complicated by the likelihood that in insects with fairly high wing-beat frequencies, parts of the thorax may also vibrate and produce complex noises; several authors are of the opinion, for example, that the changes in flight noise observable in insects such as bees in relation to various behaviour patterns may be due to such vibration. The only way of deciding such cases is by full physical analysis of the sounds and a consideration of the structures which may be concerned in producing them.

The intensities of the flight-tones and flight noises of insects are generally low, but vary a great deal. In general, soft-bodied insects with low wing-beat frequencies and insects with pliable wings consisting of hair bundles or clothed with scales, emit noises of very low intensity. The locust *Schistocerca gregaria* for example, while in level flight, emits a sound with a level probably no greater than 25 db very near the source; when making the " wing-beat noise ", however, the intensity rises and is 50 db at a distance of 2 feet from the insect. The sound output of many moths is of the order of 20 db near the source, a fact which explains such clichés as the " ghostly fluttering of a moth ". Insects with hard clear wings, such as flies and bees and beetles, and with hard bodies, produce noises of greater intensity, up to 50 or 60 db. Very few measurements of intensity have been made, and since the sensitivity of human hearing is so variable with frequency, insects with flight tones within the range 400-1,000 cycles always sound very much louder, and are reported as such, than insects which emit noises of lower or higher frequency. Since the intensity determines the range of action of the sound from a behavioural point of view it is clear that investigations of such behaviour ought to include instrumental studies of the intensity.

Many observations can be found in literature where insects emit, while in the air, noises of a nature which indicate that a mechanism other than that used for flight is in operation. Observations of the "whistling moth" *Hecatesia*, and the butterfly *Ageronia*, where distinct clicking noises were heard during flight, are cases in point, Hebard (1922) records that the Noctuid *Heliocheilus paradoxus* stridulates while in hovering flight, the noise being like the ticking of a loud watch, audible at 20 feet. Pierce (1949) attempted to investigate the noise made during flight by several Acrididae, notably *Circotettix verraculatus*, called the "snapping locust" because of these flight noises, and *Dissosteira carolina*, another locust well known for the noises it produces while flying. In the case of *Circotettix*, while in flight the sound produced consists of pulses at the rate of 5-6 per second, containing frequencies up to 6 kc/s; on the ground, the song consists of trains of pulses at about 35 per second, with frequencies up to 9 kc/s being present. *Dissosteira* performs some quite complicated aerial manœuvres, thought by some entomologists to be a courtship display, which are accompanied by acoustic emissions. The insect hovers in the air and its wings flutter very fast; a change of position occurs, generally accompanied by a gain in height, and this is accompanied by a slowing down of the wing fluttering, which, however, persists for a longer time. Pierce gives figures indicating that in both types of behaviour the sound is emitted as a series of pulses in which the principal frequency is 8 kc/s; in the fast flutter the pulse rate is about 40 per second, the emission lasting one or two seconds, while for the slow flutter the rate varies from 6-14 pulses per second but lasts from 4-6 seconds. Several other Acrididae emit noises while in flight, and as yet the exact sound-producing mechanism is not known. In some cases these insects possess one of the normal stridulatory mechanisms of the Acrididae, but others— and *Disossteira* is an example—apparently lack this.

2. SOUNDS PRODUCD BY IMPACT OF PART OF THE BODY AGAINST THE SUBSTRATE

Very little attention has been paid to this class of sounds, and most observations only go as far as recording the fact that a particular insect produces noises by impact. Probably the only published recording and analysis of impact noise is the study of the Acridid *Encoptolophus sordidus* by Pierce (1949). This insect makes sounds by stamping its tarsi on the ground; the rapidity of this motion is such that the sound is generated as a number of trains of pulses, each train consisting of 5 or 6 separate pulses. Pierce gives the principal frequency as 7 kc/s, a surprisingly high frequency if it is supposed that the material of the substrate plays some part in sound production. However, in the experiments mentioned the insect was on wire mesh, which probably modified the frequency of emission considerably, since the sound was recorded with a crystal microphone bolted to the cage. Pierce draws no conclusions as to relationship of leg movement to sound structure. In general, it is to be expected that sounds produced by body impact would be a series of distinct knocks or pulses; there would be two parts to the emission, since some energy would appear as true sound waves radiated through the air, almost certainly of low frequency, while the rest would appear as vibration of the substrate. The frequency of these latter vibrations would depend on many factors, but principally on the modulus of the material, and if this were hard such as wood, quite high frequencies could appear. In view of the amazing vibration senstivity of the sub-genual organs at high frequencies (see Chapter 3), the range of communication could be quite large, for example, in the case of wood-boring beetles, but in other cases, such as the so-called "warning drumming" of soldier termites on the earth, or the drumming of stone-flies, the considerable damping effect of the medium would almost certainly curtail the range severely. However, even here a portion of the energy will be radiated as sound waves, and Maçnamara (1926) reports that the drumming of stone-flies can be heard up to 15-20 feet on a quiet night; as in *Encoptoloplus*, the sound consisted of trains of pulses, and the pulse frequency is said to be about 30 per second, although it is not stated how this was estimated.

It is interesting to consider further the situation of insects which bore into wood, one piece of which may be infested with two or more related species; if it is accepted for the purposes of argument that acoustic emission plays a part in mating and that species discrimination is necessary, it can be asked upon what characteristics of the sound signal can discrimination be based? It cannot be frequency, because the frequency characteristics of the sound will be set for all practical purposes by the material infested, which is the same for all species. It can only be then the pulse structure of the sound, the rate of tapping, in other words, which is significant; and, in fact, as Gahan (1910) and others have pointed out, it is possible to differentiate between several wood-boring beetles on the basis of the rate of tapping they exhibit. There is as yet no clear evidence that sound signals in these beetles are of significance, but since it is likely that they possess receptors which could respond to pulsed noises, the possibility should be borne in mind in future investigations.

Amongst other insects producing impact noises almost the only comparative data is that of Pearman (1928) for certain Psocoptera, and here again the rhythm of the sounds is reported as the main characteristic, *Clothilla pulsatoria* tapping at the rate of 5-6 per second for as long as a minute, while *Lepinotus inquilinus* produces uniform pulses each lasting 3 seconds with a variable silent interval of 15-80 seconds between. Pearman had no doubt that these were " mating calls of the female ", in which case the differences may be important.

3. SOUNDS PRODUCED BY SPECIAL MECHANISMS

(a) Frictional mechanisms

This category of sound-producing mechanisms has received more investigation than any other, but despite this attention only in one group, the Orthoptera, is there any real understanding of the mode of action of the mechanisms, and only in a few species of this group has a fairly complete analysis been made of the physical nature of the sounds emitted and the behaviour which accompanies it. A start has been made on a study of the mechanisms and sounds in the terrestrial Heteroptera, and there has been isolated work on Diptera, Coleoptera and Lepidoptera. Apart from these few examples, although many so-called stridulatory mechanisms have been described covering practically all insect orders, nothing is known about the sounds which they may be capable of producing. However, a brief consideration of the mode of action of some of the best-known mechanisms will serve to illustrate the principles involved.

Frictional mechanisms in insects consist of two components; one component—which might be called the "discontinuous phase"—consists of a row of teeth, a line of hairs or a number of pegs; the other component—the "continuous phase"—consists of a single ridge or hard projection, such as a raised wing vein, and this is attached to or forms part of a relatively large area of integument. These two parts are capable of being moved relative to one another while in contact; the question of which part actually moves is immaterial, the relative motion of one part to another being the important feature. As each projection of the discontinuous phase passes in turn over the ridge of the continuous phase, it imparts or tends to impart motion to this phase. This motion causes the area of integument to which the continuous phase is attached to vibrate, the frequency being the resonant frequency of that particular system, which will clearly differ enormously between such possible areas as wings, elytra, abdominal tergites, thorax and so on. But the resonant system is not excited once only and then allowed to come to rest; it is excited by each tooth or projection of the discontinuous phase, as these pass in turn over the continuous phase. The frequency of these impacts between the teeth on one phase and the ridge on the other depends obviously on the number of teeth which hit the ridge and the speed with which the parts move relative to one another, and the number of these impacts per second has been called by Pierce (1949) the "impact frequency", for obvious reasons. The relationship of this frequency to the resonant frequency of the continuous phase component has an important bearing on the type of sound emitted by an insect, as Pasquinelly and Busnel (1955) have pointed out. There are three main possibilities; the impact frequency may be either less than, more than or equal to the resonant frequency of the continuous phase component. In the first case, the sound output will consist of a series of sound pulses; the frequency of occurrence of these pulses will be the same as the impact frequency, but the principal sound frequency present in each pulse will be that of the resonant frequency of the continuous phase part of the stridulatory mechanism. An example of an insect with such a mechanism is the Tettigoniid *Ephippiger bitterensis*, and Fig. 76 shows the relationship of the parts of the stridulatory mechanism to the sound produced. The discontinuous phase here is the file on one elytron, consisting of a number of teeth, while the continuous phase is a solid projection, the scraper, on the opposite elytron. As the insect closes its elytra together each tooth as it passes over the scraper sets up a vibration in both elytra; this results in the production of a short pulse of sound, the principal frequency of which is the main resonant frequency of the elytron. Since these latter are complex surfaces, connected to other bodies, the resultant sound has many harmonics and in fact consists of both sonic and ultra-sonic frequencies. This can be seen in the oscillograms in Fig. 76; the audiospectrogram of the sound shows that the principal resonant frequency in the sonic band is about 10 kc/s. Each tooth of the discontinuous phase produces one pulse of sound, and it can be seen that the smaller teeth at the ends of the file produce smaller pulses, and because more small teeth can fit into a given area than larger ones, the frequency of recurrence of the pulses is slightly faster at the beginning of the stridulation.

This form of sound output, occurring when impact frequency is much lower than resonant frequency, can now be contrasted to that type where impact frequency is equal or nearly equal to resonant frequency. Here, as each tooth of the discontinuous phase passes over the scraper or continuous phase, the integumental areas to which the latter is attached will commence to vibrate; they will complete one cycle of vibration, when the next tooth hits the scraper, thus keeping the continuous phase in constant motion at its resonant frequency. In this case impact frequency is equal to resonant frequency, and there will be continuous emission of a fairly pure note. Such a mechanism is found in the crickets, and Fig. 77 shows the relationship between mechanism and sound in *Oecanthus pellucens*. Each pulse of sound emitted is made by the closing of the elytra—that is, one passage of the file over the scraper. Each oscillation in the pulse is due to the impact of one tooth and, as before, because the teeth at the beginning and end of the file are smaller so the oscillations at the beginning and end of the sound are smaller. Thus one pulse of sound results from the closing together of the elytra in *Oecanthus*, and indeed in crickets in general, while in *Ephippiger* and many Tettigoniids, the closure of the elytra produces a whole series of sound pulses.

The third case envisaged, where impact frequency is higher than resonant frequency, has not yet been described from insects and so will not be further considered. There remains one further case of importance, which is in fact a special condition of the first case and arises when the impact frequency is slightly lower than the resonant frequency of the continuous phase. This is believed by some workers to be the case with the femoral elytral stridulatory mechanism widespread amongst Acrididae, and the sound output consists typically of a pulse of sound, the principal frequency of which is the resonant frequency of the continuous phase. But because the impact frequency is nearly equal to the resonant frequency, the sound will suffer great changes of phase. The sound output is related to movements of the parts of the apparatus as in crickets, that is, one movement of the stridulatory parts produce one continuous pulse of sound.

The three groups of the Orthoptera, Gryllids, Acridids and Tettigoniids also illustrate that the principal emitted frequency is related to the size of the continuous phase—the larger the area of this which vibrates, the lower the emitted frequency. In Gryllids, it seems that the whole elytron vibrates, and characteristically these insects have low principal frequencies; for *Acheta domesticus* it is of the order of 3-4 kc/s, for four species of *Oecanthus* it varies between 1·2 and 3·6 kc/s, and even for the smaller *Nemobius* the principal frequency is only 5·4 kc/s in *carolinus* and 7·5 kc/s in *griseus*. The range of the group is about 1-8 kc/s. In the Tettigoniids, however, either the elytron is reduced, as in *Ephippiger* (Fig. 9) or else only a small portion of it vibrates, as seems to be the case in several sub-families, notably the Conocephalinae and Pseudophyllinae. Fig. 8 is a drawing of the elytra of *Pterophylla camellifolia*, which is capable of emitting sounds up to 63 kc/s, and Fig. 78 is a similar drawing of *Orchelimum vulgare*, which emits frequencies of 7, 16 and 27 kc/s. The "mirror" is thought to be the high frequency resonator, and Pierce (1949) showed that if one calculated the basic resonant frequency of these areas, and also their second and third harmonics, in many species these theoretical frequencies were in fair agreement with the actual frequencies recorded from the insects. For example, in *Orchelimum vulgare* the calculated frequency was 10,600 c/s, while the actual frequency was 7,700 c/s. In *Conocephalus fasciatus* two sounds are emitted, one of 16,300 c/s and the other of about 40 kc/s; the calculated resonant frequencies were 16,600 c/s for the principal and 60 kc/s for the second harmonic. Since the calculations included very approximate figures for the elastic modulus of the elytra, this measure of agreement is quite reasonable and supports the suggestion that the mirror areas act as high-frequency resonators. Many

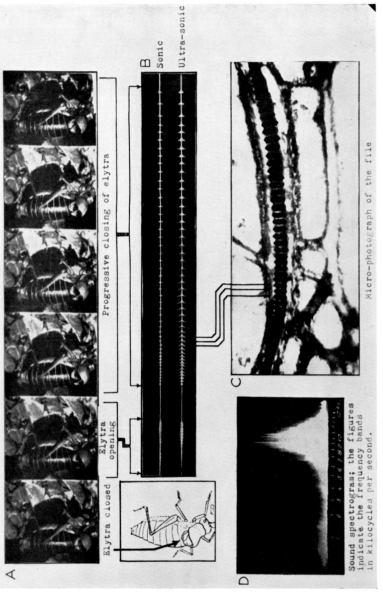

Elytra closed   Progressive closing of elytra

Elytra opening

B

Sonic

Ultra-sonic

C

Micro-photograph of the file

D

Sound spectrogram; the figures indicate the frequency bands in kilocycles per second.

Fig. 76 Stridulation of the Tettigoniid, *Ephippiger bitterensis*; (A) Film of insect showing movement of elytra (B) Oscillograms of the sonic and ultra-sonic output of the insect, showing the pulse structure. One closure of the elytra produces a whole series of pulses. (C) Photomicrograph of the file; one tooth produces one pulse. (D) The sound spectrogram, showing wide frequency spectrum. (Reproduced by permission of R. G. Busnel).

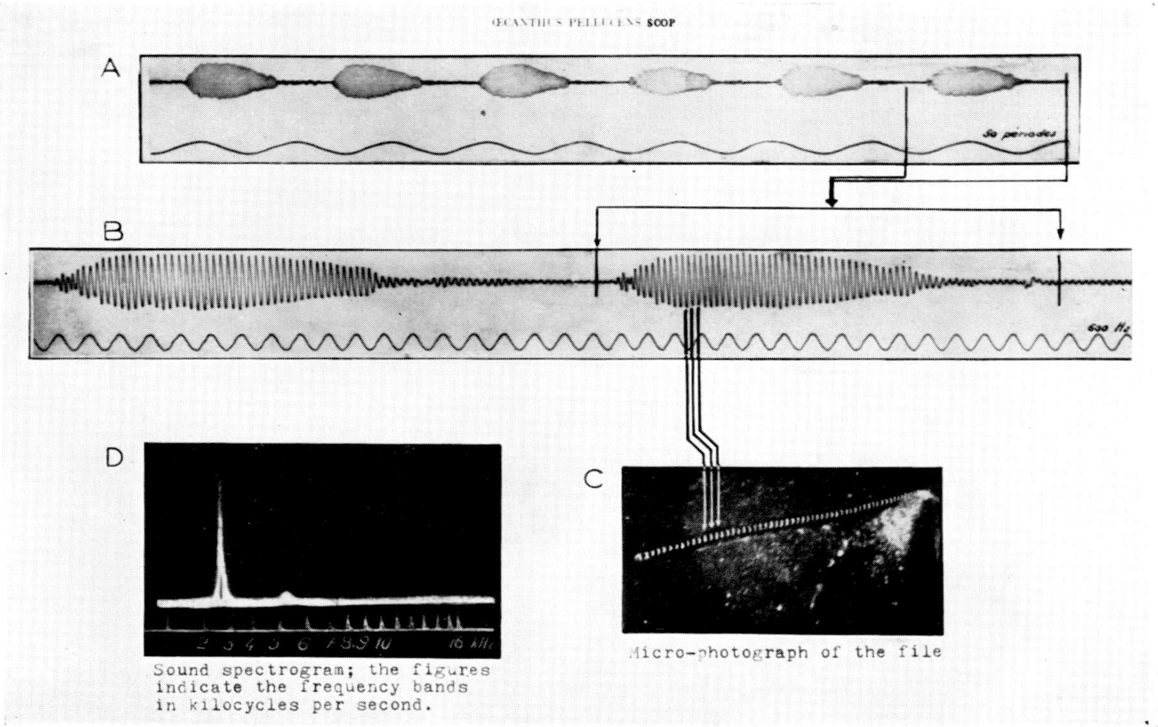

OCANTHUS PELLUCENS SOOP

A

B

C

Micro-photograph of the file

D

Sound spectrogram: the figures indicate the frequency bands in kilocycles per second.

FIG. 77 Stridulation of the Gryllid *Oecanthus pellucens*; A, & B slow and fast oscillograms of the sound, respectively. Each pulse is produced by one complete closure of the elytra. C. Photomicrograph of the file, each tooth of which produces one oscillation of the complete pulse. D. Sound spectrograph, showing almost pure tone with a small second harmonic. (Reproduced by permission of R. G. Busnel).

Tettigoniids have such wing discs, and it is therefore interesting that the group as a whole emit the highest frequencies of all Orthoptera, many of them in the ultra-sonic as well as the sonic range (e.g. *Ephippiger*, see Fig. 76). Tettigoniids rarely emit sounds of any intensity at frequencies lower than 5 kc/s and the group range may be said to be 5-100 kc/s. The Acridids seem to occupy

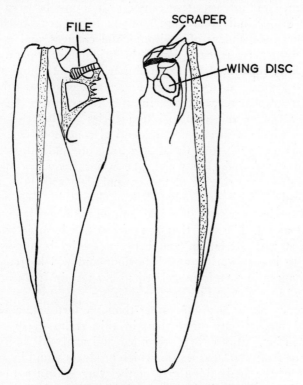

FILE

SCRAPER

WING DISC

FIG. 78. Elytra of male *Orchelimum vulgare*, showing the small wing disc areas (" mirror ") thought to be responsible for production of ultra-sonic frequencies. (After Pierce).

the mid-way position of the three, with typical principal frequencies emitted of 5 kc/s in *Chorthippus brunneus*, 9 kc/s in *Locusta migratoria* and a group range of 2-12 kc/s. Despite this seemingly neat division, the great variation and overlapping in these frequency ranges emphasizes the point that it has as yet proved impossible to specify or predict the exact mode of operation of frictional stridulatory mechanisms in terms of physical quantities because the

H

extent and nature of the resonant surfaces has not yet been discovered in any given case. It is possible to record and analyse the
sound of one or several species, but this gives no warrant for assuming similar characteristics in closely related species. In comparative
work of this sort, carried out on both insect groups and on individuals of one species, the main fact that emerges is the variation
of frequency and intensity that can occur, not only between groups
but also in one individual from moment to moment. Such variation occurs independent of environmental changes, and is clearly
related to the nervous regulation of the stridulatory apparatus. It is
perhaps best illustrated by examining a series of sound spectrographs of a group of insect songs (Fig. 79). A glance at this range
of spectrographs reveals that in the four insects concerned
frequency ranges and principal frequencies overlap enormously.
Variation within a species under identical conditions is shown in
S. lineatus (A, B, C), and variation within one individual is illustrated in *O. viridulus*, in which the wider frequency spectrum
resulting from the singing of the normal song with both femora
(E) instead of with one only (F) can clearly be seen. Overlap
between species as regards principal emitted frequency is illustrated
by E, H and J. The fact that song frequency is subject to such
fluctuation and overlap in and between species is important in
relation to insect hearing and behaviour and will be referred to
later. Changes in waveform, related to changes in frequency, also
occur, and Figs. 81A and B illustrate this.

Frequency range in groups other than the Orthoptera—indeed,
frictional mechanisms other than in this group—have received
little attention. Monro (1953) recorded and analysed the stridulation of the fruit fly *Dacus tryoni*, which produces sound by rubbing
the edge of the anal-cubital area of the wing against a row of 24
tergal bristles. The principal emitted frequency was 3 kc/s, and
the whole sound consisted of damped wave trains of this frequency
repeated at rates of about 290 per second—a pattern completely
impossible to predict from the description of the mechanism. In
the Lepidoptera, Haskell (1956) has found frequencies up to 14 kc/s
in the stridulation of the Peacock butterfly, and Alexander (1957b)
finds frequencies of 1 to 9 kc/s in certain Coleoptera, while in
terrestrial Heteroptera principal frequencies range from 6 to 12 kc/s
and even higher. Although in the latter group a very good comparative description of the structure of the stridulatory organs is
available (Leston, 1957), no attempt has yet been made to relate

the mode of action of the mechanism to the emitted sounds. While an analysis of frequency range and variation in any insect group would be of interest and importance in certain cases and as a matter of fundamental research, lack of it does not preclude us from classifying insect sounds on another basis—modulation pattern.

This term modulation here includes pulse modulation; Fig. 80

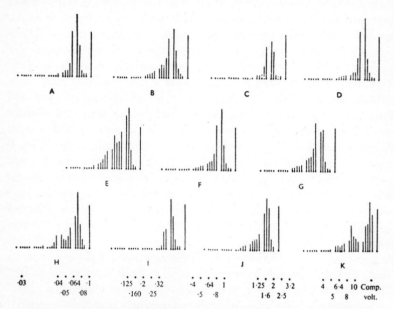

Fig. 79. Audiospectrograms of the songs of certain male Truxalinae. The key below shows the mid-point frequency of each band in kc/s; the line at the extreme right is an orientation deflection from a 1.5 volt battery. A.B.C. *S. lineatus* normal song, made by three insects under identical conditions. D. *S. lineatus*, courtship song. E.F. *O. viridulus*, normal song, sung (E) with both femora and (F) with right femur only. G. *O. viridulus*, courtship song. H. *C. brunneus*, normal song. I. *C. brunneus*, courtship song. J. *C. parallelus*, normal song. K. Imitation of *C. parallelus*, normal song.

shows oscillograms of one of the songs of the grasshopper *Omocestus viridulus*, in which the rate of repetition of the sound pulses is about 13 per second. It will be recalled that this frequency is referred to as the "pulse repetition frequency", or "P.R.F." for short. Difficulties occur in the use of this phrase, since there is as yet no agreement between biological acousticians as to terminology and a "pulse" to some indicates a very definite entity, while others use it in an altogether looser sense. The basis of using the term

"P.R.F." in acoustic analysis is that, as will become apparent, it is necessary when trying to describe insect sounds to refer to the temporal pattern of the sound units composing them. The oscillograms in Figs. 80-82 are all of sounds with very similar frequency and intensity spectra, and the main difference between them lies in the temporal distribution of "pulses"—or the P.R.F. Thus for *Stenobothrus lineatus* (Figs. 81A and B) the repetition rate is about one per second, for *Omocestus viridulus* it varies from 10-18 per second, while for *Chorthippus parallelus* it is only 5 per second (Fig. 82). These songs can be used to show the value of the concept of pulse repetition frequency. As has been said above, analysis shows that the frequency range of an insect sound can and does vary not only from insect to insect, but in an individual; but the pulse rate is much more constant and, while subject to minor variations, seems, as far as present knowledge goes, to be the most constant factor in insect song. Figs. 81A and B illustrate different wave forms, but constant modulation frequency, in two individuals of *S. lineatus*. The P.R.F. is, furthermore, independent of the longer temporal changes in structure. For example, the song of the male *C. parallelus* is shown in Fig. 82 as consisting of thirteen pulses of sound; in fact, the number of pulses in any given burst of song may vary from three to fifteen—but what does not vary nearly so much is the rate of production of the pulses, which is always approximately 5 per second irrespective of the total number of pulses. This comparatively fixed quality in sounds produced by frictional mechanisms is found also in other groups, such as certain terrestrial Heteroptera (Leston, 1957; Haskell, 1958). In some cases it may be the main distinguishing feature between the songs of closely related species as Fig. 83 shows for the Heteropterans *Kleidocerys resedae* and *K. ericae*. Here the song frequencies and intensities are almost identical, but the pulse rate of *resedae* is 8 per second, half that of *ericae*. Typical variation of these figures is 7-9 pulses for *resedae* and 14-19 in *ericae*. This inter-specific variation is nicely illustrated by the work of Alexander (1957a) on several species of the cricket genus *Acheta*. Fig. 84 shows a series of sound spectrographs of the "Vibralyzer" type of the typical calling songs of six species; it is clear that the frequency spectrum of all six overlap, but the pulse structure is very different. The two most similar are *Acheta vernalis* and *A. fultoni*, but *vernalis* has a P.R.F. of 5 per second while that of *fultoni* is 7 per second—probably sufficient for discrimination. Where one species can sing several different songs, the main differentiating quality between them has been found to be the pulse repetition frequency. Fig. 85 illustrates this in the case of the small Heteropteran *Sehirus bicolor*, where the three songs of the male all consist of a number of discrete sound pulses, the repetition rates being 1·4, 8·5, and 55 per second respectively, although in all songs the frequency spectrum and intensity are essentially similar. As will be seen this distinguishing or characteristic quality conferred by pulse repetition frequency occurs in many insects.

It is all the more interesting, therefore, to consider those types of insect sounds, produced by frictional mechanisms, which conspicuously lack any signs of an ordered nature. One such sound is the stridulation of the Reduviid bug *Coranus subapterus*, shown in Fig. 86. The stridulatory apparatus of this bug has been described many times, but only recently has the sound been recorded and analysed by Haskell (1958); it is clear from the oscillogram that it consists of an irregular train of waves, each of which is produced by the tip of the rostrum striking one tooth of the ridges of the prosternal furrow. The speed of recurrence of the waves, and the total duration of the sound are functions of the relative speed of movement of the two parts of the mechanism and even casual observation of a stridulating bug of this group will show that these are highly variable in any one individual. Sounds of this type, which are found in Hemiptera and also in Coleoptera and Lepidoptera, are therefore non-specific and cannot be used (at least in any simple manner) in a communication system. These noises —and in this case the stridulation can strictly be defined as noise— could, however, act as an alarm signal, and it may be significant that tactile stimuli are generally necessary to stimulate production of such sounds. Insects which produce such noises in response to touch, would, if seized by a predator such as a bird, at once begin to stridulate, and the noise may startle the bird into momentarily letting go. This behavioural aspect is discussed in greater detail in the following chapter; what concerns us here is the sound itself, which is characterized not only by an absence of pattern but wide frequency range and comparatively high intensity, both the latter being valuable characteristics for a defensive sound. We thus have examples of two distinct types of insect sound; one type consists of pulses or elements arranged in a definite and specific pattern, which might be called "organized" sounds, while the other type is marked by an absence of any coherent pattern and may be thought of as "unorganized" sounds. The occurrence of these two types of stridulation deserves fuller investigation, especially from the behavioural point of view. So meagre is the data on insect sounds that it is not possible to arrive at even a tentative conclusion as to the proportions of sound-producing insects which make "organized" and "unorganized" sounds. The former category has, for obvious reasons, attracted more attention, but the latter certainly occurs in various species of Orthoptera, Heteroptera, Coleoptera, Hymenoptera and Lepidoptera and merits more attention. It is, apparently, rare for an insect which normally sings "organized" songs to emit an "unorganized" sound. It is possible to argue that the development and retention of the ability to emit sounds shows them to be adaptive and of survival value; there is good evidence of this for "organized" sounds but not so far for "unorganized" ones. The behavioural aspects of these two types of sound production are discussed in the following chapter.

Some mention must be made here of frictional sound production in aquatic insects. This is well known in the water bugs, Hydrocorisae, but aquatic stridulators also occur in the Coleoptera and Odonata. In this latter group Asahina (1939) described stridulation in the larvae of *Epiophlebia superstes* as a "shrill tone made when the larvae are disturbed". However, the best known aquatic singers are undoubtedly the water bugs. The singing habits of *Corixa* and *Micronecta* have been the subject of much entomological comment, but there are few accurate descriptions of the sounds. Von Mitis (1935) describes *Micronecta meridionalis* as having two songs, one a "loud chirp" the other a rather longer buzzing noise. Walton (1938) talks of species of *Micronecta* as squeaking almost incessantly "when contented" and when feeding, both by day and night, but the songs are not described, and although he investigated their courtship behaviour no mention of stridulation is made. In Corixids, there seems to be general agreement that the males can sing at least two songs, a loud short chirp and a long-drawn grinding noise, called "knife grinding" by Schaller and Timm (1951). In *Buenoa limnocastris*, Hungerford (1924) also describes the production of two songs by the males. They move up behind a female and begin a ticking noise like a watch; when within half an inch or so of the female the ticking changes to a rapid whirring noise as the male attempts to embrace the female. Recently Leston and Haskell have recorded the songs of the Corixid *Sigara dorsalis* under water, and Fig. 87 shows two distinct songs; the first is made by males, and consists of the repetition of multiple pulses. The constituent impulses of each group number generally four or five and have a P.R.F. of about 35 per second, while the P.R.F. of the multiple pulse, also fairly constant, is 4 per second. It is not known which sex makes the second song, which is a long drawn trill of regular pulses at a rate of 10 per second. If this second song is made by the male, then the songs of *Sigara* fall into the general pattern described above for other Corixids by Schaller and Timm.

The production of under-water sounds by frictional mechanisms poses special problems in the coupling of the resonant surfaces to the fluid medium, which would be expected to exert a considerable damping effect. The loud sounds produced by such small insects as the Micronectids, for example, argues a very efficient transfer of energy from mechanism to medium; some apparatus apparently is less efficient in air than in water, as Bueno (1905) noted in *Ranatra quadridentata*, although it is difficult to see from his description of the mechanism concerned wherein the specialization may lie, although it seems possible the tracheal system and air sacs may be concerned. This particular problem is typical of many related to aquatic stridulation, an almost completely neglected aspect of insect acoustics.

This survey of the types of sounds which can be emitted by frictional stridulation mechanisms is bound to be inadequate, but it may be considered sufficient to illustrate the main points concerning such mechanisms; these are that frequency spectrum and intensity of sounds produced by them can vary not only from insect to insect but also in one individual.. The sounds may, however, have a relatively stable temporal distribution of sound pulses, occurring in a species specific pattern; this temporal distribution or modulation pattern can characterize and hence differentiate the songs of closely related species, and in species which produce more than one song enables these different sounds to be distinguished by insect hearing organs. On the other hand, certain species in several insect orders produce sounds of wide frequency spectrum in which no stable modulation pattern is present and which are hence probably undistinguishable from one another as far as insects are concerned.

(b) Vibrating membrane mechanisms

It was formerly thought that only the Cicadas amongst the Homoptera were possessed of the special sound-producing organs called tymbal organs, but the work of Ossiannilsson (1949) demonstrated that these were widespread amongst the Auchenorrhyncha. Rather similar organs have now been described from several Lepidoptera, and the basic structure of these latter and the Homopteran type have been described in Chapter 2. Owing to the work of Pringle (1954) and Ossiannilsson a good deal is known about the sounds produced by these organs, the former's work in particular showing how each component in the mechanism contributes to the emitted sound. It will be recalled that essentially the tymbal organ consists of a chitinous membrane, the tymbal, supported by a sclerotized ring; this membrane has attached to it the powerful tymbal muscle, contraction of which buckles the tymbal inwards. When the muscle relaxes, the tymbal springs out to its original position by its own natural elasticity. In clicking in and out from the resting to the buckled position, the membrane emits a pulse of sound for each movement; this pulse is an exponentially decaying damped pulse and represents the free oscillation of the membrane, and its frequency is that of the natural frequency of the tymbal membrane. This varied in the species examined by Pringle from about 4 to 6 kc/s. The tymbal rhythm during song is maintained by a myogenic contraction of the tymbal muscle, the rates of contraction varying between 170 and 480 per second in different species. The tymbals on both sides of the body contract together, and this is apparently brought about by synchronous impulses in the motor nerve to each muscle; there is some evidence to suggest the presence of a microsynaptic connection between the two nerves in the thoracic ganglion. The songs of various species, oscillograms of which are shown in Fig. 88, therefore consist of a series of short pulses of sound; since the tymbal mechanism seemed very similar in all species, Pringle examined the function of components other than the tymbal and its muscle to try and find how the various specific songs were produced. He found two further important elements in the apparatus, the first being the tensor muscles of the tymbal membrane. Contraction of these muscles increases the curvature of the tymbal, thus increasing the load on the tymbal muscle and reducing the rate of contraction and hence the pulse frequency of the sound. Owing to the greater curvature of the tymbal and the consequently larger amount of energy dissipated in overcoming this, the intensity of the sound output is raised. The tensor muscles thus enable the pulse repetition frequency and the sound intensity to be controlled. The second important component of the sound mechanism is the air-sacs; these form a cavity which

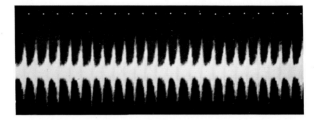

FIG. 80

Oscillogram of normal song of male *Omocestus viridulus*, timing mark 1/10 sec.

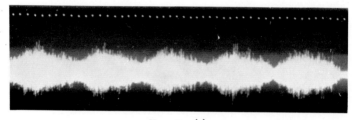

FIG. 81 (a)

Normal song of male *Stenobothrus lineatus;* timing mark 1/10 sec.

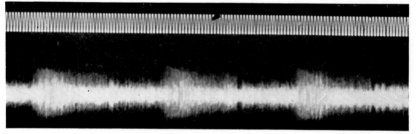

FIG. 81 (b)

Same as 81 (a) but different insect. Note differences of wave form although same modulation frequency. Timing wave 50 c/s

FIG. 82

Normal song of male *C.* parallelus; timing mark 1/10 sec.

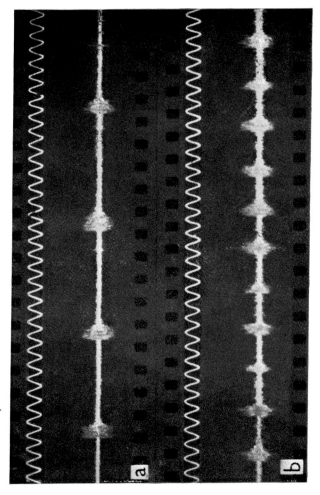

Fig. 83

One song of male *Kleidocerys resedae* (a) and male *K. ericae* (b); timing wave 50 c/s.

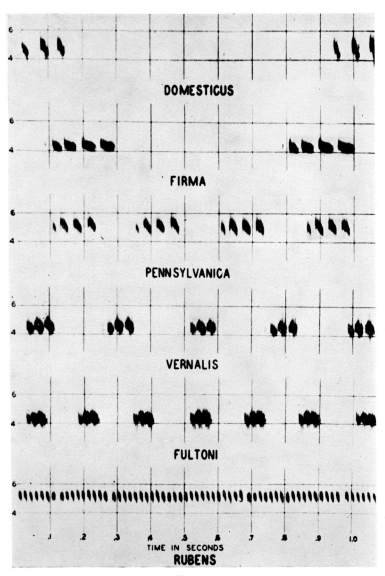

DOMESTICUS

FIRMA

PENNSYLVANICA

VERNALIS

FULTONI

TIME IN SECONDS

RUBENS

FIG. 84

Audiospectrographs of calling song of six species
of the genus *Acheta*. The figures on the ordinate
show frequency in kc/s. (From Alexander, 1957).

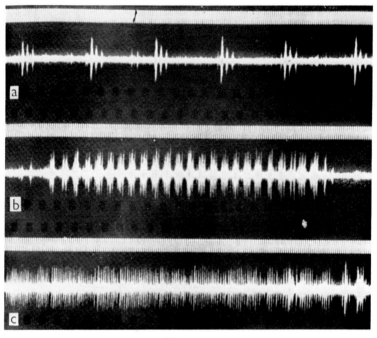

FIG. 85

Three songs of a male *Sehirus bicolor*, with pulse rates per second being 1.4 (a) 8.5 (b) and 55 (c); timing wave 50 c/s in every case.

appears to be normally resonant at the tymbal frequency, but this frequency can be controlled by expansion or contraction of the sacs themselves by movements of the abdomen. The interplay of these factors is regulated by the pattern of nerve impulses to the controlling muscles and the appearance of different songs in the species Pringle examined, all of which have apparently identical sound mechanisms, argues for the existence of an inherited central nervous adaptation which sets the song pattern for the species.

Here again we find an array of species with sound-producing apparatus capable only of producing limited and overlapping frequency spectra, whose songs can be distinguished nevertheless on the basis of pulse modulation pattern. Pringle also recorded the discharges in the tympanal nerve of a cicada on stimulation by recorded song, and found that each pulse of stimulating sound up to a frequency at least of 93 pulses per second produced a volley of impulses in the nerve. In only one species observed, *Platypleura octoguttata*, did Pringle record a distinct courtship song in a male, the other species examined appearing to have only one song. However, Ossiannilsson, in his large survey of sound production in Swedish Auchenorrhyncha, lists a number of species as having two or more songs, and Alexander and Moore (1958) have confirmed this for *Magicicada*. In a theoretical discussion on the mode of action of the tymbal organs described from many species of Auchenorrhyncha, which appear to be homologous with those in the Cicadidae, Ossiannilsson suggests two possible theories of their function. One of these is in accord with Pringle's work on Cicadas, and it seems most likely that this mode of action is almost universal in these organs. Ossiannilsson quotes the ability of some of his species in modifying the quality of the emitted sound by abdominal movements, just as described by Pringle in cicadas. The interesting and important case of *Doratura stylata* is described in greater detail in the next chapter. Using the definitions of Faber, discussed in the following chapter, Ossiannilsson described normal, courtship, pairing, rivalry and distress calls, and it is interesting that in this species complex, as in others described above, while the fundamental frequency ranges of the species may overlap, their songs are distinguished by different patterns of modulation. Ossiannilsson investigated the modulation patterns of some of these songs by using a pen recorder with a frequency limit of 200 c/s, and it is clear from some of the traces that the tymbal muscle contraction was in excess of this figure. The sounds of these small insects are naturally very weak, but the use of modern microphones and low noise amplifiers should enable them to be recorded and analysed oscillographically, when acoustic parameters could be more easily determined. The main interest in the work of Pringle and Ossiannilsson, however, from our present point of view, is to provide evidence of yet another group of insects which emit "organized" songs, distinguishable by modulation pattern, which are used in a variety of behaviourable situations.

The so-called tymbal organs of certain Lepidoptera (see Chapter 2) have not yet been investigated, and only subjective impressions of the sounds they can generate are available. Thus *Setina aurita* is said to emit a "loud crackling noise" during flight, audible over several yards, while other species are described as producing "drumming" or "buzzing" noises. Until such noises have been recorded and analysed it would be fruitless to speculate on the operation of the mechanisms or discuss its analogy to Homopteran tymbal organs.

(c) Mechanisms directly involving air movement

The best known case of sound production by direct air movement is found in the Deaths Head Hawk Moth, *Acherontia atropos*, and amongst the voluminous literature on the subject the account of Prell (1920) is probably the best and most accurate. The moth can only produce the noise when the pharynx is empty of food, since it is the pharyngeal musculature which sucks air in and out through the proboscis, and it is this air current which is modulated by movements of the epipharynx to produce the sounds (see Fig. 38). It is important to realize that this is not an organ pipe method, but a pulsed sound mechanism as in an air-blown siren. The sound is produced by the "cutting up" of the air stream by the movements of the epipharynx, and the work of Busnel and Dumortier (1959) in which the sounds were recorded and analysed have confirmed that this is the probable mechanism. Both sexes can produce the sound and there are two parts to the song; the first, produced on inspiration of air, consists of a series of transient pulses, 40 or 50 in all, repeated at a P.R.F. of 280 c/s, the whole emission lasting only about 160 milliseconds. Some hundredths of a second after the end of this part of the sound, expiration of air commences and causes the second part of the song which appears as a high pitched whistle, less intense than the preceding sound and lasting only about 60 milliseconds. The whole ensemble can be repeated rapidly and has an intensity of about 65 db several centimetres from the insect. The frequency spectrum ranges from 3·5-20 kc/s with the principal frequency of the first song about 7-8 kc/s and that of the second about 9-10 kc/s. The pulses occurring at 280 c/s are due to vibration of the epipharynx at this frequency during inspiration, while the second part of the song is perhaps a whistle with the epipharynx stationary. The constriction of the pharynx is peculiar to the genus *Acherontia*, but even so all species cannot apparently make the noise, the power perhaps being due to minute anatomical differences of the epipharynx. The moth produces the sound on tactile stimulation, but has also been recorded as chirping spontaneously, although the behaviourial context at the time was not recorded. Several other genera of moths, notably *Amphonyx*, have also been recorded as producing loud chirping noises, in circumstances which make it possible that the noise was produced by air movements. The available evidence about the production of sounds by air movement has been summarized in Chapter 2; it really amounts to very little, and the whole question of sound production by this method in insects needs thorough investigation. One exception, however, deserves quoting, and this is the work of Woods (1956, 1959) on the piping of queen honey bees. There has been a great deal of controversy as to the method of sound production in these insects; Woods reviews all the suggestions and is able, in the light of his oscillographic analysis of queen piping, to point out the difficulties inherent in all of them. Woods showed the fundamental note of the piping to be about 300-380 c/s, depending upon the condition of the insect (e.g. virgin, laying, etc.) with harmonics of this pitch present up to about 1,500 c/s. He carried out experiments and calculations which seem to dispose of several suggested mechanisms for the production of this sound—wing vibration, vibrations of thoracic sclerites, air vibration in the tracheal system and so on—and finally suggested a new hypothesis, that of a pulsed air stream, in which air expelled through the spiracles by abdominal pumping is modulated or pulsed by movements of the spiracular valves at 350 c/s. Woods points out that this explanation is in keeping with the form of the oscillograms of the sound, and also explains the apparent efficiency of the method, the sound output of a queen being about 2 milliwatts, an almost impossibly large output for any of the other methods suggested. Woods made mechanical models, based on the spiracles of a queen bee, and the performance of these was very

similar to that of the live insect. In nature, the piping appears as
a series of pulses of sound, whose duration and number seem to
vary. Hansson (1945) recorded a queen piping with 23 successive
pulses, while Woods has recorded 89 and 120. There seem to have
been no records of the rate of pulse production, which might again,
as in other insects, be of significance.

Factors affecting production and propagation of insect sounds

One of the most interesting and least investigated problems connected with insect sound production is that of the stimulus or
stimuli that provoke it. In a few cases this is clear; tactile stimulation of any part of the body will, for example, elicit vigorous stridulation in certain Heteroptera and Coleoptera and also in some
Lepidoptera under certain conditions. For various reasons, discussed
in a later chapter, this type of sound production may be thought
of as primarily defensive, and therefore it is not surprising that it
is elicited by tactile stimuli. But in a large number of insects,
including those best investigated amongst the Orthoptera,
Heteroptera and Homoptera, so-called spontaneous singing is the
rule. Indeed, as is shown later, such spontaneous singing is necessary if the sound is to play a part in bringing the sexes together.
The word spontaneous here refers only to the absence of stimulation from another insect of the same species, since clearly there
must be some stimulus which controls the onset of stridulation. It
is only the genesis of the spontaneous or normal song of insects
which is in question; the courtship, rivals duet, copulation song and
so on, are released by stimuli generated by other insects—the
responsive female, or the intruding male—which play their parts in
the behavioural complex initiated by the spontaneous song of the
male. Although the exact nature of the stimuli involved in releasing these " secondary songs ", if they may be so called, is not known,
they are clearly external to the original male and have their
origins in the behaviour of another insect, whereas the stimuli
responsible for the spontaneous song may be external, some factor
of the environment, or internal, perhaps due to hormone action or
other internal cause, or there may be an interaction of the two.
Busnel and Dumortier (1955) have shown that males of *Ephippiger
ephippiger* stridulate when sexually mature, that is when the genital
organs are in a state capable of producing a spermatophore. After
copulation the males do not sing again until the build-up of sexual
products—sperm and the secretions of the accessory glands—has

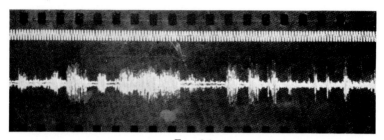

FIG. 86

Stridulation of 4th instar larva of the Reduviid *Coranus subapterus;* timing wave 200 c/s.

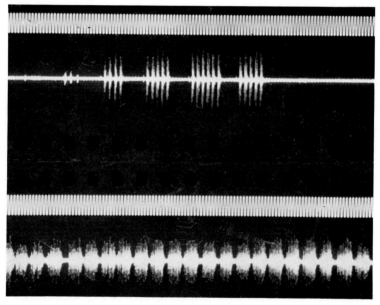

FIG. 87

Stridulation of the Corixid *Sigara dorsalis;* upper trace, one song of the male; lower trace, song of unknown origin. Timing wave in both traces 50 c/s.

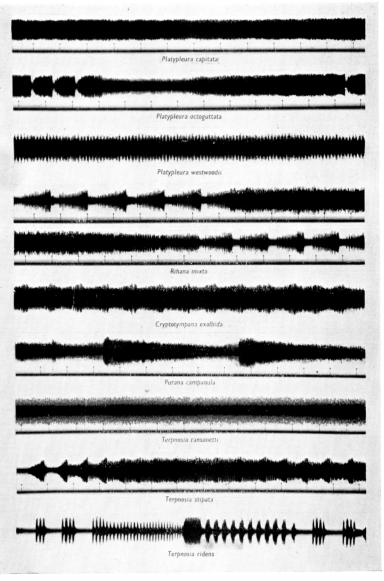

Platypleura capitata

Platypleura octoguttata

Platypleura westwoodii

Rihana mixta

Cryptotympana exalbida

Purana campanula

Terpnosia ransonetti

Terpnosia stipata

Terpnosia ridens

FIG. 88

Songs of Ceylon cicadas; time marker in all records 0.5 sec.
(From Pringle 1954).

again reached a level permitting the production of a further spermatophore (Fig. 89). This state of affairs does not hold for male Acrididae; here, not only do immature males and even occasionally third and fourth instar nymphs stridulate, but males will stridulate vigorously within a short time of having copulated. In females, on the other hand, the response stridulation is only elicited from virgin mature insects. In the Heteroptera recent work also suggests that in some bugs stridulation only occurs after sexual maturity has

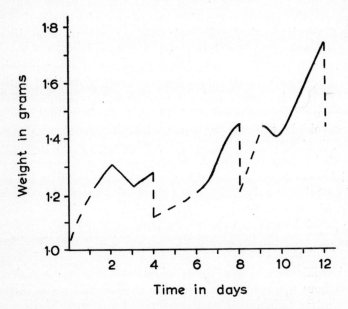

Fig. 89. Weight curve of male *Ephippiger ephippiger*, which copulated on days 1, 4, 8 and 12; broken line, silent period, solid line, song period. (After Busnel & Dumortier).

been attained. This could be the primitive adaptive state; if stridulation plays a major role in sexual behaviour then its onset might well be correlated with the state of sexual maturity. However, the Acrididae, the most advanced group of the Orthoptera, may perhaps use stridulation for semi-social purposes (see Chapter 6), and thus its appearance in this group would not be correlated exclusively with reproductive activity. There can be little doubt from the work of Huber (1955) that the ultimate nervous control of song production is sited in the higher nervous centres, most probably in the corpora pedunculata, and the most likely controlling factor in cases where song production is related to the state of the genital organs would be a hormonal one.

Dumortier, Brieu and Pasquinelly (1957) suggested this for *Ephippiger ephippiger* after a study of the environmental factors controlling the rhythm of periods of song in this insect (Fig. 90). Under natural conditions, *Ephippiger* sings most from about midnight to midday and is then silent; the rhythm persists for several days in continuous darkness and the insect can then be induced to sing in an artificially induced light-dark rhythm twelve hours out of phase with their natural rhythm. Insects with the optic nerve severed continued singing in their natural rhythm. Dumortier and his colleagues explain this and other observations by supposing that the action of light results in the formation of a song-inhibiting substance, which builds up during the hours of daylight until by midday it is in concentration strong enough to inhibit singing. After dark the concentration of this agent begins to fall, until by about midnight it can no longer inhibit song. Several rather generalized sets of observations have been made on rhythms of stridulation and the effects of environmental factors on this. Acrididae certainly sing during the daylight hours, but the onset and cessation of stridulation is not closely connected with light and dark. Richards and Waloff (1954) examined the effects of temperature, humidity and radiation on the songs of four grasshoppers, and although each species apparently responded to a slightly different set of factors no clear cut controlling influence was discovered. Tettigoniids very often sing at night, but this is not universal throughout the group, and the same may be said about crickets. Pringle (1955) observed several species of cicada; most of these sang by day in full sunlight, a few at dusk, but none at night. Annandale (1900), however, records several Malayan cicadas as singing during the night. Ossiannilsson (1949) in experimental work on certain Homoptera, found that several sang as well in darkness as in light. The effect of temperature on stridulation has long been observed. Dolbear (1897) studied its effects on the chirp rate of the cricket *Oecanthus niveus*, the so-called "thermometer cricket", and found that the number of pulses emitted in a given time bore a linear relation to the air temperature in degrees Fahrenheit. Pierce (1949) repeated this observation with *Nemobius fasciatus,* and although the results were similar the relation is only approximately linear. This marked effect of temperature seems to exist mainly amongst the crickets, since short-horn grasshoppers show no effect of

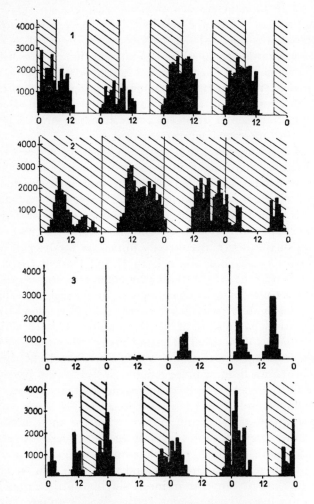

FIG. 90. Stridulatory activity of *Ephippiger ephippiger*, in relation to light. Abscissae, time in hours. Ordinate, total number of stridulations per hour. Hatching represents dark periods. 1. Natural daylight cycle. 2. Continuous darkness. 3. Continuous light. 4. Reversed cycle with artificial light. (After Dumortier, Brieu & Pasquinelly).

temperature and Tettigoniids but little. Frings and Frings (1957) studied chirp rates of *Neoconocephalus ensiger* as a function of temperature and found the relationship to be exponential; they suggest that this may be so for other species if tested with controlled temperature changes, and point out that in the field the gradual change of temperature may allow adaptation to occur. Ossiannilsson (1949) found that some leaf-hoppers had preferred temperature ranges for optimal singing and that in *Doratura stylata* the fundamental frequency of the common song of the male increased with increasing temperature.

The effect of humidity and radiation on song performance of insects has not been studied in controlled experiments and in fact much work remains to be done on the effects of environmental conditions. Such work would naturally lead on to the study of the effects of microclimate on the acoustic performance of a singing insect, for not only does environment affect the stridulation behaviour of the insect, but directly influences the propagation of the resultant sound. Both Busnel (1955) and Haskell (1955) have pointed this out, the latter showing by laboratory and field studies that the acoustic range of grasshoppers in the field was usually very much less than might have been expected on consideration of the physical parameters of the stridulation. This reduction in range is due to dissipation of sound energy due to three main causes, reflection, refraction and absorption. Any lack of homogeneity in the medium of propagation—air—increases the attenuation due to these causes. In fact, homogeneity in air is never found under field conditions because of the action of environmental factors of which temperature and wind are the most important. Temperature inversion causes layering of the air near the ground, as a consequence of which vertical temperature gradients appear. Such gradients reflect and refract sound waves and cause a diminution of the acoustic range of an insect singing on the ground. For insects which live on bushes (some Tettigoniids) or on trees (cicadas) and can sometimes get above the worst temperature layers, their range may be increased or decreased owing to circumstances. However, with these latter groups, the effect of wind is much more serious than for ground insects. Wind not only produces attenuation but also distorts the sound field. The topography and vegetation of the habitat also affects the acoustic field produced by a singing insect, especially in those which stridulate while clinging to stems of grasses, as do several Acrididae. Humidity of the air and the occurrence of rain also causes variations in intensity and range of insect sounds, and the interplay of factors is so complex that it is impossible to calculate even generally or to orders of magnitude what attenuation may occur or what specific acoustic ranges may be obtained in any given habitat. It therefore seems doubtful whether the generalizations of Busnel (1955) on the habitats and song types of Orthoptera will be found to be valid even in the widest sense. Busnel postulated that in Acridoidea, which sing on or near the ground, the lower frequencies and intensities and greater complexity of the songs are related to the higher populations and greater acoustic attenuation of their typical habitats, while in Tettigonioidea and Grylloidea, the higher frequencies and intensities but relative simplicity of the songs is related to low population densities. Clearly further investigation is needed on this question of the propagation of insect sounds, especially as regards the effects of microclimate and habitat. This question is also related to the practical aspects of recording the sounds of insects in the field, and Pasquinelly (1955) and Pasquinelly and Broughton (1955) have pointed out the difficulties which must be overcome and the limitations to be expected in this connection.

REFERENCES

ALEXANDER, R. D. (1957a) *Ann. ent. Soc. Amer.* **50**: 584-602.

ALEXANDER, R. D. (1957b) *Ohio Jour. Sci.* **57**: 101-113.

ALEXANDER, R. D. and MOORE, T. E. (1958) *Ohio Jour. Sci.* **58**: 107-127.

ANNANDALE, N. (1900) *Proc. zool. Soc. Lond.* 1900: 859-862.

ASAHINA, S. (1939) *Zool. Anz.* **126**: 323-325.

BUENO, J. R. (1905) *Canad. Ent.* **37**: 85-87.

BUSNEL, R. G. (1955) *Colloque sur L'Acoustique des Orthoptères.* *Ann. Épiphyt.* (tome hors serie): 281-306.

BUSNEL, R. G. and DUMORTIER, B. (1955) *Bull. Soc. Zool. Fr.* **80**: 23-26.

BUSNEL, R. G. and DUMORTIER, B. (1959) *Bull. Soc. ent. Fr.* **64**: 44-58.

DOLBEAR, A. E. (1897) *Amer. Nat.* **31**: 970-971.

DUMORTIER, B., BRIEU, S. and PASQUINELLY, F. (1957) *C. R. Acad. Sci. Paris.* **244**: 2315-2318.

FRINGS, H. and FRINGS, M. (1957) *J. exp. Zool.* **134**: 411-425.

GAHAN, C. J. (1910) *Entomologist.* **43**: 84-87.

HANSSON, A. (1945) *Opusc. Ent. Suppl.* **6**: 1-124.

HASKELL, P. T. (1955) *Colloque sur L'Acoustique des Orthoptères. Ann Épiphyt.* (tome hors serie): 154-167.

HASKELL, P. T. (1956) *Proc. R. ent. Soc. London.* (C):**21**:21-22.

HASKELL, P. T. (1957) *J. ins. Physiol.* **1**: 52-75.

HASKELL, P. T. (1958) *Proc. zool. Soc. Lond.* **129**: 351-358.

HEBARD, M. (1922) *Ent. News.* **33**: 244.

HUBER, F. (1955) *Z. Tierpsychol.* **12**: 12-48.

HUNGERFORD, H. B. (1924) *Ann. ent. Soc. Amer.* **17**: 223-227.

KARTMAN, L. *et al.* (1946) *J. Parasit.* **32**: 91.

LESTON, D. (1957) *Proc. zool. Soc. Lond.* **128**: 369-386.

MACNAMARA, C. (1926) *Canad. Ent.* **58**: 53-54.

MITIS, H. VON (1935) *Z. Morph. Oekol. Tiere.* **30**: 479-495.

MONRO, J. (1953) *Aust. J. Sci.* **16**: 60-62.

OSSIANNILSSON, F. (1949) *Opusc. Ent. Suppl.* **10**: 1-145.

PASQUINELLY, F. (1955) *Colloque sur L'Acoustique des Orthoptères Ann. Épiphyt.* (tome hors serie): 50-63.

PASQUINELLY, F. and BROUGHTON, W. B. (1955) *Ibid.*: 64-81.

PASQUINELLY, F. and BUSNEL, M. C. (1955) *Ibid.*: 145-153.

PEARMAN, J. V. (1928) *Ent. mon. Mag.* **64**: 179-186.

PIERCE, G. W. (1949) *The songs of insects.* Harvard Press. U.S.A.

PRELL, H. (1920) *Zool. Jahrb. Abt. Syst. Geog. Biol. Tiere.* **42**: 235-272

PRINGLE, J. W. S. (1954) *J. exp. Biol.* **31**: 525-560.

PRINGLE, J. W. S. (1955) *Spolia Zeylanica.* **27**: 229-239.

RICHARDS, O. W. and WALOFF, N. (1954) *Anti-Locust Bull.* No. 17. London.

ROEDER, K. and TREAT, A. E. (1957) *J. exp. Zool.* **134**: 127-158.

SCHALLER, F. and TIMM, C. (1951) *Z. vergl. Physiol.* **33**: 476-486.

SOTAVALTA, O. (1947) *Acta. Entomol. Fennica.* **4**: 1-117.

TISCHNER, H. and SCHIEF, A. (1954) *Verhandl. deut. Zool. Ges.*: 444-460.

WALTON, G. A. (1938) *Trans. Soc. Brit. Ent.* **5**: 259-270.

WOODS, E. F. (1956) *Bee World.* **37**: 185-195; 216-219.

WOODS, E. F. (1959) *Nature, Lond.* **184**: 842-844.

CHAPTER V

BEHAVIOUR ASSOCIATED WITH SOUND

THE behaviour associated with sound production is in many ways the most fascinating part of insect acoustics, but in common with other aspects of the field has been neglected. The realization in recent years that many insects can both emit and receive vibrations too low or too high for human ears to detect has gone some way towards restoring the interest of the entomologist in the acoustic behaviour of his subject. Whereas previously in most investigations of a behavioural situation only the modalities of vision, olfaction, thermo-reception, hygro-reception and tactile sense would be carefully studied, more notice is now taken of the possibility of distance mechanoreception playing a part in the biology of insects. Moreover, with the demonstration of the existence of numerous types of sound receptor in the group it has become probable that most insects are equipped to respond to some vibrations of their environmental medium, be this water or air, and, even if this ability is narrowly restricted in terms of frequency range and intensity, it is clear that it may still play an important part in the responses of the organism.

Already it has been demonstrated that sounds play several distinct rôles in the behaviour patterns of insects, and it seems certain that many more remain to be discovered. For the purposes of a comparative study, it is perhaps permissible to refer to the uses of sound in the insect world under three portmanteau headings. These uses are defence and warning, sexual behaviour, and sounds relating to organization in social and sub-social groups. It must be emphasized here that these headings are purely for convenience in presentation. This can be illustrated with the first category, defence and warning sounds. It is a commonplace observation that many insects produce noises on being touched or handled, and many workers have characterized such noises as "alarm" or "danger" calls. It seems probable that many Heteroptera and Coleoptera, for example, only stridulate when touched and never appear to produce their noises spontaneously. Haskell (1957b) experimented with the bug *Coranus subapterus* in which the larvae and adults of both sexes produce a loud sound when touched; the bug could never be made to produce the sound by any other than tactile stimulation. It has been suggested, although so far no concrete evidence has been produced, that this reflex sound production may serve to protect the insect if it is seized by a predator such as a bird or hunting spider, which may be so startled by the ensuing noise that it will let go its hold. The necessary conditions for this reaction are that the frequency and intensity of the sound are such as to be able to stimulate the sound receptors of the predator. In the case under discussion this is certainly so for birds and may apply to spiders, and, as Pumphrey (1955) has pointed out, it is possible to regard such sounds as in the same category of extra-specific stimuli as "warning colours". However, in many cases, especially amongst beetles (Haskell, unpublished) similar sounds are produced in a close packed group of insects when they touch one another in passing, and it seems possible that here exists some measure of intra-specific communication, although the usefulness of such signals is at the moment obscure. Further analysis of the sounds emitted in such circumstances may throw more light on the subject for the following reasons. It has been mentioned above that an extra-specific alarm signal is only of use if it can be heard by the predator; if the signal emitted is of a narrow frequency range its usefulness will be limited because of the corresponding reduction in the range of predator sound receptors it can stimulate, and it is perhaps significant that in the case of several of these so-called alarm calls (and again *Coranus* can be cited as an example), the stridulation results in the production of a true noise, that is a sound with a very wide frequency spectrum. Such a signal often has a much wider frequency range than an "organized" sound, and as such might be more effective as an alarm call. It is worth noting in this connection that the so-called "alarm call" of many Acrididae is far more variable than the "spontaneous" songs of this group. On the other hand, certain beetles, such as *Lilioceris lilii*, also appear to emit their stridulation only on tactile stimulation and for this reason their song may tend to be regarded as a defence or warning sound. But here the sound signal is organized, consisting of pulses at a fixed rate, and the signal is the same regardless of the stimulus; also, it is emitted when the beetles touch one another when crowded together. When one considers that this beetle is strictly confined to a single host plant and for that reason is often found in groups, there is some ground for thinking that the sounds in this case may be intra-specific. It is clear that facile behavioural interpretations of so-called "defence" sounds are to be avoided and that further rigorous experiment is necessary into this category of acoustic behaviour. Much the same can be said of the sounds produced by larvae, particularly those Coleopterous larvae which normally live quite deep in the ground. Once again in the absence of any real evidence, it has been suggested that stridulation may be related to seizure by moles or rabbits or other burrowing predators, but this is pure conjecture. Because of the absence of a sexual motive in this case, it has also been supposed by many that the stridulation is adventitious and meaningless, but it seems past belief that some of the elaborate structures which have evolved are useless mutations. In Passalid larvae, for example (see Fig. 26), the hind legs can act only as part of the stridulatory mechanism, which in this case certainly produces sounds, and unless and until its biological function can be shown the rôle of larval stridulation in this and similar cases must remain a challenging problem.

We are on much safer ground in assuming a purely defensive function in respect of the pupal stridulation observed in Coleoptera and Lepidoptera, since here there is no question of any advantageous communicative behaviour related to social or sexual activity. Hinton (1948) has studied pupal stridulation in the Lepidoptera, and his work makes it clear that its probable value is defence, but he points out that such a function has never been observed or demonstrated, and thus the suggestion must for the time being remain a suggestion. Pupal stridulation has been described from a few other orders, for example the Hymenoptera, where the Ichneumonid *Phytodictus polyzonias* makes quite a loud noise by scraping the end of the abdomen on the inside of the thin papery cocoon; but in all of these cases, the pupae produce the sound spontaneously and not only when disturbed, and this suggests that the sounds are truly adventitious.

Much the same attitude must be taken with regard to acoustic mimicry. It has been maintained, for example, that the noise produced by the Deaths Head Hawk Moth is very like the "piping" of a queen bee, and that this similarity enables it to enter bee hives and rob them of honey, unmolested by the workers. What is indisputable about the story is that the moth is fond of honey or syrup and lives around and about hives which it does frequently enter; it is also indisputable that many moths are found stung to death inside hives. Here again, experiment is necessary before any real progress can be made. An interesting example of audio mimicry was described by Gaul (1952); colour mimicry exists between the wasp *Dolichovespula arenaria* and the Syrphid fly *Spilomyia hamifera*, but in addition Gaul was able to show by recording their wing-beat sounds that the insects were audio mimics as well, the rate of wing beat of the wasp being 150 per second and that of the fly 147 per second. These figures are averages from several specimens, and as the variation in both is ± 2 beats per second, both wing tones will sound the same to vertebrate hearing organs. Several other flies and moths have colour and audio mimicry with poisonous or venomous insects. A further example of what may be a defensive noise was given by Williams (1922) in respect of the coffee aphid *Toxoptera coffeae*. The mode of sound production in this insect has already been described; the behaviour that accompanies it is even more interesting. These aphids collect in numerous groups on the underside of the leaves of their host plant, coffee or cocoa, and, when disturbed by moving or tapping a leaf, a greater or smaller number commence a rhythmic movement of the body which is accompanied by the emission of sound. Williams reports that the movements were synchronous and the resultant sound could be heard 18 inches from the leaf. He repeated the observations in several parts of the world, which is evidence that the phenomenon is significant and not accidental, and speculates as to whether it is useful in defence. He has one piece of evidence on this; the only time he found a colony making the sound before he himself had induced it by disturbing the insects was when two syrphid larvae were crawling amongst the colony feeding on the aphids. Unfortunately he does not record whether the larvae were frightened off by the stridulation, so once again no proof of defensive power is available.

Again, a sound whose "warning rôle" has been much discussed is the stridulation of the Peacock butterfly. This butterfly, if disturbed when settling down to hibernate or in other situations where it cannot easily take flight, opens its wings with a hissing noise and displays its "eye-spots". It will if continually disturbed repeat the manœuvre several times before becoming accommodated or fatigued. What is the use of this reaction? Again a defensive rôle has several times been suggested. Haskell (1956) recorded and analysed the sound and found an unexpected percentage of total energy radiated at high frequencies; he pointed out that among the likely predators of hibernating Peacocks were rats and mice, whose ears are particularly sensitive to such high frequency sounds. Consequently to them the butterfly noise would sound very loud and may act as a deterrent to capture. On the other hand Swinton (1877) describing in this and several other papers sound production by this butterfly, is convinced the sound plays a part in sexual behaviour, while Edwards (1889) states that the noise is made when several butterflies are in flight together, and "more particularly when a male pursues a female". Now either or both of these explanations may be true; what is frightening to a mouse under one set of circumstances may become attractive under another to a butterfly. However, the "defence reaction" theory is supported by the recent work of Blest (1957), who showed that "eye-spot" displays by some moths and butterflies were effective deterrents against several species of bird predators; it can reasonably be supposed that emission of a hissing noise simultaneously with the display would act as a reinforcing deterrent stimulus. Problems like these may be multiplied many times and can be resolved only by further observation or experiment; all that can be said without fear of contradiction is that the whole problem of "defence and warning" noises is an open one.

No such question exists about the use of sound signals in relation to sexual behaviour, where in several groups such as the Orthoptera, Hemiptera and Diptera experiment and observation have revealed the part played by stridulation in promoting meeting of the sexes, in epigamic display and in copulation; in fact the most widely accepted view of insect sound production is that which regards it as exclusively connected with reproductive activity. While it is certainly true that the great majority of available evidence relates to this sphere it will be shown subsequently that acoustic behaviour must be regarded as playing an important rôle in other connections as well. It is, however, true that the classical investigations of Regen and Faber, which really laid the foundations of the present field of work, clearly demonstrated the part played by sound signals in the mating of certain Orthoptera, and so powerful was the influence of this work that most other investigators did not attempt to look for other explanations. Poulton, talking of the behaviour of Acridids, remarks that "the sound-producing powers seemed without exception to be directed towards the females", and Swinton, referring to stridulation in butterflies, equates it with that of the Orthoptera and Hemiptera as "that stimulus of the passions". While one may now take leave to doubt these statements as too sweeping, nevertheless it must be admitted that the majority of insect sounds do play a part in sexual behaviour. The actual rôle of the sound signals varies a great deal amongst different groups of insects, as is only to be expected, but in general the acoustic behaviour serves two main purposes. These are the promotion of meetings between the sexes and the subsequent stimulation of both partners to the act of copulation. There are many important consequences of these events, such as the isolation of species and the maintenance of colony coherence to mention only two, but for the moment it will be sufficient to describe some of the actual behaviour patterns relating to courtship and copulation which are mediated by sound signals, in order to illustrate the wide incidence of the activity amongst the insects, and also its variability.

In some cases the flight noise has become a signal utilized to bring about meetings of the sexes. The most closely investigated case is probably that of the Yellow-fever Mosquito, *Aedes aegypti*, which was worked out by Roth (1948). He found that the mosquito antennae acted as an auditory organ over a certain frequency range; when a note within this range was sounded nearby, the antennae resonated and caused stimulation of the nervous receptors in Johnston's organ. The frequency preferred corresponded closely to that of the flight tone of the adult female mosquito, and Roth found he could get male *Aedes* to respond either to sounds produced by flying females or to a tuning fork giving out the same note, by flying to the source of sound and there exhibiting seizing and clasping reactions—the precursor of mating behaviour. The recent careful work of Wishart and Riordan (1959), again with *A. aegypti*, has corroborated these findings and added the following important facts. The fundamental frequency of the flight tone is the important element of the female sound, and when a male is exposed to two attractive sources of the correct frequency it chooses on the basis of intensity, moving to the loudest source. Males can distinguish the attractive sound in the presence of high background noise; attraction was only appreciably reduced when the noise was over 100 times as loud as the signal. The female flight tone can attract a male at distances up to 10 inches. Point sources were approached more closely by flying males than were diffused sources (such as loud-speakers in baffles), and while high intensity signals of atractive frequency brought males towards the signal source the high intensity near the source repelled them. Most important was the observation that presentation together of two sounds that were attractive alone virtually caused the response to disappear. This implies that attraction of a male to a female can only occur in relative isolation and not amongst a crowd or swarm. In this behaviour then, under certain conditions, the acoustic signal enables a male to orient and move to a flying female, and may in addition stimulate both sexes for mating; but this is almost certainly not the whole sequence of events nor the only stimulus involved in the behaviour. Kahn and Offenhauser (1949) have, for example, shown that a male mosquito will not mate with a female of another species even though its flight note is of the correct frequency, and this implies that other sensory modalities, such as vision or olfaction, come into play in complex mating behaviour. It is of course only to be expected that such a complicated behaviour pattern as courtship would demand the interplay of several modes of stimulation, and if we characterize such behaviour as acoustic, we mean in general that the *principal* attractive and orientative rôle is played by sound signals, although there are cases (see below) where apparently *only* auditory mechanisms are involved. Instances of acoustic attraction through the medium of the flight note could be multiplied; amongst the Diptera, the Eristalids and Tabanids show behaviour which suggests that the male courts the female with wing tones, and the same phenomenon has been described for a number of bees (e.g. *Megachile, Anthophora*) and some parasitic wasps. Sotavalta (1947) describes behaviour in the wasp *Apanteles*, where the males approached the females with a definite "song pattern" of the flight noise. But in all these cases proof of the real function of the sound is lacking because the behaviour could not be followed right through to the ultimate conclusion. Happily it is otherwise in several insect groups, particularly the Orthoptera, where a large and growing body of evidence clearly attests to the vital rôle played by sound signals in reproductive behaviour. The foundation of this study in Orthoptera was laid, as remarked previously, by Regen, who worked with the cricket *Gryllus campestris* and the long-horn grasshopper *Pholidoptera aptera* (then called *Thamnotrizon apterus*). He was able to show for the first of these insects that mature unmated females were attracted by the chirping of the males (1913); vision played no part in this attraction because females were also attracted to a telephone receiver transmitting the sound of male song. With the second insect, Regen (1926) demonstrated that the tendency for two males to sing in concert concealed a complex state of affairs; he attempted to take part in the alternation of song between two males by removing one of them and supplying the missing sounds himself with a variety of musical instruments. His first experiments were unsuccessful, but when he used as a partner a male which had not previously heard the song of its species he was able to perform a duet with it. The insect responded to noises over a frequency range of about 400 c/s to 28 kc/s, but the reaction ceased when both tympanal organs were destroyed. Here, in this classical series of experiments, was evidence of the complex behaviour underlying insect song and the challenge of further investigation and classification was taken up by Faber (1953) in Germany, who made a detailed study of song behaviour in the Acridid grasshopper genus *Chorthippus*. Faber showed that each species had a repertoire of songs which were related to a different phase of behaviour and were species specific. This discovery paved the way for a more detailed analysis of sound and related behaviour by allowing the experimentalist to concentrate on one song and its typical behavioural context, and it is difficult to overestimate its importance. Faber listed twelve types of songs related to specific behavioural patterns and gave them descriptive names; while not all workers agree with the definitions he gave, five of the song types he described have been demonstrated as occurring in a widespread manner amongst insects capable of sound production, and their names have come into general use amongst workers in this field. These song types are:

(a) The "normal" song (gewönliche Gesang), sometimes called the "spontaneous song", of males, alone or in company with other males, but with no females present.

(b) The "courtship" song (Werbegesang), also called the "serenade" of a single male in the presence of a female.

(c) The "shout of triumph" (Anspringlaute), also called the "jumping on" song of the courting male. It follows from the courtship song and immediately precedes an attempt by the male to jump on the female and engage the genitalia.

(d) The "rivals duet" (Rivalenlaute), or "rivalry song" this song is sung by a courting male who is interrupted by the intrusion of a second male. The second male also stridulates in reply, hence the term "rivals duet".

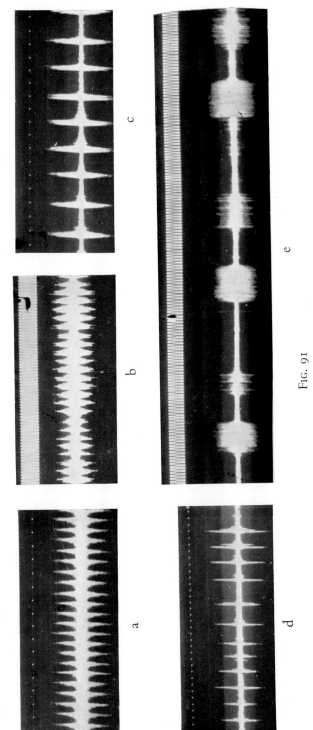

Fig. 91

Oscillograms of various grasshopper songs

(a) Normal song of male O. *viridulus*; timing mark 1/10 second. (b) Song of female O. *viridulus*; timing wave 50 c/s. (c) Courtship song of male O. *viridulus*; timing mark 1/10 second. (d) Copulation song of male O. *viridulus*; timing mark 1/10 second. (e) Alternation of stridulation between a male and female C. *brunneus*; male song occurs first, then the answering female song and so on alternately. Timing wave 50 c/s.

(e) The "copulation song" of the male (Paarungslaute). This song is sung by a male actually copulating with a female, if the latter starts moving about or becomes restless.

Fig. 91 shows oscillograms of some of these songs in the grasshopper *Omocestus viridulus*. Faber listed many other songs, as has been said, such as warning cries, produced when the insects are handled, jumping cries made just before a grasshopper leaps and so on, but these definitions and their behavioural contexts have proved very variable and have not passed into general use. The occurrence of the five songs referred to above appears to be widespread in relation to sexual behaviour in many groups of sound-producing insects, and thus the terms have become more or less universally applied. But it should be emphasized that the use of terms such as "normal" and "courtship" when applied to insect songs is at present based mainly on convenience; use of these terms does not, or ought not, to imply that the sounds so labelled are solely related to certain phases of behaviour, although in many cases they may typically be so. In short, investigation has not proceeded far enough for us to present valid generalizations on this subject; at most we can say the evidence is strongly suggestive of their general value. Frequently songs which appear to be of the same type, on detailed study of related behaviour, require to be classified otherwise. For example, Ossiannilsson (1949) studied the song behaviour of the Homopteran *Doratura stylata*; here not only the males but also the females sing. The male can emit two calls, the female only one, and the sequence of behaviour is as follows; the male emits its first song, and if a female ready to mate is within range she emits her song. As soon as this happens, the male stops singing its first song and commences its second. The female continues to sing its song, and the male, with intervals to reply with its second sound, moves towards her until they meet. Now, what is one to call the songs of the male; is the first song a "normal" song? And if so, what can one call the second, which is certainly not a "courtship" song? This illustration, which could be multiplied, should serve to show that the present terminology is for convenience only, and that no hard and fast behavioural significance can be attached to the classification. In fairness to Faber, it must be pointed out that the terms as originally employed by him in relation to certain Acridid sounds are more accurate, although even here some definitions are open to criticism. There are two other factors which have conspired to further reduce the value of this classification; first, it has now been recognized that the females of many species stridulate, and that these sounds play an important part in sexual behaviour, and secondly it has been discovered that elaborate song behaviour can occur between the males of a species, in which the so-called "normal" song, modified to a greater or lesser degree, plays an important part. In the latter case no sexual significance would seem to be involved, and it is more probable, as will be seen later, that the songs have a social significance. For all these reasons the behavioural classification of songs is most difficult, and it is to be expected that no satisfactory nomenclature will be decided on until much more data, spread over many groups of insects, are available. Despite all these drawbacks, the terminology given above is of great practical convenience when giving descriptions of behaviour associated with stridulation, and will be adhered to in this book.

As a starting point in our consideration of stridulation and sexual behaviour, let us examine in some detail the song behaviour of courtship and mating in an Acridid grasshopper *Omocestus viridulus*. The small active males of this species sing very vigorously amongst the grass of their typical habitat, particularly when the sun is high. The normal song is a rapid trill (see Fig. 91A) and can last from a few seconds to a minute or more. A female within range, and ready to mate, reacts to this song by showing signs of "attention", jerking its antennae up and turning round so as to face towards the source of sound. In many cases, but not always, the female replies with a song of her own (Fig. 91B) which is a creditable imitation of the male stridulation, although not so loud. The subsequent relative movement of the two insects depends upon the presence or absence of female stridulation. If it is absent, or if present but the male is out of range, then only the female moves, generally at a slow pace towards the singing male. If female stridulation occurs and is heard by the male, the latter orients towards the source of sound (the female) and begins to move towards it, pausing only to sing short bursts of its "normal" song. The female may likewise move towards the male, but will stridulate far less often. Due to such movements the two insects finally come within visual range; in nature this normally occurs only when they are quite close because of the restricted field of vision in the typical grassland habitat. The male then moves rapidly up to the female and typically gives a short burst of "normal" song which passes directly into the "courtship song" (see Fig. 91c). This is a quick, violent, sound pulse repeated at a rate of about 5 a second, and while so singing the male hops round and round the female in an agitated manner. Very often the male, on seeing the female and before commencing his courtship song, flexes his hind femurs in a peculiar slow movement, ending with a quick flicking motion which produces a brief "clicking" noise. This is a preliminary to a courtship song, but, as has been said, is frequently omitted. The male, then, sings this song and during it performs the hopping movements or dance; the song and dance work up to a climax, and finally the male leaps on to the back of the female and attempts to engage the genitalia. If he is not accepted the male retreats slightly and then starts his courtship song all over again, culminating with another leap on to the female. When the male is accepted, the copulating pair sit silent and immobile in the grass. Now, if the female is disturbed, or begins to move about during copulation, as some females will who wish to feed, the male sings the "copulation" song (see Fig. 91D) while still on the back of its mate, which often reduces the female to passivity once more. The copulation over, the pair separates; the experience seems to have little effect on the behaviour of the male, because after a short interval, perhaps as little as 30 minutes, he commences to sing and will again serenade, seek out and copulate with a willing female. But the behaviour of the female which has received a spermatophore has radically altered, and she no longer responds to the song of a male, at least not for a long time. However, before considering the behaviour which precedes and follows such courtship, we must first ask whether this pattern of sexual behaviour and associated stridulation can be accepted as a generalized picture for singing insects as a whole. The answer, for practical purposes, and with emphasis on the generalized aspect, is yes.

The main variation from the theme is the absence of the female song; thus in the long-horn grasshoppers and the crickets the pattern is of male normal song attracting a female, a courtship song consequent on meeting, and copulation with sometimes some form of copulation song. The behaviour of the Homopteran *Doratura stylata* has been already described above, and clearly fits the basic plan; the work of Alexander and Moore (1958) on Cicadas substantiates the same conclusion. Amongst the terrestrial Heteroptera, evidence recently presented by Haskell (1957b) indicates that here too the same behaviour pattern may be discerned, again with female stridulation as the main variant, and Schaller (1951) showed similar behaviour in aquatic Heteroptera. In the Diptera, the interesting work of Myers (1952) on the mating behaviour of the fruit flies *Dacus tryoni* and *Dacus cacuminatus* reveals the same theme; a fall in light intensity sets the male flies "calling"—emitting a high fluting note with the mechanism previously described in Chapter 2. The calling male sits motionless, but the sound stimulates females ready to mate to approach the male; in many cases Myers observed females moving from one end of the cage to the other—a distance of 12 inches—in a straight line towards the calling male. When more than one male was calling, active females flew about until apparently within range of one male, when they approached him directly. Many newly emerged females ignored the sounds. During copulation, the male fly called spasmodically. The calls of *tryoni* and *cacuminatus* were different in frequency, and females of the latter species were attracted to males of *tryoni* only in the absence of their own males; given a choice, they approached their own males first. Females of *tryoni*, however, usually moved to the nearest calling male irrespective of species, but when they touched it all further copulation behaviour ceased. Amongst other groups, such as the Lepidoptera and Coleoptera, the available data are so meagre that it would be misleading to include them at present within this scheme, although several workers, on the basis of fragmentary observations, have been convinced that meeting and courtship is mediated by sound at least in some species of these orders. Darwin, for example, describes certain observations on beetles, and concludes that sound is intimately concerned with sexual behaviour.

Whatever is finally discovered about these latter, present evidence shows that in two major groups, the Orthoptera and Hemiptera, similar sexual behaviour patterns relating to songs are found. What are the fundamentals of this basic plan? First, the male of the species sings a song which attracts a female, ready to mate, to him; secondly, the meeting accomplished, the male, with further song, copulates with the female; finally, the male may again use stridulation to prevent the disruption of copulation. With this general plan as a framework, we may now consider some of the many variations and problems associated with it. It would be fruitless, even if it were possible, to discuss every minor variation in such a large and complex behaviour pattern as that described above; the major variations, however, are of interest and importance and can be thought of in two categories, first the presence or absence of female stridulation, and secondly the variations caused by the omission of certain phases of male song. It may be as well at this point to re-emphasize that the generalization under discussion is derived from observations on comparatively few orders and indeed species, and hence must not be expected to be widely valid; it does, however, offer a framework both for description and discussion. Moreover, as will become apparent, its validity can be extended by reversing the rôles of the sexes, when patterns such as those observed in some mosquitoes and certain water-bugs, where the male is attracted by the song of the female and actively seeks her out, can be accommodated.

The problem of female stridulation has arisen acutely within the last few years because many observations of the phenomenon have been described. Faber was aware of the ability of the females of certain species to stridulate, but tended to think the noise of little significance. Jacobs (1953), Weih (1951) and Ragge (1955) noted the occurrence of stridulation in several species of Acrididae, and were of the opinion that in certain species this indicated that the female was in a physiological condition ready to mate. This finding has now been substantiated by the work of Renner (1952), Haskell (1958a) and Perdeck (1957). The last two workers, indeed, used for certain of their acoustic behaviour experiments on Acrididae only those females which responded by stridulating when stimulated by the sound of male normal song. The stridulation of most female Acridids so far examined appears to be very similar to the male normal song of the species. Fig. 91 shows oscillograms of the male "normal" and female song of *O. viridulus* and *C. brunneus* and it can be seen that the song structures as between male and female are very similar. In both these species, and in *C. parallelus* and *Stenobothrus lineatus* as well, the actual movements of the femurs of the female during stridulation appear to be closely similar in motion and timing to those of the male of the species when singing its normal song. In *parallelus*, since the female is brachypterous, no normal stridulation is produced, although a low intensity clacking noise in which the pulse structure is like that of the male can sometimes be heard. In all cases the intensity of female song is lower than that of the male, and this can readily be understood when the parts of the sound mechanism are examined in detail. It is then found that the development of the stridulatory pegs or ridge on the hind femur is much reduced in all these females.

The similarity of female song to male normal song seems to hold in most of the several species of Acrididae in which the phenomenon has been observed in detail; in none of these species has a second song in females ever been noted. It seems beyond doubt that when it occurs, the stridulation denotes that the female is ready to mate, and Haskell has called the condition characterized by a readiness to stridulate the "responsive state". Females in this condition typically respond to the normal song of the male by orientating towards the singer or source of sound, making their "response stridulation" and then moving towards the male, pausing now and then to re-orientate and to stridulate. However, the absence of such response stridulation in the female does not always indicate an unwillingness to mate—the behaviour varies between species. In *C. parallelus* and *brunneus*, for example, only rarely will a female which does not sing in response to stimulation by male normal song, allow the male to copulate. Perdeck finds the same for *C. biguttulus*. In *O. viridulus* and *S. lineatus* on the other hand, female stridulation is much rarer and is not nearly such a good criterion of the "responsive state". It has been argued, notably by Jacobs and Weih, that female stridulation is of little significance in attracting the male, but both Perdeck (1957) and Haskell (1958a) observed that the males of certain species, notably *C. brunneus* and *C. biguttulus*, reacted to the response stridulation of the female and oriented and moved towards it. Thus in these species and also sometimes in *O. viridulus*, regular alternation of song occurs between male and female (Fig. 91E), both orientating and searching for the other, a process which presumably speeds up their meeting. In other species of grasshopper such as *S. lineatus* and *C. parallelus* the female moves towards the singing sedentary male, and only at close range does the female song appear to have any effect on the male. It must be remembered that in the natural grassland habitat of these insects, visual fields are greatly restricted, and often a female may move to within a few inches of a male before he sees her, and in these cases female song may help to attract the attention of the male.

There seems to be little observation in the other groups of the Orthoptera, the Tettigoniids and the Gryllids, on the occurrence of female song, although M. C. Busnel (1953) describes the so-called warning cries of the female of *Ephippiger*, and Malenotti (1926) observed stridulation in a female *Gryllotalpa* similar to that of the male, but the behavioural significance, if any, of these sounds is obscure. Amongst the Hemiptera, however, in certain species female song plays an essential rôle in reproductive behaviour, and the case of *Doratura* investigated by Ossiannilsson has been described above. Haskell (1957b) has described stridulation related to sexual behaviour in *Sehirus bicolor*, a terrestrial Heteropteran, and the observations make it appear likely that in this species the *Doratura* pattern again occurs. Amongst the Heteroptera, Leston (1957) and Haskell have shown that frequently both sexes can sing equally well, but the significance of the stridulation in relation to particular phases of behaviour is unknown. Certainly in several beetles (Haskell, unpublished) females sing as well as males, as they do in some Lepidoptera. In this latter group, indeed, in the butterfly *Parnassius apollo*, only gravid females stridulate, but once again the significance, if any, of the sound is unknown. Finally, reference must be made to the song behaviour of queen honey bees, which according to some authorities, plays an important part in the social life of the hive, an observation discussed later on in this chapter. It is clear, then, that sound production by female insects is quite widespread—almost certainly far more so than the present data suggest—but its significance is in most cases obscure. Only in the Acrididae can it be said with fair certainty that it indicates a readiness to mate by the female concerned. Naturally these remarks on female stridulation do not apply to cases where both males and females produce sounds of sexual significance as by-products of normal activity, as in the case of the flight tones of some mosquitoes and certain other Diptera.

We must now turn our attention back to the generalized plan and consider the second major variant in the scheme. This is caused by the omission of certain phases of male song under various circumstances and by various species. For example, in the genus *Chorthippus*, the courtship song is absent in *parallelus*, which has only an "Anspringlaute", but in the related *albo-marginatus* a long and complicated serenade is used during courtship. In other species, the "Paarungslaut" may be absent or reduced and so on. Such differences are specific and fixed, but other variations may occur in song behaviour due to environmental circumstances. Thus a male and female of one species may in the field meet accidentally, without the male having sung the normal song; under such circumstances the male, as soon as he becomes aware of the female, generally starts singing his courtship song and attempts to mate with the female. If the species has no serenade, as for example in *C. parallelus*, the male sings the "Anspringlaut" song and

K

attempts to jump on the female and engages the genitalia. In these cases it is safe to say in the majority of cases that if the female is in a responsive state, mating will occur. These and similar observations show that there are two separate parts to the acoustic reproductive behaviour pattern of which the first, initiated by the male normal song, results in locomotory activity leading to a meeting of the sexes, and the second, initiated by the courtship song, results in behaviour leading to copulation. These two parts are independent, since the second can occur without the first, but for this the female must be in the responsive state, and since in this state she responds to male normal song by locomotor seeking-behaviour, it is safe to say that a female performing the first pattern will almost certainly allow copulation when she meets a male. In the field it is possible that a female performing the first part of the pattern may meet a male other than the one to whose song she is responding, and in these circumstances if the second male sings the courtship song she will probably mate with it. It therefore follows that if a responsive female is to mate only with a male of her own species, the courtship song must be a specific song as well as the normal song; in fact, a comparative study of courtship songs and behaviour of related species shows this to be true. However, it is apparent that in certain species sensory modalities other than acoustic ones come into play during courtship, which further ensures species reproductive isolation; this matter is discussed in the next chapter. The discussion above is based mainly on evidence accrued as a result of investigations by many workers into the relation of stridulation to reproductive behaviour in Acrididae.

The original premiss, it will be recalled, was that stridulation plays a dual rôle in this connection, in that it facilitates meeting of the sexes and then promotes copulation; furthermore, it appears that the two rôles are independent, in that the latter can occur, in certain circumstances, in the absence of the former. The data available shows that this is so in Acridids, Tettigoniids and Gryllids, but for other groups, notably the Homoptera and Heteroptera, the evidence allows of no clear-cut conclusion. The work of Haskell (1957b) on the Heteropteran *Sehirus bicolor* suggests that the active male finds the female by following an odour trail, and the stridulation emitted may play only a stimulating rôle during courtship and copulation; on the other hand, the probability exists that the female emits an answering song during courtship behaviour, so that sound signals could play a selective as well as epigamic rôle. While some of the evidence of Ossiannilsson (1949) in relation to the singing of certain Homoptera indicates that in some species the male has a normal song which attracts the female at a distance, this is by no means general. Alexander (1957) suggests that in cicadas individual females are not attracted to individual males, but that the songs cause aggregations of males and females, and the courtship song or some other stimulus promotes mating between individuals. This suggestion is supported by Alexander's later work with Moore (1958) on two species of *Magicicada*, where chorusing behaviour is extremely well developed and plays probably a paramount rôle in bringing both sexes together in very high density aggregations. Amongst the Diptera, as has been described above, there exist some species with behaviour patterns which fit in with the general plan, but the data are fragmentary and unsatisfactory. In other groups of insects, even those such as beetles, where sound production has been observed and commented on for a long time, virtually no satisfactory evidence is available. All that is possible to say at the present time is that some members of several insect groups display acoustic behaviour in relation to reproductive activity which appears to conform to a generalized plan.

Having carried the comparative discussion of this aspect of insect sounds as far as possible, we must now look at some further problems of this acoustic behaviour which are of general interest and importance, although the evidence relating to them has been derived from experiments on only two groups of insects—the Orthoptera and the Hemiptera. There seems no room for doubt that the most highly developed song behaviour of all insects is to be found amongst the grasshoppers, and it is in this group that the interesting "rivals duet" behaviour is most elaborated. If a male grasshopper, singing his courtship song to a female, is interrupted by the arrival of a second male who also attempts to serenade the female, the first male leaves the female, faces the interloper, and sings a song called the "rivalry song". This produces an immediate and similar response from the intruder, and the two males sing against one another; the contest may be short, when one or other leaves the field and the remaining male returns to his courtship, or so long-drawn-out that the female quits the scene herself. Pumphrey (1955) has likened these song contests to "ritual battles", and suggests they have a counterpart in the mimic contests fought by contending males in other animal groups

such as fishes and birds. Very rarely do the two contending
males come to grips, and if this does happen no damage is done.
What decides the victor has yet to be discovered; a parallel might
be drawn with the case of male Stickleback rivalry as described by
Tinbergen, where the victor is the most mature fish, which means
the fish with the most pronounced sexual colouration. By analogy
we might expect that the grasshopper which sings with the greatest
intensity would win the day, but there is no evidence that this is
so; indeed, Pumphrey records an observation in which the victor
in one of these mimic battles was a one-legged male. On the other
hand, the observations of Weih (1951) show that in certain species,
notably *C. brunneus*, the rivalry song behaviour is quite complex,
the structure of the song altering in a manner related to the distance between the two insects. It is thus possible that the song
structure presents some acoustic sign stimulus which decides the
outcome of the contest, but the matter requires much more
investigation. As has been said, such behaviour is not highly
developed amongst other insects, although Alexander (1957)
describes similar behaviour in certain crickets and suggests it may
occur in cicadas. Fighting between male crickets is of repeated
occurrence in certain species, and in Japan males are often kept
as pets and made to fight for their living, but there is only a little
evidence to suggest that the fighting is intensified by the presence
of a female. In the Tettigoniids, an intruding male may make
repeated attempts to interfere in courtship behaviour, and the only
notice generally taken is for it to be repulsed by kicks from the
hind femora of one or both of the pair when it touches them. The
existence of rivalry song thus seems to mark out the Acrididae as
a very highly evolved group—a general conclusion supported by
taxonomic and systematic studies.

   The question of a possible connection between rivalry song and
the state of sexual maturation of the insects involved now leads us
to consider the more general question of the relation of stridulation
to reproductive activity. Once again, enough evidence is available
in two groups to show a direct connection between various phases
of sexual maturation and song, whilst in others the evidence is
suggestive but incomplete. Regen observed, in his early studies, that
only adult but unmated females of *Gryllus campestris* would react
to male normal song by moving towards the source of sound. It
seems that this finding was overlooked by subsequent experimenters,
since the results obtained in later attraction experiments were very

variable. In fact, the "responsive state" of female Acrididae can be altered by two factors, as the work of Renner (1952) on *Euthystira brachyptera*, and of Haskell (1958a) on four closely related species *S. lineatus, O. viridulus, C. parallelus* and *C. brunneus*, has shown. While the findings of these observers are at variance in minor details, their general conclusions are similar and may be summed up as follows. Female grasshoppers are in the main unresponsive to the songs of the male from the time of their final moult until they become sexually mature, or more precisely until the first eggs are ready to pass into the oviduct. They then become responsive and stimulation by male normal song elicits the typical behaviour of orientation

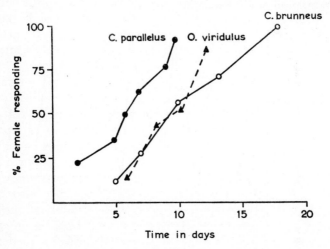

Fig. 92. Graph illustrating return of the "responsive state" in groups of six females of three species as a function of the time of acoustic isolation in days.

and locomotion to the source of sound, with stridulation responses also present. In this state the females will allow males of their own species to copulate without the preamble of the normal song, provided the latter sings the courtship song. Once copulation has taken place and a spermatophore is implanted in the female, the latter becomes unresponsive to male song. In *Euthystira*, Renner found that this unresponsive state was terminated by oviposition, but Haskell found with his species that this was not always so. He found that in the majority of females the responsive state was rarely regained during the remainder of the life span provided the insects were able to hear male normal song; acoustic isolation of the females from the song of their own species, however, secured a return of the responsive state in a time dependent on the species. Fig. 92 shows some typical figures for three species. Renner and Haskell also found that the responsive state of a female was terminated by approaching oviposition; the response disappeared about 24 hours before oviposition and returned in a short time, generally 2-3 hours, after the act was completed. Both workers agree that the essential factor in the termination of the responsive state by copulation is the transfer of the spermatophore; prolonged copulatory contact without the passage of sperm does not cut off the response. These general findings on the relation of female response to maturation and copulation are of great importance experi-

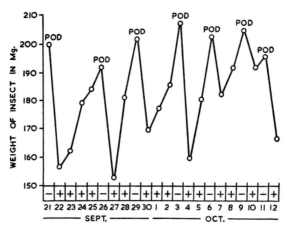

Fig. 93. Relationship between oviposition and response to male song in a virgin *C. brunneus*; +, responsive and −, unresponsive to song.

mentally, and also in the relation of stridulation and its associated behaviour to other aspects of the life of the insect. This latter aspect is discussed at length in Chapter 6, but something must be said here about the experimental importance of these findings. From this point of view, it is clear that in carrying out behaviour experiments relating to the effects of song on females, it is essential that the full sexual history of the insect be known in order to determine its physiological state. Moreover, if the female be other than newly moulted, data on her oviposition cycle must be available in order to be able to predict the disappearance of the responsive state caused by egg laying. Such prediction may be accomplished in some species by using a daily weight chart, and Fig. 93 shows such a chart together with the related changes in song response behaviour in the case of a virgin *C. brunneus*. Another useful criterion of female responsiveness, used by both Perdeck (1957) and Haskell (1958a), is that of female response stridulation; if this can be elicited from a female by stimulus with male normal song then that female is in the responsive state.

This dependence of the responsive state of females on maturation and oviposition and its termination by copulation has not been as extensively studied in other groups as it has in Acrididae. In the Tettigoniids, however, the evidence of Regen (1913, 1923) and of Busnel *et al.* (1956) shows that copulation terminates the responsive state; the fact that in these insects the spermatophore is attached externally to the female and the sperm only passes in some time after the pair has separated, enabled Busnel to show that it is in all probability the passage of the sperm which causes the change in behaviour, since removal of the spermatophore a short time after the end of copulation, but before the sperm has passed into the female, leaves the insect in the responsive state. As yet no evidence is available for Tettigoniids as to the reappearance of the responsive state, or of the effect of oviposition on song behaviour. In Gryllids, the observations of Regen suggest that a similar regime occurs here, and in several other groups evidence exists which makes it likely that the responsive behaviour of females is related to their state of sexual maturity. The mating behaviour of *Aedes aegypti*, described previously, relates essentially to mature males and females and the stridulation of certain Lepidoptera, for example *Parnassius* as described by Jobling, only occurs when the females are gravid; evidence of this suggestive but unsatisfactory nature is available for the females of some species from almost all groups which contain sound-producing insects. The same can be said about males, although the evidence here is even more meagre; there are, however, data which shows that in two groups, the Acridids and the Tettigoniids, acoustic and reproductive behaviour are inter-related differently. Male Acridids exhibit the full range of song behaviour when immature and often in the nymphal instars. Weih, Jacobs and Haskell all report nymphal stridulation in the genus *Chorthippus* from the third instar onwards, although attempts to copulate by nymphs are rare. Adult but immature males, however, do attempt copulation but are rarely successful in these attempts, and even if the genitalia are joined no spermatophore is passed and so no change occurs in the female. Adult, mature Acridid males are always apparently ready to copulate, and their emission of normal song is only interrupted for a short period, perhaps an hour or two, when they copulate fully and sucessfully with a female. Sometimes males will finish copulating with one female and immediately court and copulate with another; however, there is no evidence to show that in the second of such copulations a full spermatophore is passed. Nevertheless, the regime of their song behaviour is not materially altered by copulation, while in Tettigoniids the song of the male is dependent on mating behaviour. In this group, as Busnel and Dumortier (1955) have shown for *Ephippiger ephippiger* and *E. bitterensis*, the male only sings when it is ready to copulate, which in turn means that both testes and accessory glands are replete with material for the formation of a spermatophore. After a successful copulation, the male falls silent and takes no notice of females placed near it; this state of affairs lasts until the reproductive organs are again replete, when the male once more commences to sing the normal song. Fig. 89 shows a weight graph of a male of *E. ephippiger*, showing loss in weight relating to copulation, and consequent silent periods. In this group then, singing by a male is dependent on the state of the gonads, and the same relationship would seem to be true for Gryllids. In other groups, very little evidence relating male song to sexual state is available, although in the Heteroptera what data there are suggest that in certain species the male stridulates only when mature. Certainly this is so to a large extent in Corixids; according to Schaller (1951) the effect of male song on females is to make the latter swim vigorously but erratically, generally in circles. Since males ready to copulate always swim towards large objects moving in the water, such swimming by the females attracts the males. Male Corixids can generally sing two songs, and it is suggested that the second song is a courtship one, although this has yet to be confirmed. Leston (unpublished) finds that in the water-bug *Arctocorisa germari* both sexes stridulate during the February-March mating period, while another Corixid, *Sigara distincta*, does not commence singing in the south of England until late March, when its mating normally commences. Haskell (1957a) suggests that in the terrestrial bugs *Kleidocerys resedae*, *K. ericae*, *Piesma quadrata*, and probably in *Sehirus bicolor*, the onset of stridulatory activity commences at sexual maturity. As regards other groups of stridulating insects, there have been many suggestions that male song is related to sexual maturity, although the evidence is rarely satisfactory. Thus the tapping of certain wood beetles and the drumming of Psocoptera is said to occur mainly after the occurrence of maturation, but there is no evidence available as to whether male song and copulatory behaviour in these and other groups follows the Acridid or Tettigoniid pattern.

Enough has now been said to show that a large proportion, and probably the greater part, of insect acoustic behaviour is closely related to reproductive behaviour, and that it is possible to discern in this behaviour a generalized pattern applicable to many groups. There is now left the final heading of the three under which we are considering insect song and behaviour—sounds relating to organization in social, sub-social and gregarious insects. Certain manifestations of group sound behaviour may have additional significance as being defence or warning sounds. For example, Bristowe (1925) observed that if colonies of the termite *Cornitermes similis* are disturbed, the soldiers will commence to tap with their heads on the ground and may continue for half a minute. This tapping is rhythmical and in unison, and is said to act as a warning to the remainder of the colony. Very similar observations have been made on ant colonies; Gounell (1900) describes the concerted noise produced by ants of the genus *Camponotus* tapping with their heads in rolled-up leaves of bamboo. He also quotes observations by Forbes on ants of the genus *Polyrachis* in Sumatra, which produce noises by striking the leaf surface with their head; Forbes claimed that this rhythmical synchronous tapping could be heard over very large areas where the colony has spread, but that disturbing the ants in one part of the area caused the whole colony to stop tapping. In these and other cases the rôle of the sound signal is to act as a colony alarm, but of more interest is the use of sound signalling in maintaining the coherence of a colony of insects and in regulating its behaviour. Eggers was of the opinion that swarms of midges and mosquitoes maintained their coherence by means of reactions to one another's flight tone, and many observations in agreement with this view have been made; it is of course of particular importance to crepuscular or night flying insects. It should be noted, however, that such swarming behaviour is also in many species basic to reproduction. Wesenberg-Lund describes the copulatory behaviour of *Culex pipiens*; the males gather into little swarms and "on still evenings, the females fly to the males and are at once seized by them". In the Acrididae, observations suggest that the gregarious behaviour which is so marked a feature of the behaviour of certain species may be partially mediated by sound. Haskell (1957a) investigated the possibility that the fantastic cohesion observed in the Desert Locust, which makes it possible for migrating swarms to cover thousands of miles without serious reduction in numbers, was due to the wing-beat noise of the insects, a hypothesis advanced by Pumphrey in 1948. While it is true that flying locusts can hear the wing beats of their fellows over fair distances, it seems that this is only one factor of many which contribute to cohesion. However, in rather similar studies of the colony coherence of grasshoppers, Haskell (1958b) amasses evidence to show that here stridulation and associated behaviour clearly play an important part; a good deal of this evidence relates to the song behaviour of males, and this is of general interest for two reasons. First, because it is clearly unrelated to reproductive behaviour, and, secondly, because similar behaviour is also observable in other groups.

When detailed studies began to be made of the stridulation and song behaviour of male grasshoppers by such workers as Jacobs and Weih, it was soon evident that certain songs were used by males in communication with each other, and such stridulation was given the general title of "responding song". Responding behaviour between two male *C. brunneus* for example, consists in the alternate singing of a song which seems very similar to the single pulse normal song; but the essence of the behaviour lies in the rapid alternation and the perfect maintenance of the rhythm between the two insects. Weih studied in some detail the structure of the normal, responding and rivalry songs in this species, and came to the conclusion that the main difference between them was the rate of utterance of the chirps, which in turn depended on the distances between the two insects. If separated by about 2 metres or more, the males sing the normal song, emitting a pulse about once every 2 seconds; if the distance between males was $\frac{1}{4}$ to 1 metre they sing the responding song, the pulses being emitted about once every 1·0-1·7 seconds. At distances less than $\frac{1}{4}$ metre, rivalry behaviour commences and the song is emitted much more rapidly, about 1 pulse every 0·5 seconds. In other species of Acridid this stridulation behaviour between males takes the form of a group of males which sing the normal song either concurrently as in *O. viridulus*, or synchronously as in *S. lineatus*. Normally in such groups no locomotor movement takes place and the insects may not all be within visual distance of one another. Haskell (1957c) observed, however, that after a period of isolation of 24 hours or more males of these species would, on being placed just within acoustic range of such a group, move towards it and join in the stridulation. Periods of isolation thus enhanced the reactivity of the males to the stimulus provided by group singing. Haskell in a later paper (1958) speculates as to the effect of this in the field, and concludes that it may tend to group the males together, and thus be part of a mechanism evolved to maintain the coherence of the colony. Similar "song concerts" occur amongst Tettigoniids, although here the structure of the group is rather different, in that one insect commences to sing and is answered by several others. M. C. Busnel (1953) in her study of this phenomenon calls the stridulation of the first insect the "leader's song" and remarks that it is "particularly shrill". Amongst certain Gryllids, male song behaviour is different again and is most interesting, once more bringing in the idea of "distance apart", but in a different way. In *Oecanthus pellucens*, and probably in other crickets which are arboreal, the males appear to mark out a "territory" which they patrol; the appearance of another male near the borders of this territory evokes the so-called "warning stridulation" from the male in occupation. This interesting phenomenon seems analogous to the territory marking of certain song-birds, which is established by the male by singing at the territorial boundaries prior to the commencement of the mating season. The experiments of Regen relating to the "concerts" of males of *Pholidoptera aptera* have been described above; these observations point to the existence of learning behaviour in this insect, since males which had already sung with their fellows could never afterwards be induced to sing in alternation with artificial noises; such behaviour would tend to preserve the species group. There is some evidence from unpublished observations of Leston and Haskell that similar group singing of males occurs in certain bugs, but in other insects acoustic communication solely between males, if it occurs, seems to have gone unreported. Such behaviour is clearly not primarily connected with reproductive behaviour (although it may be a precursor to it), and it may have repercussions on the distribution and ecology of the species; this aspect will be discussed in Chapter 7.

As a final example of song behaviour related to the organization of a group or colony we shall consider the acoustic behaviour of honey-bees. Sound production by drone bees is apparently limited to noises produced by the wings, but queens and workers are capable of producing piping sounds, the origin of which has been discussed already. Several observers, including Armbruster, Orosi-Pal and more recently Woods have investigated the origin and significance of these various sounds, and have come to the conclusion that they are related to the economy, prosperity and health of the hive. Woods (1959) has suggested that the wing sound of workers is related to disturbances in the hive, such as failure of queens to lay or the approach of swarming. In such circumstances the sound output of the massed workers alters from the normal steady tone to a warbling note, and Woods claims that by noting the alterations in the sound, bee-keepers can check the condition of their hives. According to MacKeown (1937) the wasp *Polistes variabilis* also shows a variation in the nest note on disturbance. The piping of queens appears to be more complicated in its behavioural significance, but might perhaps be a " territorial response ", since it seems to be related to the appearence or insertion of a new or virgin queen in the hive. Woods has detailed observations which make it probable that the direct stimulus to piping is olfactory; for example, when requeening a hive, if an old and new queen in mesh cages are put next to one another the new queen usually pipes vigorously, and if a laying queen is left a short time in a new cage and then replaced with another queen, the latter becomes agitated and pipes. On the other hand queens from twin cells, presumably with a common odour, will never pipe at one another but will do so at a strange queen. This piping between queens recalls the rivalry behaviour of grasshoppers; if the outcome of rivalry depends on sexual maturation or some other function connected with reproduction, the two behaviour patterns may be even more similar, because the queen piping seems to be related to the egg laying potential of the queens. Virgin queens pipe best, but as the ovaries develop the power wanes, and when queens are egg laying their piping performance is both difficult to elicit and very inferior when evoked; as egg production is reduced however, perhaps prior to swarming, the acoustic powers of the insect return. Woods is of the opinion that under normal beekeeping conditions the only piping heard is that of virgin queens. In hives ready to swarm but prevented from escaping, the piping observed was shown to be that of virgin queens which had already supplanted the old queen.

Other observations on acoustic behaviour of Hymenoptera include many on ants, with the suggestion that acoustic signals initiate certain behaviour reactions, but the data are in general unsatisfactory. However, Santschi (1926) details some interesting observations on the ant *Megaponera foetans*, which suggest that the marching columns of these insects are led by a single individual, the "ant-guide", and the latter leads or entices the column by stridulatory signals. In support of this idea of acoustic communication in this species, Santschi describes the experiment of Callant; a worker was taken from a *Megaponera* column and trapped in some sand 50 cms from the band. The observer at once heard stridulatory noises, and at the same time the column of ants changed direction towards the trapped ant, and on reaching it quickly disengaged it from the sand. This interesting observation has now received support from the work of Wilson and Grinnell at Harvard on *Pogonomyrmex badius*. I am indebted to Professor Wilson for the following account of their unpublished work. Workers of this species only stridulate in a very specific stimulus situation, that is when they are trapped in a closely confined space. They do not respond to mechanical stimulation inside or outside the nest, nor to chemical stimuli, nor to the invasion of the nest by fire ants (*Solenopsis saevissima*). All of these stimuli induce an alarm reaction which is communicated olfactorily to other ants, but stridulation is only elicited by confinement, as least as far as present experiments show. Wilson and Grinnell raise the hypothesis that in nature workers stridulate when trapped in cave-ins, and the sound causes digging on the part of free workers, which are perhaps led to the scene by release of mandibular-gland secretion by the trapped ant.

Santschi further describes experiments he made with a species of *Messor*, in which he claimed that foraging ants which found a pot of honey near the nest attracted the attention of other workers by stridulation and then conducted them towards the food. This observation of Santschi's is paralleled by that of Rose (1948), who found that when foraging honey bees arrive at a food source some distance from the hive they emit a noise of ultra-sonic frequency, in the narrow band 20-22 kc/s; the intensity of the noise seemed to vary with the degree of agitation of the bees. In view of their advanced social behaviour, the possibility of acoustic signalling in bees and ants is of great interest, and is a field which both requires and deserves further study.

To conclude this chapter we must draw attention to several modes of acoustic behaviour in insects which do not fall within the main categories discussed above, but which are important as indicators of the new fields of research awaiting attention. It seems impossible to imagine that the Ichneumonids which parasitize other wood-boring hymenopterous larvae—locating them accurately enough for oviposition through perhaps an inch of bark—can do so by the use of any senses other than that of mechanoreception. The Chalcid wasp *Choetospila elegans*, which is a parasite of the beetle *Sitophilus granarius*, was shown by van den Assem and Keunen (1958) to locate the beetle larvae by detecting mechanical vibrations—including air-borne sounds—probably with antennal receptors. Again we may refer to the work of Richard (1952) on the feeding responses of ant lions, which react to their prey through vibrations of the substrate, detected by receptors on or in the first thoracic segment. The water-bug *Notonecta* also detects its prey by vibration location. Rabe (1953) showed that blinded bugs used certain hair organs on the hind legs to detect the vibration set up by the swimming prey; these organs also enabled the bug to locate a source of sound accurately over considerable distances. Lastly there is a recently discovered ability in the night-flying moth *Prodenia eridania*, which may use an echo-location system to avoid obstacles during flight. The tympanal organs of this moth have been investigated by Roeder and Treat (1957), who found them to be particularly suited for the reception of short pulses of high-frequency sound. These workers also discovered that during flight, the moth emits such a pulse of sound, very short in duration and high in pitch, and investigation showed that this sound could be detected by the tympanal organs of another moth over a range of at least 8 inches. Because of the characteristics of the wing sound and the tympanal organ, it is possible that the system could act similarly to the echo-location obstacle avoidance mechanism already found in bats, the sound pulses being reflected from objects in the flight path and being detected by the insect, causing it to take avoiding action. The acoustic organs of this moth are also capable of detecting the ultrasonic emission of flying bats, and there is some evidence to suggest that this may enable the insects to avoid capture by the mammals by settling as soon as they detect the bat squeaks. This suggestion is supported by the work of Schaller and Timm (1950) with other species of moths. Another suggestion is that moths may keep in contact, or attract one another, through the agency of this mechanism. It seems appropriate to end this chapter on behaviour associated with insect noises with this series of suggestions and speculations, because it sums up the present position quite well.

We know that insects make noises, that they can hear them, and in some cases we have quite detailed knowledge of the behaviour concerned with these abilities. But clearly this research only touches the fringe of the field; there must be much experiment, much speculation and very much more detailed observation before we can begin to define the possible rôles that sound emission and reception can play in insect behaviour.

REFERENCES

ALEXANDER, R. D. (1957) *Ohio Journ. Sci.* **57**: 101-113.

ALEXANDER, R. D. and MOORE, T. E. (1958) *Ohio Journ. Sci.* **58**: 107-127.

ASSEM, J. and KUENEN, D. J. (1958) *Ent. exp. et appl.* **1**: 174-180.

BLEST, A. D. (1957) *Behaviour.* **11**: 209-255.

BRISTOWE, W. S. (1925) *Nature, Lond.* **115**: 640-641.

BUSNEL, M. C. (1953) *Ann. Épiphyt.* **3**: 333-421.

BUSNEL, R. G. and DUMORTIER, B. (1955) *Bull. Soc. zool. Fr.* **80**: 23-26.

BUSNEL, R. G., DUMORTIER, B., BUSNEL, M. C. (1956) *Bull. biol.* **90**: 219-286.

EDWARDS, H. (1889) *Insect Life.* **2**: 11-15.

FABER, A. (1953) *Laut und Gëbardensprache bei Insekten. Orthoptera, (Geradflügler) Teil* **1**. Stuttgart.

GAUL, A. T. (1952) *Psyche.* **59**: 82-83.

GOUNELL, E. (1900) *Bull. Soc. ent. Fr.* 1900: 168-169.

HASKELL, P. T. (1956) *Proc. R. ent. Soc. Lond.* (C) **21**: 21-22.

HASKELL, P. T. (1957a) *J. ins. Physiol.* **1**: 52-75.

HASKELL, P. T. (1957b) *Proc. zool. Soc. Lond.* **129**: 351-358.

HASKELL, P. T. (1957c) *Brit. J. Anim. Behav.* **5**: 139-148.

HASKELL, P. T. (1958a) *Anim. Behav.* **6**: 27-42.

HASKELL, P. T. (1958b) *Insectes Sociaux.* **5**: 287-298.

HINTON, H. E. (1948) *Entomologist.* **81**: 254-269.

JACOBS, W. (1953) *Z. Tierpsychol, Beiheft I.* 228 pp.

KAHN, M. C. and OFFENHAUSER, W. (1949) *Amer. J. trop. Med.* **29**: 811-825.

LESTON, D. (1957) *Proc. zool. Soc. Lond.* **128**: 369-386.

MACKEOWN, K. C. (1937) *Austr. Mus. Mag.* **6**: 183-185.

MALENOTTI, E. (1926) *Atti. Ac. Agr. Sci. e Lett. Verona.* **3**: 177-184

MYERS, K. (1952) *Aust. J. Sci. Res.* (B). **5**: 264-281.

OSSIANNILSSON, F. (1949) *Opusc. Ent. Suppl.* **10**: 1-145.

PERDECK, A. C. (1957) *Behaviour,* **12**: 1-75.

PUMPHREY, R. J. (1955) *Colloque sur L'Acoustique des Orthoptères. Ann. Épiphyt.* (tome hors serie) 320-337.

RABE, W. (1953) *Z. vergl. Physiol.* **35**: 300-325.

RAGGE, D. R. (1955) *Brit. J. Anim. Behav.* **3**: 70.

REGEN, D. J. (1913) *Pflügers. Arch. ges. Physiol.* **155**: 193-200.

REGEN, D. J. (1923) *S.B. Akad. Wiss. Wien.* (1): **132**: 81-88.

REGEN, D. J. (1926) *S.B. Akad. Wiss. Wien.* (1): **135**: 329-368.

RENNER, M. (1952) *Z. Tierpsychol.* **9**: 122-154.

RICHARD, G. (1952) *Bull. soc. zool. Fr.* **77**: 252-263.

ROEDER, K. and TREAT, A. E. (1957) *J. exp. Zool.* **134**: 127-158.

ROSE, M. *et al.* (1948) *C. R. Acad. Sci. Paris.* **227**: 912-913.

ROTH, L. M. (1948) *Amer. Mid. Nat.* **40**: 265-352.

SANTSCHI, F. (1926) *Bull. (Ann.) Soc. ent. Belg.* **66**: 327-330.

SCHALLER, F. (1951) *Z. vergl. Physiol.* **33**: 476-486.

SCHALLER, F. and TIMM, C. (1950) *Z. vergl. Physiol.* **32**: 468-481.

SOTAVALTA, O. (1947) *Acta. Entomol. Fennica.* **4**: 1-117.

SWINTON, A. H. (1877) *Ent. mon. Mag.* **13**: 169-172.

WEIH, A. S. (1951) *Z. Tierpsychol.* **8**: 1-41.

WILLIAMS, C. B. (1922) *Entomologist.* **55**: 173-176.

WISHART, G. and RIORDAN, D. F. (1959) *Canad. Ent.* **91**: 181-191.

WOODS, E. F. (1959) *Nature, Lond.* **184**: 842-844.

CHAPTER VI

SOME PHYSIOLOGICAL ASPECTS
OF ACOUSTIC BEHAVIOUR

I n the last chapter an outline was given of various types of behaviour associated with insect sounds. These behaviour observations, particularly when detailed, have thrown up a number of associated problems, mostly physiological in nature, some of which, being of general interest in relation to insect acoustics, will be separately and briefly considered in this chapter.

The first problem is whether acoustic signals alone are concerned in the observed behaviour or whether other modalities such as vision and olfaction play a part. Busnel (1956) and Haskell (1958) have both experimented on the rôle of vision in this connection. The former found that a female *Ephippiger*, with compound eyes and ocelli covered with black paint, was still capable of finding a singing male over the usual distances, and that even when close to the male the movements of the female were still clear and definite. In contrast to this, Haskell, repeating the same experiment with certain grasshoppers, found that although the original orientation to, and movement towards, a singing male was as definite as in normal grasshoppers, the nearer the female came to a male, the less definite became her movements, so that often the female took some time finally to "find" the male acoustically. Often the search was ended by the male himself, who, seeing the female when the latter had approached to close range, moved rapidly to her and began courtship behaviour. The resulting copulatory behaviour was normal. Haskell, by blinding the male as well as the female, was able to show that vision played a part in the behaviour of these grasshoppers. In these circumstances, although the approach of the female was at first normal, when she came within a few inches of the male orientation failed, and this time, since the male was unable to help, the two insects would move aimlessly to and fro and were a very long time in making contact if they did so at all. There is thus evidence that in these two groups of the Orthoptera acoustic signalling is in one case aided by vision. Jacobs (1953) indeed is of the opinion that in the grasshopper *Stenobothrus* vision is as important or almost as important as sound in bringing the sexes together.

The above contrasting observations on Tettigoniids and Acridids may perhaps be related to the directional characteristics of the different types of tympanal organ possessed by these groups, which have been described previously. With any displacement receiver, the fundamental orientation properties will diminish as the receptor moves nearer the source of sound, since the latter grows relatively larger and is no longer a point source. However, the "scanning" mechanism in Tettigoniids would enable these insects to retain their powers of acoustic orientation when quite near to the source of sound, and from the behaviour reported above it seems they can do so. A comparison of orientation power between a long-horn and short-horn grasshopper, each with only one tympanal organ functional, bears this out; both can still orientate and move towards a sound source, although with greater difficulty than when both receptors are functional, but the orientation of the short-horn breaks down almost completely when near the sound source.

But, as we have seen earlier, insects have more than one type of sound receptor; what rôle, if any, do receptors other than tympanal organs play in insect acoustic behaviour? Clearly, in certain species of Diptera and terrestrial Heteroptera, where behavioural evidence hardly leaves room to doubt that acoustic signalling plays a part in heterosexual aggregation, we must allow that receptors other than tympanal organs mediate and control the reactions observed. The mating behaviour of mosquitoes has already been described, and here orientation to a sound source has been demonstrated and shewn to be mediated by Johnston's organ, but it seems likely from other evidence that in this group vision also plays an important part in the behaviour. Olfaction is an obvious supplementary modality which is almost certainly used in some cases, probably in the latter stages of behaviour when males and females are close together. In the bug *Sehirus*, Haskell (1957b) thinks that the male follows the female by olfaction and that sound may play only a stimulating rôle in reproductive behaviour. There is evidence (Norris, 1954, Loher, 1958) that olfaction as well as sound plays a part in the courtship of *Schistocerca gregaria*, and it is fairly safe to predict that it will be found to be concerned in much reproductive behaviour even if only in an accessory rôle, and perhaps more especially in those insects which do not appear to possess well-developed acoustic receptors. As to insects with tympanal organs, in many species of several orders these receptors would seem to be the main mediators of acoustic reproductive behaviour. Schaller (1951) in his experiments with the water-bug *Corixa striata* found that communal stridulation between males and the reactions of females to male stridulation all ceased if the tympanal organs of the insects were destroyed. This is also the case in Tettigoniids and Gryllids according to Busnel and Regen. In short-horn grasshoppers, however, the situation is more complicated, since Haskell (1958) has described experiments in which female *C. parallelus*, with both tympanal organs destroyed, made typical stridulation movements in response to high intensity playback of the male normal song. This reaction was apparently mediated by certain abdominal hair sensillae, since smearing these organs with vaseline caused the response to disappear. But Haskell also obtained a response from a female *parallelus* which had both tympanal organs destroyed and the abdominal sensillae vaselined, but only when stimulation was from a loud-speaker on the floor of the insect cage. This response he attributed to the sub-genual organs in the legs, and it seems that these organs may play a subsidiary rôle in stridulation behaviour.

This is also a possibility in some Tettigoniids, Busnel and his co-workers (1956) having made observations on the courtship behaviour of *Ephippiger bitterensis* which seem to point to the use of these receptors. In this species the male lives in bushes and sings his normal song there; responsive females are attracted by the song, move towards the bush and eventually begin to climb it. When a female begins to ascend a bush the male often displays a form of behaviour called by Busnel "tremulation". This consists of rapid vertical movements of the whole body at a frequency of about 25 per second, for perhaps ½ to 1½ seconds. During this movement the female remains still, but as soon as it ceases she commences to climb again; when the male repeats the tremulation, the female stops moving, but resumes her progress when the vibration ceases. If during her progress the female stops for some time, the male then recommences singing his normal song, which seems to have the usual stimulatory effect on the female, who starts to move; the tremulation is then resumed, if necessary with bouts of stridulation interposed, until the insects meet. This remarkably vibratory movement can be elicited from a singing male by the appearance on its bush of another male, or even another insect. Thus, as Busnel points out, it is only a response to mechanical vibration and is not specific; for the female, however, it may constitute a specific signal, since the frequency of oscillation seems fairly constant. Tremulation in the female has also been observed, but is rare. Thus there is evidence in these insects of rather complex acoustic signalling, partly mediated by the tympanal organs and partly, presumably, by the sub-genual organs. It seems possible that such vibratory phenomena may exist in the stridulation behaviour of other species especially over short distances; for example, Haskell (1955) has shown that the act of stridulation by a male *C. parallelus* sets up vibrations of the substrate which can be detected by this grasshopper over distances of the order of 15 cms.

Although the stimulus and its reception in insect reproductive behaviour mediated by sound may both be complicated, the evidence, in every case where detailed observations have been made, strongly suggests that there is one main receptor system, which if destroyed puts an end to the behaviour in the great majority of cases. In groups with tympanal organs such as certain Orthoptera, Homoptera, Lepidoptera and some aquatic Heteroptera, these receptors appear to mediate both the initiation and maintenance of reproductive behaviour; in groups without tympanal organs where observations are available, such as Diptera, Johnston's organ seems to be the main sensory organ used.

From the moment it became obvious that acoustic signals were concerned in reproductive behaviour and that a certain specificity of stimulus and response was present, it has been tempting to assume that the rôle of stridulation could also include the function of species isolation. Species reproductive isolation certainly occurs in many groups of singing insects where several closely related species live together in one habitat, for example, in Gryllids, Acridids and in some Homoptera and terrestrial Heteroptera. As far as certain grasshoppers are concerned the influence of song on isolation has been put beyond doubt by the work of Perdeck (1957), who has shown that the sole barrier to interspecific mating between *Chorthippus brunneus* and *C. biguttulus* resides in their stridulation behaviour. There is strong evidence that this is so in other singing insects, and this matter is more fully discussed in the next chapter. Here we must consider the question, " What features of the stridulation characterize the essential part of the signal which enables one species to recognize its own song amongst others? "

This problem can be tackled in two different ways; one is to stimulate the insect with recorded song and then alter one by one all qualities of the sound until elimination or alteration of one characteristic nullifies the response; the other is to use artificially generated sounds for stimulation, the characteristics of which are accurately known. Both methods have been used and have produced equivocal results which are not yet reconciled. Probably the first detailed experiments using artificial sound as a stimulus were those of Regen on *Pholidoptera*, described previously. By selecting young male insects, he was able to get them to sing in concert with signals from a variety of musical instruments, but he was unable to elicit responses from males who had already sung together with other males. Some element or elements of the natural signal was thus acting as an essential character differentiating it from the other stimuli used, and it is clear that this essential character could be intensity, frequency, modulation or the rate of change of any of these. Modulation, in this sense, also applies to the structure of a whole song, and this includes also the special case of duration of the signal. It is clear that whatever feature or combination of features constitute the specific element, it will appear in all natural signals of the species concerned. It should be possible then by analysis of natural signals to arrive at some common specific factor, and thus we find modern experimenters making instrumental analyses of the intensity, frequency range and spectrum and duration of many insect songs. This was most exhaustively done in the case of the Orthoptera, and quickly led to the conclusion that none of these qualities was important in itself. Naturally the song has to be of a frequency, intensity and duration such that the receptor organ of the insect concerned can respond to it, but this gives wide limits for variability which were indeed found in the stridulation examined. Thus M. C. Busnel (1953) showed that in *Locusta migratoria*, the intensity of emission of the copulation song could vary from 26 to 39 db, that the frequency spectrum was variable by several kilocycles, and that the principal frequency was likewise variable between 7 and 9 kc/s in the insect examined. Furthermore, variation of these parameters could occur rapidly in some insects, when either one or both femurs were used for singing. It is now known that such variations in intensity and frequency are common to the songs of many insects, and it is probable that these qualities do not constitute the essential, information-bearing element of the signal.

In 1951 Weih published his work on stridulation and behaviour in several species of *Chorthippus*; he used a simple machine which produced noises whose timing could be altered at will, and he found, particularly with *C. brunneus*, that the temporal structure of the song was of great importance. This effect of timing was also noted by Busnel and his colleagues (1953, 1954) in their experiments with *C. brunneus* and *C. biguttulus*. They used a variety of artificial noises, varying from pure sine waves to imitation bird calls, and Loher also used imitations of the grasshopper songs made by mouth. Further experiments by Busnel and his co-workers carried out on both Acrididae and Tettigoniidae confirmed that frequency was not an essential quality of the successful stimulus—the stimulus, that is, that was capable of releasing behavioural responses in the form of song and locomotor movements from the experimental insect. Provided that the frequency of the stimulating sound was such that it fell within the frequency range of the tympanal organs, the insect responded. Fig. 94 is an oscillogram showing responses by a male *C. brunneus* to an imitation of its normal song made by mouth. The disparity of fine structure of the natural and artificial sounds which reflects differences in the principal frequency and in frequency spectrum, can easily be seen. This finding applied to both Acrididae and Tettigoniidae, but in other factors the two groups differed considerably. In Acrididae, some anomalous effects of intensity were noted; for example in *C. brunneus* some males responded to signals from a Galton whistle of 55-70 db by singing their normal song, but an increase of intensity to 75-80 db produced a "supra-normal" response, the insect singing a new louder song of its own. The repetition frequency of the stimulus was important, and here the findings of Weih were confirmed, since an increase in repetition frequency evoked the faster "rivalry song" in response. When artificial signals consisting of trains of square-wave pulses emitted from a loud-speaker were used, the duration of each train being 100 milliseconds, it was found that the signal was effective providing that the interval between each adjacent pulse in a train was 20 milliseconds or less. Experiments with Tettigoniids, mainly of the genus *Ephippiger*, produced variable results; Galton whistle signals produced responses generally only when they were repeated at intervals of one or two minutes, and under these conditions the number of responses from the insect to each whistle signal gradually increased, until finally the insect could be induced to sing continuously. The intensity of the signals used had to be high, about 80-85 db, and the modulation pattern could be variable. The duration of the signal and the time elapsing before the insect responded was unimportant in some species, very important in others. On the basis

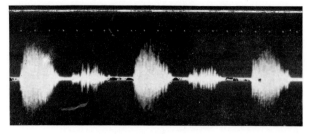

FIG. 94

Oscillogram showing response by male *C. brunneus* to imitation of its normal song made by mouth by the experimenter. Imitation pulse occurs first, followed by response of insect and so on alternately. Timing mark 1/10 second.

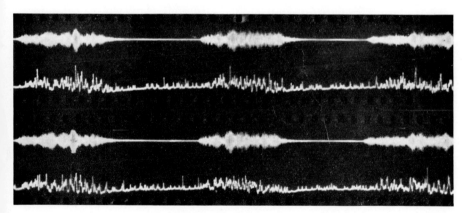

FIG. 96

Two records of responses in the tympanal nerve of a male *C. brunneus* (lower oscillogram trace) to repetitive stimulation by identical sound stimuli (upper trace). See text also.

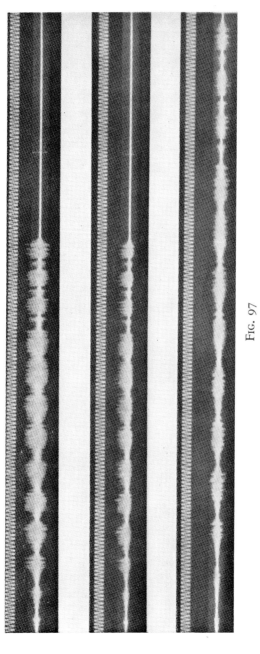

Fig. 97

Oscillogram showing changes in waveform and modulation of part of a recording of the normal song of a male C. *parallelus*; for behavioural changes related to the sound see text.

of their experience with grasshoppers, Busnel and his co-workers have advanced the theory that the important feature of those artificial stimuli which are capable of eliciting a response from the insects is the presence somewhere in the signal of a "transient"— a rapid build up or decay of sound amplitude. A signal of the type shown diagrammatically in Fig. 95 (trace I), where build up and decay of amplitude is relatively slow, is said to be ineffective in producing acoustic responses, whereas if the same signal is bisected (trace II) producing two signals each of which contains a transient, both these parts, a & b, act as successful stimuli; trains of square

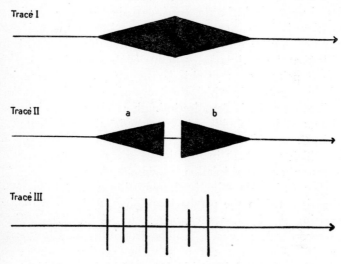

FIG. 95. Illustration of Busnel's "transient" theory; for explanation see text.

waves (trace III) will also be effective for the same reason. Busnel (1955) invokes the theory of differential perception to explain these results, and suggests the hypothesis may be found to hold in many groups of insects and also in certain vertebrates.

Haskell, in several papers (1956a, 1956b, and 1957a), has denied this view, and on the basis of observations of the actual nerve responses of insect tympanal organs has proposed that the pulse modulation of the sound is the important element therein. Fig. 96 shows one of the more important experiments. The normal song of a male C. brunneus was recorded on a length of tape, the ends of which were joined to give an endless belt which on passing through the recorder produced repetitive identical sound stimuli. The nerve impulses in the tympanal nerve of a grasshopper produced by such repetitive stimulation were then recorded, and the figure shows part of the resultant oscillograms. The upper trace is the stimulus, which is identical in both records, and the lower trace shows the corresponding impulses in the tympanal nerve which are different in every case. It will be seen that the responses to the transients that occur in the first pulse of the stimulus are quite different in the successive records. Haskell argues that if the responses to identical stimuli themselves differ, it does not seem likely that any internal feature of the natural stimulus, which is itself variable as between individual insects, could be the species specific factor on which discrimination is based. He suggests that since tympanal organs respond to modulation patterns of the stimulating sound, it is most probably that the modulation structure of the songs is the key character, and points out that this is the most constant quality of stridulation, and one in which the songs of species differ markedly, thus affording a basis for discrimination. Haskell performed an experiment which upholds this hypothesis; the recorded normal song of a *C. parallelus* male was played back to males of the same species which were kept in isolation (Fig. 97, upper record). This treatment enhances stridulation response, and 72% of males in 50 trials responded to the stimulus by emitting normal song. A filter was then inserted in the playback amplifier, which had the effect of distorting the frequency characteristics of the signal (Fig. 97, middle record). On playback, a slight drop in the number responding, to 68% of 50, was noted. Finally the experiment was repeated with the filter removed, but with the tape played at half its normal speed; this distorted the frequency spectrum as before, but also reduced the pulse repetition frequency by half (Fig. 97, lower record), and under these circumstances the number of males responding dropped markedly to 28% in 50 trials. Strong evidence that in crickets of the family Oecanthinae the pulse rate of the male normal song is the significant factor in specific discrimination by responsive females has been produced by the experiments of Walker (1957), who demonstrated positive phonotaxis to conspecific songs in four species. One of the most interesting aspects of this work is the fact that the female receptor mechanism apparently has some temperature compensating mechanism, since the females responded to the male song over a range of temperature which caused the male pulse rate to alter appreciably. Against such evidence as this, however, several facts ought to be recalled. One is that until single fibre discharges in the tympanal nerve have been studied in more detail it is not possible to dismiss the idea that differential intensity perception is involved in the discrimination process. Again, the work of Katsuki and Suga (1958) and of Horridge (1960) referred to in Chapter 3, does in fact suggest that some very rudimentary form of frequency analysis—between sounds containing high and low frequency elements—may be possible due to differential neurone sensitivity in insects with tympanal organs—and such a faculty would be an aid to discrimination, although it could hardly be the whole story. In this connection one must remember the Diptera, where discrimination does appear—at least in many mosquitoes—to be based on frequency as detected by Johnston's organ, although here again other modalities such as vision and olfaction almost certainly play a part in the process of discrimination. Further, even when using artificial signals in which the modulation pattern is the same as that of natural song, there is always a proportion—sometimes a high proportion—of insects which are not deceived by the imitation. It is probably considerations of this sort that have led Pumphrey (1955) to suggest that the power of song discrimination depends in some way on the functional importance of the stimulus situation. This means in effect that the insect uses other features of the situation, besides acoustic ones, to aid in song discrimination, and that other sensory modes play a part in initiating the responses, and it has already been shown above that other modalities are concerned in some behaviour associated with stridulation.

The situation is further complicated by the fact that in some species, the power of discrimination is either absent or poorly developed, since inter-specific acoustic behaviour is seen. Weih (1951) described inter-specific acoustic responses between various Acrididae, and Busnel and his co-workers (1956) have shown that in certain species of *Ephippiger*, not only is there inter-specific acoustic communication, but that this can and does lead to copulation and passage of a spermatophore. Busnel points out, however, that the species of *Ephippiger* displaying this behaviour were brought together artificially for the experiment, and that normally they live in widely differing habitats, and postulates that here at least habitat preference maintains the isolation of the species. It is clear that any experimental approach to the question of song discrimination should therefore have regard to the natural relationships of the species concerned, such as their ecological distribution and ability to inter-breed.

Another aspect of stridulation behaviour related to discrimination and recognition is the question as to whether the behaviour is instinctive or learned. There can be little doubt that stridulation itself—the power of sound emission—represents an inherited and adapted system of motor movements. But what of the behavioural responses to stridulation? Are these inherited or learnt? No modern work has been done on this aspect of insect song, and the one piece of experimental evidence seems to be that of Regen (1926) relating to the responses of *Pholidoptera* males to artificial sounds. It will be recalled that Regen was able to make newly-moulted males sing in concert with several artificial noises, but males which had once sung with other males could not be induced to sing in this fashion; this clearly suggests learning had occurred. No similar phenomenon has been reported in more recent investigations, and indeed the evidence suggests not only that stridulation is instinctive but also the behaviour associated with it is as well. Several authors, notably Jacobs (1953) and Weih (1951), have commented on the power of some of the early instars of Acridid grasshoppers to stridulate like males; Haskell reared males of *C. parallelus* in isolation from hatching and found that they could stridulate quite normally. However, the frequency of occurrence of spontaneous stridulation in these isolated males was much lower than that of males reared crowded with other males, but was permanently increased when the experimental insects were put with normal males, an observation which could be explained on the basis of learnt behaviour. Nymphal stridulation also occurs in several other groups besides the Orthoptera, notably the Homoptera and Heteroptera, but its significance and the relationship of instinct and learning in acoustic behaviour must await further research.

It is implicit in all the behavioural work done on acoustic signalling and communication in insects that some higher nervous centre or centres must be concerned in the process. The inter-play of song discrimination, orientation to the sound source and locomotor responses in, say, the grasshoppers or the mosquitoes, shows that integration of a mass of sensory data is involved. The experiments and observations of Huber (1955a, 1955b) have gone some way towards showing that, in Orthopteroid insects at least, such functions are probably carried out in the corpora pedunculata of the brain. In the cricket *Gryllus campestris* motor control of the muscles involved in the stridulatory mechanism resides in the second thoracic ganglion, but this is in turn controlled by centres in the protocerebrum and the normal, courtship and rivalry songs can be induced by mechanical stimulation of certain brain areas with glass needles; subsequent histological examination showed that the punctures which produced song reactions were localized in the corpora pedunculata and the central body of the brain. Huber (1952) was also able to show in the same insect that the last abdominal ganglion and the ventral nerve cord must be intact for mating behaviour to progress normally, and he is of the opinion that the presence of a ripe spermatophore is signalled to the brain via the last ganglion, and that this condition is an essential precursor to normal courtship. The observations have been repeated on the Acridid *Gomphocerus rufus* as far as the higher centres controlling stridulation are concerned, and in this species again these appear to be the corpora pedunculata.

REFERENCES

BUSNEL, M. C. (1953) *Ann. Épiphyt.* 1953(3): 333-421.

BUSNEL, R. G. (1955) *C. R. Acad. Sci. Paris.* **240**: 1477-1479.

BUSNEL, R. G., BUSNEL, M. C. and DUMORTIER, B. (1956) *Ann. Épiphyt.* 1956 (3): 451-469.

BUSNEL, R. G., DUMORTIER, B. and BUSNEL, M. C. (1956) *Bull. biol.* **90**: 219-286.

BUSNEL, R. G. and LOHER, W. (1953) *C. R. Acad. Sci.* **237**: 1557-1559.

BUSNEL, R. G., LOHER, W. and PASQUINELLY, F. (1954) *C. R. Acad. Sci. Paris.* **148**: 1987-1991.

HASKELL, P. T. (1955) *Nature, Lond.* **175**: 639.

HASKELL, P. T. (1956a) *J. exp. Biol.* **33**: 756-766.

HASKELL, P. T. (1956b) *J. exp. Biol.* **33**: 767-776.

HASKELL, P. T. (1957a) *Brit. J. Anim. Behav.* **5**: 139-148.

HASKELL, P. T. (1957b) *Proc. zool. Soc. Lond.* **129**: 351-358.

HASKELL, P. T. (1958) *Anim. Behav.* **6**: 27-42.

HORRIDGE, G. A. (1960) *Nature, Lond.* **185**: 623-624.

HUBER, F. (1952) *Verh. dtsch. Zool. Ges.* 1952: 138-149.

HUBER, F. (1955a) *Z. Tierpsychol.* **12**: 12-48.

HUBER, F. (1955b) *Naturwiss.* **20**: 566-567.

JACOBS, W. (1953) *Z. Tierpsychol. Beiheft.* **1**: 1-288 pp.

KATSUKI, Y. and SUGA, N. (1958) *Proc. Jap. Acad.* **34**: 633-638.

LOHER, W. (1958) *Nature, Lond.* **181**: 1280.

NORRIS, M. J. (1954) *Anti-Locust Bull.* No. 18, 44 pp.

PERDECK, A. C. (1957) *Behaviour.* **12**: 1-75.

PUMPHREY, R. J. (1955) *Colloque sur l'Acoustique des Orthoptères. Ann. Épiphyt.* (tome hors serie): 320-337.

REGEN, D. J. (1926) *S. B. Akad. Wiss. Wien.* **135**: 329-368.

SCHALLER, F. (1951) *Z. vergl. Physiol.* **33**: 476-486.

WALKER, T. J. (1957) *Ann. ent. Soc. Amer.* **50**: 626-636.

WEIH, A. (1951) *Z. Tierpsychol.* **8**: 1-41.

CHAPTER VII

SOUND IN THE INSECT WORLD

I N the preceding chapters an attempt has been made to give an outline of present knowledge relating to insect sounds—the mechanisms by which they are generated and detected, some of their typical patterns, the part they play in certain behaviour patterns and some of the problems to which these phenomena give rise. In this concluding chapter this outline will be assessed in its relation to the insect world as a whole—its evolution and survival. It has frequently been said above that acoustic behaviour is a very neglected aspect of insect ethology and one of the reasons for this is the technical, practical difficulties attendant on the experimental approach. Entomologists have known about the powers of sound production in insects for a very long time, but it is only in recent years that some part of the rôle it plays in insect behaviour has been appreciated, and only as this knowledge grows can its importance in such spheres as survival and speciation be assessed. But there are already sufficient data on which to base some interesting hypotheses, which contain an exciting challenge for future research.

It is clear, for example, that the powers of sound production must have evolved several times over in certain groups, a fact which suggests some potential survival value in the accomplishment. Leston (1957) has shown that in the terrestrial Heteroptera, sound-producing mechanisms have appeared no less than eighteen times, including a possible five times in Aradidae. In the water-bugs or Hydrocorisae, stridulatory organs have evolved independently about twelve times. The evolution of sound-producing organs in the Orthoptera has been discussed by Zeuner (1934, 1939) and Ander (1939), and the conclusion that the power has evolved independently on several occasions is also arrived at here. It is often difficult and always dangerous to speculate on the effects which have followed the evolution of some new organ or function in a species or higher group of animals, and if we here indulge it is because it is part of the purpose of this book to throw out some hypotheses to stimulate further research.

As far as the direct survival value of stridulation is concerned, there are two main aspects of this; one is the possibility that insects can frighten off, or escape from, predators by the use of sounds, and the second is that by use of sound signals meetings of the sexes are brought about and mating facilitated. A third aspect of the survival value of stridulation, which may be thought of as indirect, concerns its effect on the ecology of certain species. It should be stated at once that there is very little, if any, direct evidence of the power of stridulation in frightening off predators. This aspect has been discussed in an earlier chapter, and so the evidence, such as it is, need not be presented again. But the widespread evolution of pupal stridulation in the Lepidoptera, for example, which can apparently have no possible significance other than that of defence, and the audio mimicry of wasps by certain flies, does suggest that under certain conditions sounds can have a defensive and hence a survival value. But the question of how widespread and how effective such powers are must of necessity remain a question for the moment. One further aspect of this defensive rôle of stridulation must be mentioned, and that is the opposite, disadvantageous possibility that a singing insect may attract the attention of predators, particularly those accustomed to using acoustic orientation methods in hunting, such as small mammals, birds and perhaps amphibians. Marler (1955) has commented on this possibility, and points out that the frequencies of a large number of insect songs lie in a range that is above that of the maximum sensitivity of most birds. Haskell (1958a), however, has pointed out that in certain grasshoppers the opposite is true, and that their song may well be easily located by birds. Unfortunately, the auditory ability of the typical predators mentioned above is but little known, so that even an approximate assessment of the "predator attraction" of insect songs is at present impossible. But the possibility of the existence of this disadvantageous effect ought to be remembered when discussing the rôle of stridulation in the life of the insect, particularly in any consideration of the so-called "defensive sounds" on which so many naturalists have commented. It is clear, of course, that such a disadvantage would only occur in those species which sing spontaneous songs.

On the second aspect of the survival value of stridulation, which is concerned with the facilitation of courtship and mating, a great deal more evidence is available. There can no longer be any reasonable doubt that in several groups of the Orthoptera, meetings of the sexes and epigamic display leading to mating is initiated and controlled by acoustic stimuli, and it appears highly probable that a similar arrangement exists amongst certain Diptera, Homoptera and Heteroptera. Further than that at present it seems unwise to go, for the evidence is meagre and for the most part rather subjective. This may be thought an over-cautious approach, but when one considers the possible part played by sound signals in such behaviour, particularly in the present context of survival value, there is evidently need for care: for it is widely accepted that specificity in courtship and mating behaviour has the special function of reproductive isolation. Tinbergen (1951, 1954) points out that the balance of available evidence supports the common assumption that interspecific copulation produces inferior progeny as compared with intraspecific mating, and that reproductive isolation has definite survival value. In the present context then, evidence for the survival value of insect songs must derive from cases where it can be clearly shown that the sole or at least the principal isolating mechanism is song specificity and song discrimination; at present such evidence is available for only one or two species, although the probability exists in many more. The best evidence so far is that deriving from the work of Perdeck (1957) on the isolating value of stridulation in two species of grasshopper *Chorthippus brunneus* and *C. biguttulus*. These closely related species are sympatric, and viable offspring result from their hybridization. They are not separated by ecological or morphological barriers, but in nature seem to remain almost completely separate, since the incidence of natural hybridization is very low. The most striking difference between the species lies in their stridulation, and Perdeck was able to show that this difference forms almost their only effective isolating mechanism; he further suggests that this is a primary mechanism, that is, the song patterns have not developed to perfect a species isolation already brought about by other factors, but have developed independently.

Of other evidence available on the isolating and hence survival value of song none is as critical as Perdeck's. Thus, although Walker (1957) was able to show specificity of oriented locomotor responses in females of certain tree crickets to the normal song of their conspecific males he has nothing to say about the effect of song in courtship behaviour, which in sympatric species lacking ecological and morphological barriers is most important. In fact, Walker's work only shows that song is one factor in the production of reproductive isolation in the tree crickets; it gives no information about its value relative to other possible factors. Similarly the work of Alexander and Moore (1958) on the sympatric species of the seventeen year cicada, *Magicicada septendecim* and *M. cassinii*, while showing the importance of sound production and reception in the life history and behaviour of the two species, does not allow of a critical assessment of the value of the acoustic behaviour in species reproductive isolation. This is the situation in regard to all other similar evidence; probably the first serious suggestion that stridulation could be involved in species isolation came from Fulton (1952), who in a series of papers on the ecology, behaviour and speciation of crickets used song as a taxonomic character, although Allard (1910) had long since noted geographic variation in the songs of field crickets. More recently Alexander (1957a) has used song characters in a taxonomic study of crickets of the genus *Acheta*, and although these characters are clear cut his data on the ecology and hybridization of the various species make it unlikely that song could be the prime cause of isolation and speciation. Similarly Haskell (1958) comments on the striking song differences between the closely related bugs *Kleidocerys ericae* and *K. resedae*, which are almost impossible to separate morphologically. Here, however, the possibility of an ecological barrier exists, and even if song could be shown to be of importance in mating behaviour, it might only prove to be of secondary value for isolation purposes.

The interesting work of Busnel *et al.* (1956) on interspecific song relationship in the Tettigoniid genus *Ephippiger* underlines the importance of factors other than song. In species collected together artificially from normally distinct habitats, Busnel and his co-workers were able to show that the normal songs of a given insect were not specific, but were capable of releasing behavioural responses from both males and females of other species. Moreover, such behaviour could lead with some species both to meeting of the sexes and to copulation, accompanied by transfer of a spermato-phore in the normal manner as when con-specific partners mate. These observations emphasize the importance of ecological and environmental barriers in the separation of the species of this genus; this importance is further underlined by an experiment in which Busnel released a female *Ephippiger bitterensis* in a situation where she had an equal choice of moving towards a singing male of her own species or of *E. ephippiger*. In 63% of cases the female moved towards the *ephippiger* male, thus only in 37% responding " specifically ". While the effect partially depended on song intensity, further experiment showed this was not an overriding cause. We therefore are confronted with the interesting situation where a female *E. bitterensis* is more attracted by the song of a male *E. ephippiger* than by the song of a male of its own species. On examination of oscillograms of the songs of the males of the two species, it is evident that they are rather similar, both in frequency range and in pulse rate; this being so, we should expect a female *ephippiger* to be attracted by the song of a male *bitterensis*, the converse of the above situation, and this in fact occurs. However, in this case the behaviour does not terminate in copulation, and Busnel was unable to induce mating with these partners. This suggests the existence of some further barrier, unrelated to song, operative in these circumstances. With problems of this nature unsolved, the rôle of stridulation in reproductive isolation needs clarification; valuable information could be obtained by pursuing studies, such as those of Perdeck mentioned above, of the songs of naturally occurring hybrids and by producing hybrids in the laboratory and examining their acoustics (von Hörmann, 1955).

The final rôle which stridulation may play in the insect world concerns its possible effect on ecology, which is here taken to refer to the distribution of the insects in their habitat and their movements in relation to changes in that habitat. M. C. Busnel (1955) describes the territorial behaviour of the cricket *Oecanthus pellucens*; the male lives in vegetation, typically bushes, about 50 cms. above the ground and stays for the whole or at least the great majority of its life confined to a small area about 50 sq. cms. It moves about this territory and sings its normal song for a more or less fixed period of time; if during the course of this tour it encounters another intruding male, it sings a type of song characterized by M. C. Busnel as "the warning song". If confined in a laboratory cage, the same acoustic behaviour applies to a much smaller territory of about 2 or 3 sq. cms. Although Mme. Busnel gives no account of the subsequent behaviour between the males, Alexander (1957a) describes similar behaviour in *Acheta assimilis*, and states that although the contest that ensues between the two males may be one of song only, fighting can take place; in either case, one male eventually retires. It is clear that such behaviour would produce a spacing effect in the distribution of males, and this is a concept referred to by several orthopterists, although experimental and observational evidence for it is meagre. It is said to occur in

Tettigoniids, but certainly does not apply to Acrididae, where the distribution of males and females is not of a dispersed type even in a uniform habitat but rather of a group nature. The territorial behaviour described in crickets is reminiscent of "rivalry" in grasshoppers, the difference being in the releasing stimulus.

Opposed to this type of territorial behaviour, leading to spatial distribution of the males, is the congregational behaviour of cicadas. Alexander (1957b) mentions this as a distinguishing feature of cicada song, "that the males and females congregate into close proximity during the daily singing period". However, Pringle (1955) mentions that although the species may congregate, mass singing does not always occur; in *Terpnosia ridens*, for example, an individual insect sings for about 30 seconds only and then the song is taken up by another cicada, so that a wave of sound passes over the habitat. The rôle of song in this species is obscure; it probably does not bring about the grouping, although it may tend to preserve it once formed. However, Alexander and Moore (1958) describe the remarkable congregational chorusing of the seventeen years cicadas *Magicicada septendecim* and *M. cassinii*, and conclude that it plays an important rôle in aggregating the species. In the Heteroptera, Leston (1957) has referred to one function of stridulation in the group as that of tending to form "heterosexual aggregations", and Haskell (1958) has reported that in several Heteroptera (e.g. *Kleidocerys* species) the insects will, if confined in a small space so that they commonly touch one another in moving about, stridulate at every contact. It is possible that such behaviour is a recognition signal which may prevent dispersal of such a group if formed by acoustic behaviour in nature, but no clear evidence on this point is available. In the case of certain Acrididae some observations have been made on the rôle of stridulation in ecology. There are several sympatric grasshoppers in England, and their tendency to form groups, even in a relatively uniform habitat, has been commented on by several workers, notably Clark (1948) and Chapman (1952). Indeed, so noticeable is this effect that Richards and Waloff (1954) in their detailed study of the ecology of five sympatric species, used the word "colony" to denote restricted areas within the general habitat wherein the grasshopper density was much higher than in the intervening areas and which appeared to be persistent breeding sites. However, their study also made it clear that such population centres tended to shift with a change in the vegetation of the habitat. The maintenance of grouping in certain of these grasshoppers, noticeably *Chorthippus brunneus* and *C. parallelus,* is remarkable. Clark (1948) showed that about 70% of marked groups of males and females were in the same place 10 days after release, and 95% were within 5 metres of the point of release at this time. Both Clark (1948) and Chapman (1952) refer to this coherence as the result of "social reactions", although they do not amplify this statement or adduce any direct evidence. Haskell (1958a), however, has reviewed this and other evidence in relation to the stridulation behaviour of these grasshoppers, and proposes the hypothesis that acoustic behaviour plays a dual rôle in these species. It promotes meetings of the sexes and forms the basis of courtship and copulation behaviour and also serves to maintain the grouping of a colony, preventing dispersion of the latter during movements occurring in relation to changes in the vegetation of the habitat. This second suggestion is based largely on observations relating to the group singing and assembly of males, on which more data are desirable, but the hypothesis may form a suitable working basis for future research.

It is clear that these few considerations cannot encompass all the possible rôles that sound emission or reception may play in the life of the insect. Many other aspects come at once to mind—the use of sounds in the oviposition of certain parasitic insects, the use of sounds in hunting, in feeding, in social life—all these are subjects of potential interest to those working on insect acoustics which have only been briefly mentioned in the preceding chapters, but so little evidence is available on these matters that it is pointless to enumerate it.

There is, however, one remaining aspect of the subject which must be mentioned, and that is the possible practical benefits which may accrue from the fundamental research which has been outlined above. As early as 1935 Schwarz, Kranz and Sicke described an apparatus, consisting of an amplifier and associated equipment, designed to detect the larvae of the House long-horn beetle *Hylotrupes bajalus* both in samples of wood and in the timbers of buildings. Colebrook (1937) produced a similar apparatus in England, and although the limitations of the method were great, it clearly had some promise. Lately, attention has been re-directed to this problem both in England and the United States, and the technical advances in amplifiers and microphones which have been made in the intervening period, together with the much greater knowledge of the types and possible specificity of insect sounds, make it possible that a device of real value in the detection of infested timber, both in growing trees and in buildings, can be perfected. In several types of boring beetle infestation the very long larval life which the insect can pass tunnelling in the wood makes early detection difficult, and this generally comes about by observation of the emergence holes of adult beetles and the powder or chippings they produce in making these holes. An apparatus which would detect larval activity in building timbers in an early stage would therefore be of great value, particularly as it would seem likely that the simplicity of use would encourage the making of periodical checks. The problem is partly technical and partly biological; the apparatus and the observer must be capable of distinguishing between larval feeding and locomotor noises, and also be able to recognize noises characteristic of sexes and species. This clearly entails a great deal of fundamental research at the outset into the sound emission and related behaviour of wood-boring insects. Feeding noises have already been utilized by Adams *et al.* (1953, 1954) to localize infestations of larvae of the granary weevil *Calandra granaria*, and once again with further technical development the method may become even more useful.

There have been many suggestions that high intensity or high frequency sounds could be used to kill insects, and Frings *et al.* (1948) have shown that this is in fact possible, but point out that the cost of the process is prohibitive, and the method is out of the question for practical control. Other suggestions for sonic insect control have included the use of ultra-sonic beams to disrupt swarms of locusts and prevent aggregation of biting-flies; such notions do not bear critical scrutiny, and it is clear that the contribution of acoustics to any form of insect control will probably be in the sphere of attraction and detection. The two best examples of insect control involving acoustics exploit just these principles. The first concerns mosquitoes, the second bees. In 1945 Kahn, Celestin and Offenhauser published a paper on the sounds produced by certain disease-carrying mosquitoes. As a result of their studies, coupled with what was already known about the acoustico-sexual behaviour of mosquitoes, they believed it would be possible to design a sonic-baited trap for mosquitoes. This they did, and carried out field trials of the apparatus in Husillo swamp, Cuba. The apparatus as described by Kahn *et al.* (1949) consisted of a loud-speaker through which could be played the recorded female flight note of the species it was desired to attract; surrounding this was a metal grid connected to a very high voltage source. When the female flight note was played, males in flight within acoustic range flew towards the source of sound, hit the screen and were electrocuted. The field trials were only a partial success; certainly the song recordings used proved to be species specific, and of all mosquitoes of responsive species electrocuted 90% proved to be males—an essential point, of course, in the fundamental control aimed at, the reduction of multiplication rate of the species. However, two main snags were found; one was that the recorded sound could not be played back at very high intensities, otherwise it became repellent, and this reduced the effective range of the trap. Secondly and more seriously, the female flight note was not able to induce flight responses in male mosquitoes during the time when they were not normally active. These drawbacks are of course serious, and the work has unfortunately not been followed up; but it seems possible that more research may supply answers which would increase the efficiency of the trap. For example, a sound stimulus might be found which could induce flight in normally inactive males, and by alternating this with the attractive female song a higher proportion of males in the effective trap area would be killed. The basic idea may in any case be more effective with other species.

The other practical use of sound referred to above is a device called the "Apidictor", developed by E. F. Woods (1959) in England over the past ten years. This device enables an apiarist to detect the probability of swarming in a hive of honey bees by measuring their acoustic reaction to a stimulus. Woods, in the course of experiment and observation, had recorded and analysed the sound output of a hive—caused by wing movements of the workers—during various stages in the growth of a colony. He noticed that a short time prior to swarming, the bees reacted to the stimulus of a sharp tap on the outside of the hive by a sound output of a markedly different frequency spectrum from the normal. He developed the "Apidictor" to facilitate the easy recognition of this change. It is basically an audio frequency amplifier, driven by a very small crystal microphone which is inserted between the combs of the hive. The output passes through crystal filters and operates a meter; by selection of the filters the frequency spectrum giving maximum output can be measured and thus changes in the acoustic response of the bees to the tap stimulus can be observed. This device has undergone field trials, and all the indications are that it can facilitate the early detection of swarming. Since this condition and its detection is the most expensive single factor connected with large scale bee-keeping, the desirability of such an instrument is clear.

It is probably in indirect methods such as these that the greatest future for acoustic control of insects will be found, but as in the case of the Apidictor, the pre-requisite is an accurate knowledge of the sound output and associated behaviour of the insects concerned. The preceding chapters have given an outline of the present state of knowledge in the field, and it is obvious that the foundations of the study have only just been laid. Years of patient research lie ahead before even an approximate assessment can be made of the part played by acoustic signals in the life of an insect. This research is difficult and can be costly in a technical sense, because of the equipment required for the recording and analysis of sounds. However, in April 1956 the International Committee for Biological Acoustics was formed, and in 1957 an offshoot of this, the Committee for Biological Acoustics, was started in England. The aim of these bodies is to foster research into all aspects of biological acoustics, and one of the principal aims is the foundation and operation of a library of recorded animal sounds. There are, of course, already in existence several collections of this kind, but the proposed library will be for international research purposes with wide terms of reference, and, when established, should be of enormous assistance to all those carrying out work in this fascinating field. One can also add " this neglected field ", particularly when talking of insect sounds. But there is now evidence that this phase is nearly over, and that, in the future, insect acoustics will get the attention it deserves, not only as a fascinating branch of study in its own right, but as an essential factor in life in the insect world.

REFERENCES

ADAMS, R. E. *et al.* (1953) *Science.* **118**: 163-164.

ADAMS, R. E. *et al.* (1954) *Cereal. Chem.* **31**: 271-276.

ALEXANDER, R. D. (1957a) *Ann. ent. Soc. Amer.* **50**: 584-602.

ALEXANDER, R. D. (1957b) *Ohio Jour. Sci.* **57**: 101-113.

ALEXANDER, R. D. and MOORE, T. E. (1958) *Ohio Jour. Sci.* **58**: 107-127.

ALLARD, H. A. (1910) *Ent. News.* **21**: 352-357.

ANDER, K. (1939) *Opusc. ent. Suppl.* **2**: 306 pp.

BUSNEL, M. C. (1955) *L'Acoustique des Orthoptères. Ann. Épiphyt.* (tome hors serie): 175-202.

BUSNEL, R. G. *et al.* (1956) *Ann. Épiphyt.* 1956 (3): 451-469.

CHAPMAN, K. (1952) *J. ent. Soc. S. Afr.* **15**: 165-203.

CLARK, E. J. (1948) *Trans. R. ent. Soc. Lond.* **99**: 173-222.

COLEBROOK, F. M. (1937) *J. Sci. Inst.* **14**: 119-121.

FRINGS, H. *et al.* (1948) *J. cell. comp. Physiol.* **31**: 339-358.

FULTON, B. B. (1952) *Evolution.* **6**: 283-95.

HASKELL, P. T. (1958a) *Proc. zool. Soc. Lond.* **129**: 351-358.

HASKELL, P. T. (1958b) *Insectes Sociaux.* **5**: 287-298.

HÖRMANN, S. VON (1955) *Naturwiss.* **42**: 470-471.

KAHN, M. C., CELESTIN, W. and OFFENHAUSER, W. (1945) *Science.* **101**: 335-336.

KAHN, M. C., CELESTIN, W. and OFFENHAUSER, W. (1949) *Am. J. trop. Med.* **29**: 811-825.

LESTON, D. (1957) *Proc. zool. Soc. Lond.* **128**: 369-386.

MARLER, P. (1955) *Nature, Lond.* **176**: 6-8.

PERDECK, A. C. (1957) *Behaviour.* **12**: 1-75.

PRINGLE, J. W. S. (1955) *Spolia Zeylanica.* **27**: 229-239.

RICHARDS, O. W. and WALOFF, N. (1954) *Anti-Locust Bull.* No. 17. London.

SCHWARZ, KRANZ and SICKE (1935) *Deutsche Bauzeitung.* 1935: 392-393.

TINBERGEN, N. (1951) *The study of instinct.* Oxford.

TINBERGEN, N. (1954) In *Evolution as a process.* Ed. by Huxley, Hardy and Ford. London.

WALKER, T. J. (1957) *Ann. ent. Soc. Amer.* **50**: 626-636.

WOODS, E. F. (1959) *Nature, Lond.* **184**: 842-844.

ZEUNER, F. (1934) *Nature, Lond.* **134**: 460.

ZEUNER, F. (1939) *Fossil Orthoptera Ensifera.* London.

Almost all the papers referred to in this book up to about years 1957-8 are collected in an analytical bibliography, *Sound Production and Sound Reception by Insects. A Bibliography.* Mable Frings and Hubert Frings, The Pennsylvania State University Press, U.S.A., 1960.

INDEX